HINDUISM

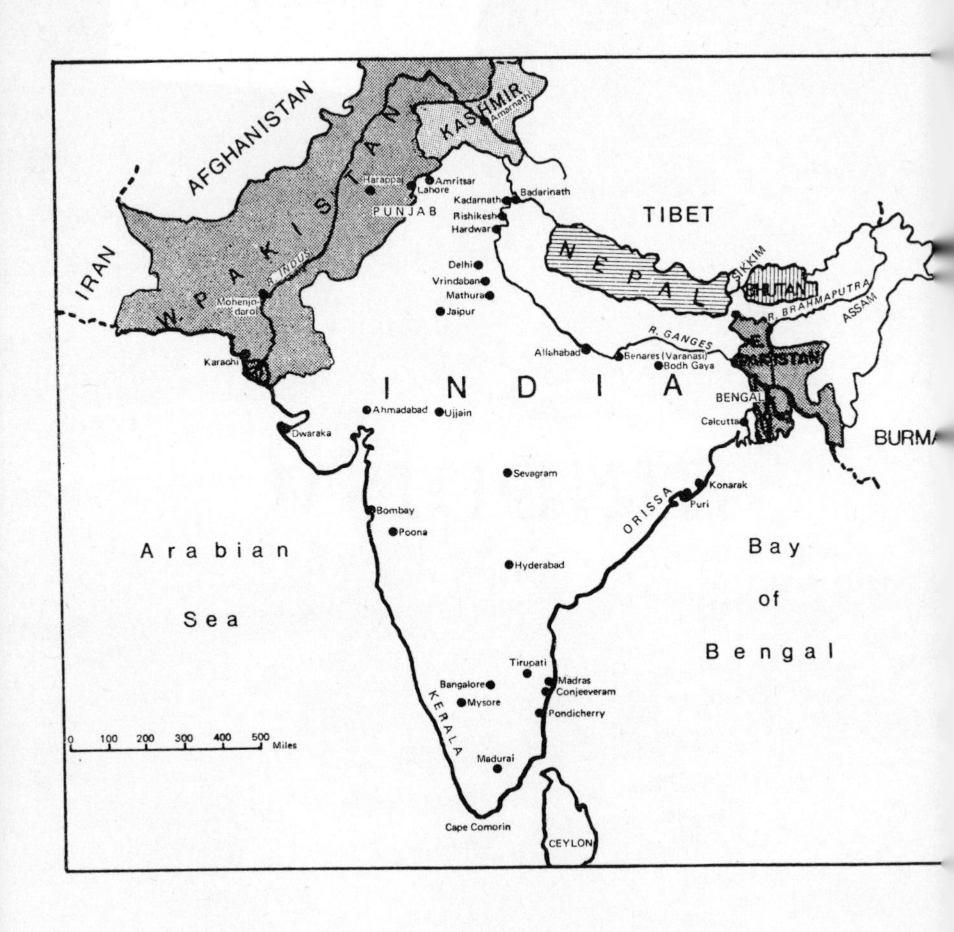
AFGHANISTAN
IRAN
W. PAKISTAN
KASHMIR
Amarnath
Harappa
Lahore
Amritsar
PUNJAB
Badarinath
Kadarnath
Rishikesh
Hardwar
TIBET
NEPAL
SIKKIM
BHUTAN
R. BRAHMAPUTRA
ASSAM
R. INDUS
Mohenjo-daro
Delhi
Vrindaban
Mathura
Jaipur
Karachi
R. GANGES
Allahabad
Benares (Varanasi)
Bodh Gaya
E. PAKISTAN
INDIA
BENGAL
Ahmadabad
Ujjain
Calcutta
Dwaraka
BURMA
Sevagram
Konarak
ORISSA
Puri
Bombay
Poona
Arabian Sea
Hyderabad
Bay of Bengal
Tirupati
Madras
Bangalore
Conjeeveram
Mysore
Pondicherry
KERALA
0 100 200 300 400 500 Miles
Madurai
Cape Comorin
CEYLON

WORLD RELIGIONS IN EDUCATION

HINDUISM

Edited by
John R. Hinnells
Lecturer in Comparative Religion
University of Manchester
and
Eric J. Sharpe
Senior Lecturer in Religious Studies
University of Lancaster

ORIEL PRESS

First published 1972

Reprinted 1973

ISBN 0 85362 116 0 Hard Cover
ISBN 0 85362 137 3 Paper Cover

Library of Congress Catalog Card No. 72-127067

Acknowledgement
The editors wish to express their gratitude to Miss R. Orpin and Mr. L. S. Cousins for help in proof reading and to Mr. J. Parry for the indexing.

Published by
Oriel Press Limited
27 Ridley Place
Newcastle upon Tyne
England NE1 8LH

Distributed by Routledge and Kegan Paul Limited
Broadway House, 68-74 Carter Lane
London EC4V 5EL and
9 Park Street
Boston, Mass. 02108, USA

Printed in Great Britain by
Redwood Press Limited, Trowbridge, Wiltshire

CONTRIBUTORS

To Part One

E. G. Parrinder (EGP), Professor of Comparative Religion, King's College, University of London.

E. J. Sharpe (EJS), Senior Lecturer in Religious Studies, University of Lancaster.

W. Weaver (WW), Lecturer in Comparative Religion, University of Leeds.

To Part Two

D. G. Butler (DGB), Headmaster, West Denton High School, Newcastle upon Tyne.

W. O. Cole (WOC), Head of Religious Studies, James Graham College of Education, Leeds.

E. G. Parrinder.

Mrs. E. Wilson (EW), Primary school teacher, Huddersfield.

To Part Three

W. O. Cole.

E. J. Sharpe.

Ninian Smart (NS), Professor of Religious Studies, University of Lancaster.

E. Wilson.

CONTENTS

The Editors gratefully inscribe this book
to the memory of
Mr. and Mrs. H. N. Spalding
founders of the Spalding Trust
whose trustees have generously
supported
The Shap Working Party on World Religions in Education

EDITORS' INTRODUCTION

THERE IS A growing desire among teachers and pupils alike that religions other than Christianity should be included in syllabuses of religious education. This book seeks to make available to teachers and students of education some of the academic and educational material necessary for a course on Hinduism. It is intended primarily to be a tool for the teacher, providing concise information on Hinduism and suggestions on how the information might be conveyed and the pupil stimulated, together with guides to general and advanced reading, a glossary and index, and a survey of the audio-visual aids available for use in the classroom (records, films, filmstrips, slides and children's books). It has been produced in response to the demand for such a work evidenced at the first (1969) Shap conference on *The Comparative Study of Religion in Education* (proceedings published by Oriel Press, 1970), and has grown out of material delivered at the 1970 Shap course on Hinduism organized by the Department of Adult Education, University of Newcastle upon Tyne.

Clearly other choices of subject might have been made. Judaism, Islam and Buddhism are equally deserving of detailed study, and it is hoped that future courses and books will be devoted to them, though not necessarily in that order. But there are good reasons why Hinduism should be first on the list. For two centuries or so, there have been practical and political links between the West and India, and the appeal of India to the West has often centred on the Hindu religious tradition in one form or another. The study of Indian history, languages and culture—all indespensable to a thorough understanding of Hinduism—has been cultivated in Western universities for many years, though perhaps somewhat less intensively of late. Parallel to this academic study there has been the less formal, though no less intense, fascination which India (or perhaps the image of India) has always seemed to exercise on the Western mind. That India is 'spiritual' while the West is 'materialistic' is of course a myth; but like many another myth, it has proved extraordinarily tenacious, particularly in the context of a generation in revolt against much of what the West is assumed to stand for. A further reason for taking Hinduism first is the complete lack of any suitable book for the teacher.

The study of Hinduism is not easy. It is certainly fascinating; but its complexity increases the closer one approaches it. Not only is it in many respects the direct antithesis of the Western tradition in which we have been reared; it contains within itself so many paradoxes, anomalies and apparent contradictions that the unwary student may, by studying only one 'Hindu' tradition, construct for himself an entirely false picture of the nature of Indian religion. In order to facilitate understanding, to try and avoid the presentation of Hinduism as one unified tradition and to present the teacher with material in a useable form the survey of Hinduism is broken down into a number of units, each approximately 1000 words in length. The earlier period of Hindu history (down to the nineteenth century A.D.) is covered in so far as this is necessary for a proper understanding of contemporary Hinduism; emphasis is, however, placed on modern Hinduism and on those practices which the Editors believe will be of particular interest to teachers and, indeed, to a wider public.

The subsequent articles on the teaching of Hinduism on various educational levels do not pretend to express anything other than the convictions of practising teachers—convictions arrived at in the light of many years' experience. They are offered not as norms but as possible and *practical* approaches to an increasingly important but immensely difficult task: the teaching of world religions.

JOHN R. HINNELLS
ERIC J. SHARPE

April 1971

PART ONE

HINDUISM PAST AND PRESENT

I

INTRODUCTION TO HINDUISM

THE WESTERN STUDENT approaching Hinduism for the first time is faced with what may seem to be insurmountable obstacles to understanding. Not the least of these is the question of definition. What exactly *is* Hinduism? Is it a religion, or many religions and many philosophies? Certainly it is kaleidoscopic in its variety, and a slight change of approach or emphasis may well give the observer the impression that all its elements have shifted—some merging into others, others again standing out with renewed colour and clarity. The historian sees one thing, the mystic another, the sociologist something quite different.

Perhaps, therefore, the first question which we ought to ask is whether the single English word 'Hinduism' is at all appropriate to describe the phenomenon we are trying to study. It is not merely a matter of diversity. Christianity, Islam and Buddhism are also very diverse religions; but in these cases the problem may in part be resolved by making reference to the teachings of a founder and to the beliefs and practices of a historic community of believers. Judaism is capable of fairly close definition on similar lines, through Moses, the Law, the Prophets and the community. However, in the case of Hinduism this approach simply will not work. It is not a 'founded' religion. It has no creeds—except in some unusual cases, and these are as a rule accepted only within the group which has produced them. Its holy scriptures are of immense size and staggering diversity. It has nothing even remotely approaching a central organization (or ecclesiastical authority), and would not know what to do with it if it had one. In short, whatever it is, and whatever its unity, that unity is neither doctrinal nor organizational. Not surprisingly, then, one modern Western observer, whose opinions must always be treated with respect, has written that 'The term "Hinduism" is . . . a particularly false conceptualization, one that is conspicuously incompatible with any adequate understanding of the religious outlook of Hindus.'[1]

The stages by which this term came into popular use in the West to describe the traditional religion of India are interesting, but we cannot go into them now. It is worth mentioning, however, that the words 'Hindu' and 'Hinduism' are basically geographical, derived, *via* Persian, from the name of that river now called the Indus. A 'Hindu' was originally a dweller in the land of the Indus who did not happen to have made his submission to Islam (and this of course dates the term to the Middle Ages). Hindu*ism*, then—Europeans love 'isms'—is the European blanket term which is used to cover the religion of all those Indians who do not happen to be Muslims, Christians, Parsis, Jains or Buddhists. In other words, it is a term originally applied by those who are not members of this particular tradition (or these particular traditions) to those who are. It would not be surprising to find that it had loopholes and other shortcomings.

Indians themselves, if they belong to the Hindu tradition, have a variety of ways of referring to it. One classical expression is *arya dharma*, the noble order, or noble law; another is *sanatana dharma*, or eternal law; a third is *hindu dharma*, which we can only translate as Indian law or Hindu law. What these all have in common is the word *dharma*, which means a variety of things, but which may perhaps be summed up as the sacred order, or law. *Dharma* is both the way things are and the way they should be, the only appropriate order for the universe and for man in it. This includes the various manifestations of what we call religion: ritual, devotion, myth and doctrine; it also includes social order (as *varnashramadharma*, the caste system as a form of sacred law) and philosophical theories of man and the universe. Like all laws, *dharma* may be observed, or it may not; but whether or not it has followers, it will remain inviolate and inviolable.

From the Hindu point of view, then, there is a strong *prima facie* case for avoiding the term 'Hinduism' altogether and using instead *hindu dharma* or some such expression more in line with Hindu usage. But the term 'Hinduism' has become too deeply entrenched in Western vocabulary to be easily dislodged. Moreover, it is now widely used by Hindus themselves whenever they have to express themselves in English. For instance, the first chapter in Morgan's book *The Religion of the Hindus*, written by a leading Indian historian, is called 'The Nature and History of Hinduism'.

Hinduism is admittedly not an ideal term; but provided that we do not suppose that all Hindus share identical religious beliefs or observe identical religious practices, it may serve. One thing which it does unquestionably do is to emphasize the closeness of the links which bind Indian religion to the totality of Indian history and Indian culture. All Hindus do not live in India; nor are all Indians Hindus. But since a fruitful understanding of the diversity of Hinduism depends to a large extent on our understanding of the diversity of India and the Indian people, we must take a little time to look at the motherland of the Hindu people.

India is popularly called a sub-continent, and it is certainly advisable to think of India in continental, rather than in national terms. To envisage India as a country is almost certain to be misleading, since it encourages an impression of overall unity, a unity which may exist as an ideal in India's case, but which does not correspond to the actual situation. India has been effectively cut off from the remainder of the land mass of Asia by the Himalaya and other mountains to the north, north-east and north-west; and by the sea on its other two sides. It is a land of vast distances, at least by British standards, measuring approximately 2000 miles from north to south, and about 1800 miles from east to west at its widest point. Its area is about one and a quarter million square miles, or twelve times the size of Great Britain; in fact the area of India and the area of continental Europe (excluding the U.S.S.R.) are virtually the same. The population of India in 1961 was calculated to be some 442 millions, and since then it has grown to over 500 millions. The difficulties involved in supporting such a large population are well known, although India, when viewed as a whole, is not quite such a poor country as is sometimes supposed. The problem is one of sheer size and distribution, centring in the majority of cases on the supply of water. The question of the distribution of wealth is not one which we can discuss here, but the dimensions of the problem may perhaps be envisaged by reflecting that there are ten times as many people in India as there are in Great Britain, and two and a half times as many as in the United States of America—and this despite the fact that in area, the U.S.A. is almost three times the size of India.

Despite this enormous population, there were at the last census only seven cities in India with a population of more than a million—Ahmedabad, Bangalore, Bombay, Calcutta, Delhi,

Hyderabad and Madras. In 1961, 82 per cent of the people of India were listed as 'rural', that is, living in villages and small towns and making their living either directly or indirectly from agriculture. This is a fact of some importance for the understanding of Hinduism, since it is in precisely this section of the population that so-called 'popular' Hinduism is observed in all its many forms. And explain it how we will, it is an uncomfortable fact that although the West claims to know a fair amount about Hinduism, what is known best is the sophisticated religion and philosophy of a rather small minority, while the actual beliefs and practices of the overwhelming majority of Hindus remain virtually unknown.

We have said that not all Indians are Hindus. More precisely, at the last census 85 per cent of the people were returned as Hindus—more than 375 millions in all. For purposes of comparison we may note that other important religious groups in India include Muslims (10 per cent), Christians (2·3 per cent and Sikhs (1·7 per cent).

A further measure of the continental diversity of India is to be seen in the inter-related areas of race and language. India has many distinct racial types, and a bewildering variety of languages. Methods of computing language diversity vary, of course, but if we reckon simply in terms of numbers of speakers, there are between a dozen and twenty 'major' languages, and more than two hundred 'minor' ones, not counting dialects. These languages correspond broadly to racial differences, and fall into three main classes. The major northern languages are derived from Indo-European sources, being descended more or less directly from Sanskrit. Examples of these are Hindi, Bengali and Marathi. In the south, the main languages, such as Tamil, Telegu and Malayalam, are Dravidian. A third class comprises languages of Tibeto-Chinese origin. It cannot be emphasized too strongly that the difference between the Hindi-speaking north and the Tamil-speaking south is not merely one of dialect. It is equally a difference of race, of culture, and of atmosphere—which is why Tamils object so strongly to official attempts to make Hindi into a language for the whole of India. Whatever good the British may or may not have done in India, they did at least provide the sub-continent with a language of universal communication.

Much of the cultural and religious diversity of India becomes more understandable when viewed against the background of the history and geography of the land. Indian history will be dealt with (at least in so far as it has a bearing on religion) in what follows; but a few words must be said at this point about the geographical structure of India.[2]

Stretched like a huge barrier across the extreme north of India are the Himalaya mountains, with their eastern and western offshoots. Their presence has meant that the would-be invader from the north has not been able to enter India without great difficulty; invasions have, however, taken place, usually through the passes of the north-west frontier. In the Himalaya arise the two great rivers of north India, the Indus in the west and the Ganges in the east. The Indus in particular, thanks to its extensive system of tributaries (*Panjab* = the land of the five rivers), supported a notable civilization before the coming of the Indo-Europeans in the second millennium B.C. The region between the two rivers, frequently the scene of great battles, was once the heartland of classical Indian culture (*Aryavarta*). Now it is very largely barren, though still densely populated. This is the hottest part of India, and very poorly watered.

South of the great northern plain is a highland area, culminating in the Vindhya mountains, which in the past have acted as a barrier between the north and south of India. South of these again is the dry Deccan plateau, bounded on each side by a range of hills, the Western and Eastern Ghats respectively. The small area between the Western Ghats and the sea includes some of the most fertile country in India, including the extraordinary state of Kerala, while from the Eastern Ghats to the sea there is the broken plain of Tamil Nadu leading down to the southern capital and port of Madras. On the plateau between the two ranges there are cities like Bangalore, which, apart from being one of the most 'Western' of Indian cities, has a type of climate, with hot days and relatively cool nights, which is among the best in India.

Otherwise the chief climatic feature of India (apart from heat) is its almost total lack of rainfall for eight months of the year, from October to May. From October to February temperatures are not extreme; but between March and May they rise steadily, particularly on the plains. All being well, in June the monsoon begins, and the country comes to life again. But after a long period of drought, all too often there is severe flooding. India never seems to be able to do anything by halves!

How far the geography and climate of India have left traces

on the religion of the country is a matter of some complexity. Some of its features are more simple than others—for instance, the prevalence of a religion based on the fertility of the earth in a land of agriculturalists, and a land in which seasonal cycles count for so very much. But the historical relationship between the emphasis of 'popular' Hinduism on fertility, and the religion of the Indo-European peoples, with its pantheon of mainly celestial deities, is a question which has never been satisfactorily settled. And variations between Hindu patterns of belief and practice from one part of the country to another are also, to say the least, disturbing to the would-be student. All the features of India which we have attempted to outline here have their place and their influence within the overall structure of Hinduism, and each is deserving of close consideration when we attempt to describe what Hinduism is, and what it is not.

We might perhaps sum up by saying that the word 'Hinduism' is both elastic and potentially unclear, and that it is possible to make out a good case both for its abandonment and for its retention—provided, in the latter event, that it is defined with some accuracy. The difficulty which commentators find in hitting upon an adequate definition is notorious, and possibly insoluble. Its connection with the land and life of India must be our starting-point, but we must on no account use the word as though it indicated one fixed system of religious beliefs and practices. One of our foremost interpreters of India, the historian A. L. Basham, defines a Hindu (notice, not Hinduism) as '. . . a man who chiefly bases his beliefs and way of life on the complex system of faith and practice which has grown up organically in the Indian sub-continent over a period of at least three millennia'.[3]

Following on from this, we might provisionally define Hinduism as 'the traditional socio-religious structure of India in so far as it rests on belief in the authority of certain Vedic, post-Vedic or other scriptures, and is contained within the institution of caste'.

In the pages which follow, we shall attempt to trace the historical development of Hinduism from its beginnings in the Indus Valley Civilization and the Indo-European peoples, through its great formative periods, down to modern times.

It will be necessary during the course of this book to make rather frequent reference to Sanskrit names, titles and technical terms. The Sanskrit alphabet is much more elaborate than the Roman, and can be transliterated into Roman only with the aid of diacritical marks. A fully transliterated Sanskrit alphabet will be found in the Appendix (48), but in the body of the book, diacritical marks have been omitted. The Glossary and Index contains the majority of these words *with* diacritical marks.

Where there are common Anglicized forms of Sanskrit or other Indian words, these have been used.

EJS

Footnotes

[1] W. Cantwell Smith, *The Meaning and End of Religion*, Mentor edition, 1964, p. 61.

[2] See also P. Spear, *India, Pakistan, and the West*, London, 1967[4], pp. 13–32.

[3] *The Concise Encyclopaedia of Living Faiths*, ed. R. C. Zaehner, London, 1959, p. 225.

2

THE INDUS VALLEY CIVILIZATION

In 1920 archaeologists announced the discovery of extensive urban ruins in the Indus Valley which pre-dated the earliest literary sources and which caused scholars working on the ancient texts to re-examine their views on the different phases of Indian culture. The *Rig Veda*, which speaks in such derogatory terms of the enemies subdued by the Aryan tribes, gives the impression that they were all savage barbarians. In fact, some of them had developed a highly sophisticated way of life which compares favourably with that of contemporary urban civilizations in Egypt and Mesopotamia.

The extensive excavations carried out at the two principal city sites, Harappa and Mohenjo-Daro, both situated in the Indus basin, indicates that this pre-Aryan culture was well established by about 2500 B.C. and subsequent discoveries have revealed that it covered most of the Lower Indus Valley. What we know of this ancient civilization is derived almost exclusively from archaeological data since every attempt to decipher the script used by these people has so far failed.

The Indus cities were carefully planned and well constructed with wide streets, fired brick buildings, well-equipped private dwellings, enormous granaries, and even an elaborate drainage system for the disposal of sewage. In contrast to Egypt and Mesopotamia where a great many temples and religious monuments have come to light, the Indus cities seem to have had very few public buildings. The only one of any note is the Great Bath at Mohenjo-Daro which appears to have been used in the performance of certain rituals. Nothing that can be clearly identified as a temple or a shrine has yet been discovered.

The people depended upon agriculture and trade for their livelihood. Wheat, barley and the date palm were cultivated; animals were domesticated; and cotton textiles, ivory and copper were exported to Mesopotamia, and possibly China and Burma in exchange for silver and other commodities.

Evidence of the religious beliefs and practices of these people is slight, since the Indus script cannot be read and, apart from the bath at Mohenjo-Daro, there appears to be no religious architecture. A certain amount of information has been derived from scenes depicted on seal-amulets and from the terra-cotta figurines found at different sites throughout the area; but such evidence is open to wide interpretation. The predominance of female figurines and seals depicting a horned goddess in association with the sacred pipal tree are generally regarded as evidence of the worship of a mother-goddess who presided over fertility and birth and who may have acted as guardian and protector of the dead.

In some of the mother goddess cults of the Ancient Near East, the Great Mother who symbolised the power of fertility came also to be associated with the renewal of human life after death. In her role as mistress of the blessed dead she protected and revived those committed to the earth from whence this new life sprang. It is impossible to say, on the basis of the existing evidence, whether or not the Indus Valley goddess was concerned so intimately with the fortunes of the departed; although it is worth noting that a good deal of care and attention was given to the dead.

It would seem that inhumation was the most common method of disposing of the corpse. Some were buried in a fully extended position and provided with an assortment of grave goods, including pottery vessels which may have contained food and drink offerings. In addition, many examples of 'fractional' burials have come to light. The provision of grave goods may indicate that life in the hereafter was thought of largely as a continuation of the present mode of existence so that through burial the dead were transported to their subterranean abode presided over by the goddess.

Reference has already been made to the great bath at Mohenjo-Daro. It is certain that this strange monument was not constructed merely for the purposes of hygiene since all the private dwellings were equipped with excellent bathrooms. Since so many elements of the Indus culture appear to have found their way into early Hinduism it is possible that ancient purification rites were taken over and reinterpreted by members of the brahmin caste. If this is so the later practice of constructing *pushkaras* or artificial lotus ponds may be very ancient indeed.

These lotus ponds were used during historic times for various purification ceremonies concerned with kingship and the priesthood. What is perhaps more significant from the point of view of the religion of the Indus Valley dwellers is the suggestion by D. D. Kosambi[1] that the bath was probably used in the mother goddess cult. In a number of references these lotus ponds are said to be the abode of a group of feminine water deities known as the *apsaras* and renowned for their beauty and musical talent. If this ancient belief associating goddesses with sacred baths is derived from pre-Aryan sources, then the cult at Mohenjo-Daro may have involved some form of ceremonial bathing as a prelude to ritual cohabitation with female representatives of the goddess, carried out in the small ante-chambers adjoining the bath. Although there is no direct evidence to substantiate this theory, the practice of sacred prostitution associated with the mother goddess cults elsewhere lends some support to the suggestion.

In contrast, the deities of the invading Aryans were predominantly male and little attention is paid in the *Rig Veda* to the veneration of female powers. In later Hinduism these two distinctive elements are drawn together, so that the great god Shiva, whose character owes so much to the old Vedic gods, is provided with a female consort, known by various names, who represents the *shakti* or the vital force of the god.

It would appear that the religion of the Indus Valley dwellers was not confined exclusively to the worship of the goddess. One seal uncovered at Mohenjo-Daro depicts a three-faced, male god with arms outstretched, seated on a low platform in a cross legged position (similar to that adopted by the later yogis). His arms are adorned with bangles and his head is crowned with a fan-shaped head-dress from which two horns project. The fact that he is surrounded by a number of animals and fertility symbols suggests that, like the goddess, he was concerned primarily with the promotion of fertility. This remarkable figure has been interpreted as a prototype of the later Shiva in his forms as *pashupati* 'Lord of Beasts' and 'Prince of Yogis', but until more evidence is forthcoming this must still remain a matter for speculation.

The end of the Indus Valley Civilization seems to have been fairly abrupt and violent. Mohenjo-Daro was set on fire and its inhabitants massacred. But long before the end came there seems to have been a gradual process of internal decay and stagnation.

WW

Footnote

[1] *The Culture and Civilization of Ancient India*, pp. 66–68.

Bibliography

B. and R. Allchin, *The Birth of Indian Civilization*, Harmondsworth, 1968.
E. O. James, *The Cult of the Mother Goddess*, London, 1959.
E. Mackay, *Early Indus Civilizations*, London, 1948.
S. Piggott, *Prehistoric India*, London, 1950.
H. M. Wheeler, *Civilizations of the Indus Valley and Beyond*, London, 1966.
The Indus Civilization, Cambridge, 1968[3].

3

THE ARYANS

IN THE MIDDLE of the second millennium B.C., sometime between 1,750 and 1,200 B.C., the Aryan-speaking tribes who entered India from the north-west established themselves in the Punjab and gradually advanced eastwards. This movement was not an organized invasion of India; it was rather part of a whole series of ethnic waves or movements that affected both Europe and Asia. These early Indian settlers belonged to the same racial group as the tribes that established themselves in Persia, now known as Iran—the land of the Aryans.

The religion of that branch of the Aryan peoples which eventually settled in India and Iran (the Indo-Iranians) can be partially reconstructed from the evidence of the ancient Indian texts, the *Vedas* (see unit 4) and the ancient Iranian (Zoroastrian) Bible, the *Avesta.*

The imagery surrounding the gods was drawn from the daily life of the Aryans. They were warriors and their deities, too, are described as warriors (e.g. Indra in India, Mithra in Iran), they battle with the demons and destructive spirits. Although the gods are described in human terms with heads, eyes and hands, although they dwell in mansions and ride forth on chariots (e.g. Varuna), rarely do we find mythical stories about them. The notable exception is the god Indra whose conflict with Vritra (the demon of drought) is the central theme of many Vedic hymns. Mythical imagery is used to describe the gods, but rarely do they have adventures, never do they have love affairs. All the imagery is used to express the character of the god, who may in fact be the personification of an abstract concept, thus Mithra (Indian Mitra) is the word for Contract, Aryaman = Hospitality, Verethraghna = Victory. The imagery expresses the concept in vivid terms, so Mithra unites countries and Verethraghna/Victory is described as an ironclad boar or as a stallion. The Aryans were nomads and their descriptions and understanding of the gods are inspired by nature, so we read of storm gods (Maruts), of a hymn to the dawn and the moon. In nature they observed a certain regularity, or order, *rita*, an order which they believed pervaded the whole cosmos, upholding the worlds, of gods and men, the universe, the social order and human ethics. On a number of occasions the sacred altar is said to be the 'seat' or 'womb' of *rita*, implying that the principle which sustains the cosmos is itself strengthened or reborn at the sacrifice. The sacrificial ritual formed the focal point of the Aryan religion. To this day the sacred fire remains an important part of Hindu ritual and the centre of Zoroastrian devotion. One of the main Aryan rituals was the *soma* (Iranian *haoma*) ritual, in which the pressing of the sacred plant was interpreted as the death of the god (Soma/Haoma) from which men received life mediated through the ritual consumption of the sacred drink. In some of the Vedic hymns the concept of sacrifice is fairly rudimentary. Through its performance the gods could be persuaded to offer their protection and bestow upon man all the benefits essential for a long and happy life—health, good fortune, children and cattle. Sacrifice was also a means of purification and expiation, and it served as a link, uniting the living members of the clan with ancestors who had departed to the realms beyond.

From the Vedas we can construct a picture, albeit blurred, of the settlement of the Aryans in India. Hymns to Indra and Agni praise the gods for the terrible devastation that they wreak upon the *dasas* (or *dasyus*), the dark-skinned enemies who already inhabited the land. Exhilarated by the offerings of the intoxicating Soma juice Indra dispersed the foes of the Aryans and rent in pieces their mighty fortresses (R.V. IV, 16, 3). Similarly, with the appearance of Agni; 'the dark hued races scattered abroad, deserting their possessions.'[1] There is also ample evidence in the *Rig Veda* to indicate that the Aryan tribes fought amongst themselves and that some of them enlisted the support of the *dasas* in these inter-tribal hostilities. Thus not all the *dasas* were slaughtered or driven out; in some cases the new inhabitants dwelt alongside the old in a peaceful co-existence that gained strength through intermarriage and trade.

The *Rig Veda* makes no mention of permanent settlements or towns. The people were simple village dwellers whose wealth was derived from their cattle and from looting the settlements of defeated enemies. After establishing themselves mainly in the Punjab area some of the tribes moved eastwards in the Ganges valley and along the Himalaya foothills to southern Nepal, and southwards through the region of modern Bihar. It is along this route that the earliest Aryan cities appear.

When the Aryans arrived in India their tribal structure was already organized on a patriarchal basis. The small village communities, comprised largely of family units, maintained contact with their fellow tribesmen through the *sabha*. The word denotes both the tribal assembly and the meeting hall where the men gathered for council and recreation. The tribal leader, or *raja*, was elected from among the men of leading families on a non-hereditary basis and his authority was restricted by the tribal assembly. This state of affairs seems to have continued until about the sixth century B.C. when some of the more powerful *rajas* annexed the weaker tribes and began to carve out for themselves small kingdoms.

Scholars who have attempted to investigate the origin and development of caste have sought for evidence of class differentiation in the early Vedic period. A. L. Basham has suggested that a simple bi-partite division which distinguished the nobility from the ordinary tribesmen was an established feature of the Aryan tribes before their settlement in India. After a careful analysis of Indo-European mythology Georges Dumézil concluded that the Aryan social structure was based on a threefold class distinction made up of priests, (*brahmins*), warriors and rulers (*kshatriyas*) and ordinary tribesmen (*vaishyas*). (Dumézil has also sought to establish such a tripartite structure of the divine world.) As some of the tribes moved eastwards these divisions of society became more distinct. The successful mastery of the land required the services of another group—the *shudras* or slave class which was made up largely of conquered pre-Aryan peoples. The *shudras* were not recognized as full members of the tribe; this privilege was reserved for those belonging to the three highest classes of society. The steps by which the ancient priestly families emerged as the powerful brahmanic class of the later Vedic period are not set out clearly in the Vedic hymns, although there is clear evidence that the priestly function was becoming more and more indispensable.

WW/JRH

Footnote

[1] R. V. VII, 5, 3. All translations of the Rig Veda are taken from. R T. H. Griffith, *The Hymns of the Rig Veda.*

Bibliography

B. and R. Allchin, *The Birth of Indian Civilization*, Harmondsworth, 1968.
I. Gershevitch, *The Avestan Hymn to Mithra*, Cambridge, 1959.
D. D. Kosambi, *The Culture and Civilization of Ancient India*, London, 1965.
C. Scott Lyttleton, *The New Comparative Mythology*, California, 1966.

4

THE RELIGION OF THE RIG VEDA

THE SACRIFICIAL SYSTEM which developed in India after the settlement of the Aryans was so complex that a considerable body of priests each specializing in one aspect of the ritual, had to be employed. In one Vedic hymn seven classes of priests are named. The most important of these was the *Hotar* who recited the hymns and the *Adhvarya*, 'the officiating priest', who attended the sacrificial fire and organized all the paraphernalia of the ritual. Although the *Udgatar* or 'singing priest' is not mentioned in this particular list his liturgical chants formed an important and integral part of the ceremony. In the course of time a large number of verses were gathered together, nearly all from the *Rig Veda*, and arranged in a manual for the use of the *Udgatar*. This collection is known as the *Sama-Veda*. Similarly, the *Yajur-Veda* is a compendium of the formulas and prayers, composed partly in verse and partly in prose for the guidance of the *Adhvarya*. With the formulation of these two manuals the *Rig Veda* tended to become the official veda of the *Hotar* priests. All three *Vedas* were considered divinely inspired.

The *Rig Veda* must be seen for what it is; a collection of hymns composed by different poets at different times; as a source book for Vedic religion it is both fragmentary and incomplete. Some of the oldest hymns bear traces of the quasi-nomadic life of bygone days, while others reflect Indian surroundings and conditions. Some of the old Aryan gods have disappeared altogether; others are in the process of decline as new deities rise to take their place.

When the poets were moved to sing the praises of one particular god they freely ascribed to him the qualities and titles of other gods. Some of the later sages went further and declared that all the gods were simply different manifestations of one Supreme Spirit. 'To what is One, sages give many a title; they call it Agni, Yama, Matarisvan.' (R.V. I, 164, 46).

The Vedic deities are almost entirely male and benevolent. Indra, to whom nearly one-quarter of the hymns are dedicated, is a good example. He is frequently referred to by the title '*Vritrahan*' (slayer of Vritra). Vritra has been variously interpreted as a force which holds back the light or the rains, or as the power of the *dasas* to resist the Aryan invaders. In fact he appears to be a combination of all these so that Indra appears in a dual role as the god who restores order and balance to the natural world, and as the powerful war lord of the Vedic Aryans. In the Vedic hymns Indra has already taken over some of the royal prerogatives of the god Varuna. Originally a sky god, Varuna is honoured with the title 'universal monarch'. From his exalted position in the heavens Varuna fixed the laws of the physical universe. The sun, moon and stars were all subject to his 'ordinances' and under his direction the rivers followed their appointed paths. Although all gods are 'guardians of *rita*' (see unit 3) the title has special significance when applied to Varuna, where it has a distinctly ethical as well as cosmic content. As guardian of the moral law Varuna is concerned with human behaviour and conduct; he inflicts sickness as a punishment for sin (R.V. VII, 89); he observes all the deeds of men (R.V. I, 25); and he binds the sinner with fetters (R.V. V, 85). At the same time he is ready to forgive those who are truly penitent and to protect those who worship him aright.

The gods may also have an ambivalent character; Rudra, for example, is constantly implored not to slay his devotees yet he also brings healing and comfort. It is from this ancient storm god that Shiva, one of the greatest gods of Hinduism, is thought to have evolved. It has even been suggested that there was a dark side to the character of Varuna, for he could be symbolised by the night, stagnant waters and a black bull. 'Good' and 'evil', or 'creativity' and 'destruction' could, then, be seen as two sides of the one coin.

Arrayed against the gods were the hosts of darkness, the daemonic powers who sought to disrupt the order of the cosmos and to afflict mankind with terrible calamities. At times it becomes impossible to distinguish between supernatural and physical enemies, largely because the poets themselves are not concerned with this distinction. The opposition of the *dasas* is viewed as one aspect of a battle which is constantly being waged at all levels. The fact that all the demons are smitten either singly or collectively by the gods suggests a general spirit of optimism. This optimism is further reflected in the attitude of the Vedic Indian to life in the present world and to his status in the hereafter. The hymns are concerned primarily with the means of securing a long and happy life and little is said about the nature of death and the abode of the departed. From what is said, however, it is clear that the old belief in the subterranean kingdom of the dead was gradually being replaced by the more attractive 'World of the Fathers'; a celestial realm where the dead were freed from the pains of suffering and old age. The ancestors were not thought of as being completely cut off from their living relatives, for on certain auspicious occasions the Fathers left their heavenly abode in the company of Agni and Yama to take up their allotted place at the sacrifice.

Isolated references indicate that some distinction was made after death between the righteous and the wicked. The 'World of the Fathers' is contrasted with the 'House of Clay' and in R.V. IV, 5 and VII, 104 the wicked are said to be cast into a 'deep place' or 'a pit'. Apart from these two references, however, the idea of post-mortem judgement finds no place in the *Rig Veda*, and even here other interpretations are possible.

The beginnings of some of the later philosophical movements, both orthodox and heretical, may be indicated by different attitudes expressed in the Vedas. In R.V. II, 12, for example, reference is made to those who deny the existence of the gods, particularly Indra. A much more common tendency, although it was expressed in various forms, was to seek a unifying principle, an original first cause, to account for the multiplicity of the gods and to reduce to a single souce the variety of created forms. Rather than elevate a well established god like Indra to a position of unrivalled supremacy, a common feature of divinity was selected, an epithet like *vishva-karman* (maker of everything) or *praja-pati* (lord of living beings) which can apply to any god, and personify this as the supreme creative force. In other hymns the quest for unity expresses itself in the form of pantheistic monism where distinctions between creator and creation disappear altogether. Thus, Prajapati is both the originator of the universe and at the same time he is the universe itself (R.V. X, 121). The same idea is conveyed in the *Purusha sukta* (the hymn to Purusha, R.V. X, 90) where the Cosmic Being is, himself, the whole universe since it arose from the dismembered parts of his body. The sun comes from his eye, the earth from his feet, the great gods Indra and Agni from his mouth. Similarly the classes of men come from his body: the brahmin from his mouth, the warrior from his arms, the worker from his thighs and the slave from his feet. Thus behind all life there is but one ultimate source or being. In what is perhaps the finest hymn of the whole collection (R.V. x, 129) the universe is traced back to the single, impersonal '*Tad Ekam*', That One. At this point the luxuriant mythology of the early Vedic period with its variety of gods and its optimistic outlook on life has given way to a feeling of uneasiness and uncertainty, out of which emerged India's great philosophical movements.

WW

Bibliography

M. Bloomfield, *The Religion of the Veda*, London, 1908.
R. T. H. Griffith, *The Hymns of the Rig Veda*, Benares, 1920–26.
A. B. Keith, *The Religion and Philosophy of the Veda and Upanishads*, 2 vols, Harvard, 1925.
A. A. Macdonnell, *Vedic Mythology*, Strassbourg, 1887.

5

BRAHMANAS, ARANYAKAS AND UPANISHADS

As some of the Aryan tribes moved eastwards the class divisions within Vedic society became more pronounced. The priestly class, now organized into a number of distinctive schools, each with its own tradition, was steadily emerging as a sacerdotal aristocracy determined to show that priestly power was superior even to that wielded by the monarch. One priestly text of the period states quite explicitly: 'That king who is weaker than the brahman is stronger than his enemies.' (*Shatapatha-Brahmana* 4, 4, 15). The priests asserted that the created order which had proceeded from an original act of sacrifice needed to be maintained by its constant repetition; and since they alone possessed the specialized knowledge and skills necessary to ensure the continued validity of the sacrifice, it followed logically that all things in heaven and on earth became dependent upon their sacred functions.

In the course of time the traditions of the various priestly schools came to be embodied in a collection of prose writings which worked out this theory of sacrifice in all its intricate details. These commentaries or treatises are known as the *Brahmanas*. Although for sheer prolixity the Brahmanas have few equals in religious literature, they are nevertheless an invaluable source for the study of religious practices and priestly institution during the later Vedic period.

At the end of the Brahmanas there appears a group of texts known as the *Aranyakas* or 'Forest Treatises'; so called because their teaching was delivered in the solitude of the forest. Attached to these are further philosophical treatises, the *Upanishads*. The division between the two is not a sharp one, since some of the oldest Upanishads are incorporated into the Aranyaka texts. Although the themes of the Aranyakas are by no means consistent, they do tend to subordinate the performance of ritual to the deeper meaning or spiritual significance that lies behind it. In this respect the Aranyakas form a bridge between the Brahmanas with their emphasis upon *brahman* as a magical force to be manipulated and controlled, and the Upanishads with their idea of *brahman* as the life-force of the universe with which the real self of the individual is identified. The association between ritual and meditation as it occurs in the Aranyakas may indicate that asceticism was a natural growth or development within Brahmanism and not a reaction to it. The Sanskrit word *tapas*, which means literally 'heat' or 'fervour', occurs in some of the later hymns of the *Rig Veda* as a creative principle. The term soon came to be applied to the austerities practised by certain individuals who may have been stimulated in the first instance by the desire to acquire abnormal or miraculous powers. Soon, however, asceticism became part of the discipline, referred to in the Upanishads, by which the true nature of self could be discovered. Reference is made to an ancient order of ascetics in one of the Vedic hymns (R.V. x, 136), where it is stated that the *Munis* or 'Silent Ones', 'girded with the wind, wear garments soiled with yellow hue. They, following the wind's swift course, go where the gods have gone.' (R.V. x, 136, 2). The hymn goes on to describe how the *Muni*, during his period of austerities, soars above the desires and limitations of the earthly life and attains fellowship with the gods of the air.

The practice of asceticism found a place in the scheme which gradually evolved whereby life was divided into four stages or *ashramas;* The first stage was that of student, when the boy attached himself to a teacher for instruction in discipline and the Vedas; the second was the life of a householder when, after completing his studies, the young man married, raised a family and performed the prescribed rituals; this was followed by the life of retirement when as an older man he withdrew into the forest for meditation, and last of all was the life of renunciation when through asceticism and meditation the man devoted himself completely to the search for self-knowledge.

The Upanishads point to the final goal to be achieved by those willing to follow the prescribed disciplines. The word Upanishad seems to denote the idea of 'sitting down near' [*upa* (near) *ni* (down) and *sad* (to sit)] and may refer to the method by which spiritual truths were communicated, *i.e.*, by a teacher or *guru* whose pupils gathered around him to receive instruction. The texts themselves indicate that the content of this teaching was a closely guarded secret. Of the vast number of Upanishads that have come down to us, almost two hundred, the oldest or classical Upanishads number about a dozen. These are thought to have been composed in the period between the eighth and sixth centuries B.C.

When we speak of the philosophy of the Upanishads it must not be thought that the texts set out one clearly defined system; rather, they give a variety of answers to central metaphysical problems. They are concerned with the nature of man and his relationship to the phenomenal world and the Reality that lies behind it; a few recurring themes stand out most prominently.

Most Upanishads express the conviction that behind the world of multiplicity and change there is a principle that remains constant; a Reality that is beyond all vicissitudes and change. This principle is most frequently referred to as *Brahman*, a word which seems originally to have meant 'sacred knowledge' or 'utterance'. By the time of the Brahmanas it had acquired the meaning of 'mysterious power'. In the Upanishads Brahman has become the essence of everything; the All-encompassing Absolute from which everything proceeds. The *Chandogya Upanishad* (III, 14) defines Brahman as that which emits, sustains and reabsorbes the world; and by a series of vivid metaphors the *Mundaka Upanishad* shows that the material universe rises from the eternal Brahman which itself remains ever complete and undiminished (I, 1.7).

In other sections of the Upanishads Brahman is represented as the Impersonal Absolute which can neither be defined nor attributed with personality since this would imply limitations. It is simply 'It' or 'That', and because this ultimate Reality is beyond the capacity of the human mind it can be described only in negative terms.

The earliest Upanishads do not teach that the phenomenal world is unreal, since it is shown to be an aspect of manifestation of the eternal Brahman; but they do suggest that the world can be deceptive. The man who sees only the externals—the world of multiplicity and change—misses the Reality that lies behind it. 'Just as those who do not know the field walk again and again over the hidden treasure of gold and do not find it, even so all creatures here go day after day into the Brahma-world and yet do not find it for they are carried away by untruth.'[1] There is at the same time, the conviction that untruth can be banished by right knowledge. The *Brihad-aranyaka Upanishad* contains the ancient prayer; 'From the unreal lead me to the real, from the darkness lead me to the light, from death lead me to immortality' (I, 3, 28).

When man understands his true nature, then everything else is seen in its correct perspective. So, it is often pointed out that the great achievement of the Upanishads is the so called Brahman/Atman equation. The 'self-existent Brahman', the one Reality, is also called Atman. The term seems to be derived from *an*, 'to breathe', and it is frequently used to denote the real self of the individual, which is distinguished not only from the physical body but from the inner feelings or emotions and the mind as well. In certain passages the Upanishads teach that the Atman in man is identical with the Atman in the universe; that the self of the individual is of the same nature as Brahman, the ideal principle of the universe. The same truth is expressed in the formula *tat tvam asi* (That art thou), which summarizes briefly what these ancient philosophers regarded as the climax of the spiritual quest. But what actually results when the goal is achieved is expressed in different ways. One passage from the *Brihad-aranyaka Upanishad* seems to suggest that liberation results in the total subjugation of the individuality within the All: 'Having arisen out of these elements (the self) vanishes again in them. When he has departed there is no more (separate or particular) consciousness.' (*Brh. Up.* IV, 5). In contrast, the *Taittiriya Upanishad* describes the spiritual goal as a state of bliss or joy (*ananda*) in which the self, freed from all limitations, moves freely throughout the universe (III, 10, 5).

Whatever descriptions are used by the different sages to express the idea of *moksha* or liberation, the fact remains that it was thought to be comparatively rare. The vast majority of people were forced to endure the troubles and sufferings of earthly existence not merely for the duration of a single life span but for a whole succession of future lives. It is in the Upanishads, then, that we first meet two doctrines that were destined to occupy a central place in the religious thought of India; the belief in *samsara* or the constant stream of births and deaths, and the law of *karma* which determined the status of the individual in each new life. In the priestly texts *karma* appears as a technical term for a religious rite; it was believed that each ritual act produced automatically the result or 'fruit' for which it was intended. The Upanishads add a further dimension to the notion by extending its operation to cover all deeds and actions and by relating it directly to the concept of *samsara*. The status of the individual at each new birth, then, is the direct result of his conduct in former lives.

'Those whose conduct here has been good will quickly attain a good birth (literally womb), the birth of a Brahman, the birth of a Kshatriya, the birth of a Vaishya. But those whose conduct here has been evil, will quickly attain an evil birth, the birth of a dog, the birth of a hog or the birth of a Candala' (*Ch. Up.* v, 10, 7). By suggesting that a person's present position on a scale that begins with the highest form of human life and descends to the lowest form of animal existence is due to his conduct in past lives, the Upanishads provide an incentive for right living. Their main concern, however, is not to ensure that the individual attains to the highest form of birth; but, rather, that he ceases to be involved in the whole process which leads to reincarnation.

It should be pointed out, finally, that there are important Upanishads in which the Ultimate Reality is seen in personal terms, and in which the whole idea of impersonal Brahman is rejected. The greatest of these is the theistic *Shvetashvatara Upanishad*, which served as one of the main sources of the later doctrine of *bhakti*, or loving devotion.

WW

Footnote

[1] *Chand. Up.* VIII. 3. 2. Translations from the Upanishads taken from S. Radhakrishnan, *The Principal Upaniṣads*.

Bibliography

P. Deussen, *The Philosophy of the Upanishads*, Edinburgh, 1919.
M. Hiriyanna, *Outlines of Indian Philosophy*, London, 1967.
R. E. Hume, *The Thirteen Principal Upanishads*, Oxford, 1934.
S. Radhakrishnan, *The Principal Upaniṣads*, London, 1953.

6

THE EARLIEST SECTS

SO FAR, we have been concerned almost exclusively with what might be called the main stream of religious development in ancient India; that is, the beliefs and practices associated mainly with the priestly class that are embodied in the earliest written texts-the *Vedas*, *Brahmanas* and *Upanishads*. The great 'heresies', Buddhism and Jainism, which arose in the sixth century B.C. and reacted against some of the main principles of Brahmanism—notably, the sacrificial cult and the caste system, indicate that there were other currents of religious thought quite separate and distinct from the main tradition. We have observed, too, that as the Aryan tribes penetrated further into the Indian sub-continent they came into contact with different local faiths and cults which resulted in a process of mutual influence. The increasing appeal of Buddhism and Jainism to the ruling classes partly explains why the brahmins sought to bring more of the aboriginal cults under their sphere of influence by finding a place within their scheme for popular religious movements. Brahmanism, then, provided an elastic framework into which almost any cult and social class could be fitted; and out of this fusion the great gods and goddesses of Hinduism were born. The startling results of this interaction which took place gradually over a period of many years became apparent when Brahmanism again found favour with the ruling classes from about the beginning of the Sunga period i.e. from about 185 B.C. The old Vedic gods and even the ritual itself had become overshadowed by a powerful group of new deities, of much more concrete individuality than the gods of the Rig-Vedic pantheon, who were worshipped by their followers with passion and devotion. Two gods in particular stand out most prominently. These are Vishnu and Shiva who were later associated with the more colourless Brahma to form the famous Hindu triad (*Trimurti*) in which Brahma appears as creator;

Vishnu as preserver; and Shiva as destroyer. As the worship of Vishnu and Shiva spread throughout all India the popular gods of local cults came to be regarded as aspects or manifestations of one or the other. This tendency which led eventually to the proliferation of a variety of religous and social groups (designated by the terms Vaishnavism and Shaivism) is usually referred to as sectarian Hinduism. Under the directing genius of the priestly class some of the well established principles of Brahmanism (the idea of caste, the *atman* doctrine, and the belief in *karma* and *samsara*) became intertwined with the worship of the numerous manifestations of Vishnu and Shiva to form a loose connecting link between the various sects. This complex cultural pluralism that came to be denoted by the title Hinduism (a term coined originally by the Muslim Arabs of the eighth century) defies all attempts to be fitted into clearly defined categories.

Although it is impossible to trace the origins of the earliest cults with which Vishnu and Shiva came to be associated it is clear that by the fourth century B.C. devotional cults were already well established. The worship of the god Vasudeva (later associated with Krishna and eventually identified with Vishnu) is attested to by Heliodorus, the Greek ambassador to King Kasiputra Bhagabhadra. Heliodorus was so impressed by the worship of Vasudeva that he erected a column in the god's honour at Besnagar in central India. In the inscription he declares himself to be a devotee of Vasudeva. Krishna was an influential deity in his own right long before he became the most important '*avatar*' or manifestation of Vishnu. When the Greeks invaded north India in the fourth century B.C. they identified a god worshipped in that region (generally assumed to be Krishna) with their own Herakles. This cult is also noted along with that of Shiva by Megasthenes who visited India in about 300 B.C. as commissioner of Seleucus Nicator. Megasthenes reported that Dionysos (Shiva) was worshipped in the hills, while the worship of Herakles (Krishna) prevailed in the Ganges valley.[1]

In addition to these influential religious movements which attracted the attention of the foreign diplomats there were hundreds of other cults connected with isolated villages and tribes about which nothing is known. Yet, all of them, both great and small came under the impact of Brahmanism. Regional gods were either renamed (thus Vasudeva was called Vishnu) or, as in the case of Krishna, regarded as manifestations of a brahmanized god. Important goddesses like Parvati, Kali and Durga became the consorts of Shiva while those less important became the forms of manifestation of these goddesses. Shiva became lord of demons and spirits and so encompassed the whole range of primitive tribal and village worship. New scriptures were composed to provide a sort of theological apologia and local rituals were brought into line with Brahmin standards. So, the whole process of assimilation and syncretism multiplied and accelerated.

WW

Footnote

[1] This is, however, disputed territory. A case can be made out for Megathenes' 'Herakles' having been Indra rather than Krishna; the identification of 'Dionysos' as Shiva is also questionable.

Bibliography

See under units 6, 15 and 16.

7

THE EPICS

THE TWO GREAT epics of India, the *Ramayana*, 'The Story of Rama' and the *Mahabharata*, the 'Great Story of the War of the Bharatas' have exercised a profound and lasting influence upon the religious life of India. It is largely from the epics that we learn of the developments in Indian religion outlined briefly in the two preceding sections. They contain so much of the essence of Hinduism that Swami Vivekananda described them as 'the cherished heritage of the whole Hindu world' and 'the basis of its thought and its moral and ethical ideas'[1]

The sacred literature of Hinduism falls roughly into two categories (a distinction made by the brahmins). The first is *shruti* which means literally 'hearing' and denotes that which has been revealed directly by God. This category comprises the sacred Veda in its threefold aspect—the hymns and chants, the sacrificial commentaries (*Brahmanas*), and the 'forest treatises' (*Aranyakas*) which merge into the *Upanishads*. The epics along with the later *Puranas* and philosophical and legal writings are designated by the term *smriti* or 'memory' and are revelations only in a secondary or limited sense. Although technically inferior to the Veda, whose saving knowledge is restricted to members of the highest castes, the epics reflect popular religion and declare the message that God's love is available to all men irrespective of caste differences.

The heroic exploits of Rama and the stories contained in the Mahabharata became familiar to the population at large, even the most illiterate, through recitations given by professional storytellers; and poets, dramatists and artists of succeeding generations drew their inspiration from these tales of India's national heroes.

It is impossible to date the epics precisely since in their present form they have been carefully edited and worked over by the brahmins, a process that probably occurred between

200 B.C. and A.D. 200. Unlike the Mahabharata, which evolved over several centuries at the hands of several sages, the original form of the Ramayana is attributed to the poet Valmiki and may have been composed as early as the fourth century B.C. The poem is written in about 24,000 Sanskrit couplets and deals with the adventures of Rama, in which the hero, after being dispossessed of his right to the throne, retired into exile and performed many daring feats; the most outstanding was the rescue of his wife Sita from the clutches of the demon Ravana. The poem is not just a fascinating tale; it is a moral discourse as well, setting out the ideal qualities of human life. Rama is the embodiment of all virtues. He is truthful, brave and honourable and prefers to suffer the loss of his kingdom rather than renounce his honour. Sita, too, expresses the ideals of Indian womanhood by her faithfulness and devotion.

In two sections of the Ramayana which are generally acknowledged to be of later composition than the rest, Rama is represented as an *avatar* (incarnation) of Vishnu.

The Mahabharata is a very much longer work (about four times the length of the Ramayana) and takes as its main theme the fortunes of the descendants of King Bharata. It describes the family feud that arose between the sons of Dhritarashtra, called the Kurus, and the sons of Pandu, the Pandavas. When Pandu died his brother Dhritarashtra inherited the throne and brought up Pandu's five sons along with his own hundred sons. The Kurus, jealous of the heroism and virtue of their cousins conspired to bring about their deaths but the Pandavas learned of the plot and retired to the forest where they lived disguised as brahmins. Arjuna the third son of Pandu and a skilled bowman, won the hand of the princess Draupadi at an archery contest and she eventually became the common wife of the five brothers. In the course of time the kingdom was divided between the two groups of cousins and although the Pandavas inherited only the most desolate parts, they laboured hard and long to make their lands rich and fruitful. Once more, their success aroused the anger and jealousy of the Kurus who plotted to take the kingdom for themselves by enticing Yudhishthira, the eldest of the Pandu brothers, into a game of dice with the condition that the loser must spend twelve years in exile, and thereafter live unrecognized in a city for one year. If his identity were discovered during that time the period of exile would begin all over again. Yudhishthira lost the game and set out with his four brothers and Draupadi to fulfil the obligation. With the assistance of Dharma they successfully passed the thirteenth year unrecognized and returned to reclaim their kingdom. When the Kurus contemptuously refused to return even one village to each of the five brothers they prepared to fight, and after eighteen days of terrible conflict Yudhishthira became the undisputed ruler of the entire land. Eventually, the brothers, along with their wife Draupadi, retired to the Himalayas where they practised severe austerities before setting out on the great journey to the heavenly abode.

It will be obvious to the reader that a work of such magnitude contains many subsidiary themes in addition to the main story. These digressions take the form of legends, fables and discussions of moral, political and religious principles so that, viewed as a whole, the Mahabharata forms a kind of encyclopaedia of Indian culture.

One small section of the poem known as the *Bhagavad Gita*, 'The Song of the Lord' contains so many elements of Hindu thought, and has become so influential in its own right that it will be discussed separately in the following section.

WW

Footnote

[1] *The Complete Works of Vivekananda*, vol. IV, p. 97.

Bibliography

G. J. Held, *The Mahabharata*, Amsterdam, 1935.
E. W. Hopkins, *Epic Mythology*, Strassbourg, 1915.

8

THE BHAGAVAD GITA

THE *Bhagavad Gita* ('The Song of the Adorable One'), which forms a section of the sixth book of the *Mahabharata*, is the most popular of all Indian sacred writings. It probably reached its final form between the second century B.C. and the second century A.D. It is indebted to the Upanishads, it may contain elements of Buddhism, and it alludes to certain ideas which later became crystallized within the six orthodox schools. An attempt is made to draw these threads together and to mould them into a comprehensive synthesis.

The poem takes the form of a dialogue between the prince Arjuna and his charioteer, the god Krishna, whose true nature as an *avatar* of Vishnu gradually becomes apparent. The scene is set on the battlefield of Kuru, where the forces of the five sons of Pandu (one of whom is Arjuna) are preparing to do battle with their cousins, the sons of Dhritarashtra. Arjuna's nerve suddenly fails him; he is appalled by the fact that he is preparing to slay his kinsmen. He asks Krishna's advice, and is told that it is his duty to fight (he is a *kshatriya*), but the discussion soon moves on to topics that have no direct bearing on this issue. The author of the *Gita* takes up and develops many themes that have already appeared in the Upanishads, and adds to these the notion of *bhakti* (loving devotion)—the adoration of God as a means of salvation.

When the Upanishads consider the one Reality which lies behind the phenomenal world they alternate between a view of Reality as the transcendent 'That' which defies description, and a view which sees Reality as an immanent and omnipresent Lord. Both these attitudes are represented in the *Gita* (VII, 3–5). The Supreme has a twofold nature: a lower (*apara*) which encompasses and controls the world of change, and a higher (*para*) which is the life force of all creation but which remains completely transcendent and unaffected by the changing world order (IX, 9). This double position is enforced by the position of Krishna, who is both immanent as an *avatar*, and transcendent as the one Reality. The foolish and ignorant see only the human form and fail to realize the Reality that is hidden behind it (IX, 11). The wise see the Supreme in Krishna, and follow the way of *bhakti*, which brings about a deliverance from the round of rebirth (XVIII, 65).

According to the *Gita*, the truly spiritual man is characterized by tranquillity and balance. He has transcended the realm of matter (*prakriti*) with all its apparent contradictions, and is no longer tossed about by his passions and emotions. The soul (*purusha*, *atman*) resembles matter only in so far as both are indestructible, but for the purposes of the *Gita's* argument it is held captive by matter, passing through endless rebirths. However, it is unaffected by what happens to matter: even when the body is slain, the soul is untouched (II, 19–25).

This tranquillity in the midst of change is, however, not to be gained by withdrawing from the world, but by living in a spirit of non-attachment within the world. This the *Gita* calls *karma-yoga*, and also *nishkama karma* (desireless action). Although *karma* normally leads to retribution, where there is no desire there is no retribution, and hence all actions should be undertaken free from desire for reward or result. Since desire binds man to matter, it is this selfish motivation which should be renounced by the wise man. However, such renunciation is not easy: the senses are always liable to attract man back into their grip. So on the one hand the *Gita* recommends the practice of technical *yoga* (VI, 10 ff.), culminating in the centring of the mind on the Lord (VI, 14). Concentration on Ishvara is known in all forms of Yoga, but in the *Gita* concentration passes over into loving devotion, through which salvation may be obtained.

Mention has already been made of Krishna as an *avatar* of Vishnu. In the *Gita* we find the normative statement of the *avatar* doctrine: whenever the law of righteousness declines, then the Lord generates himself on earth in one or another form. It is of the essence of the doctrine that *avatars* may occur just as often as they are needed, in succeeding *kalpas* (ages of the world) (IV, 7–7).

The *Gita* culminates in a great theophany, in which Krishna, at Arjuna's request, reveals his true nature to him. Arjuna is unable to see Krishna's nature with normal vision, and is given a 'celestial eye', with which he then beholds the entire universe converging in the body of the Supreme Lord. Krishna is also revealed as Lord of Time, with many mouths, into which the warriors of the original battle-field (which now seems rather remote) rush, to be ground to powder. 'Time am I,' says Krishna, 'wreaker of the world's destruction' (XI, 32). At this point Arjuna ceases to regard Krishna as his charioteer and comrade: he bows down and does worship, and prays that Krishna will return to his more familiar form. Krishna does so, reminding Arjuna that the sacrificial practices of the Vedas, the asceticism of the *munis*, the giving of alms, are all inadequate for the obtaining of such a vision: only by *bhakti* can Krishna be seen in such a form (IX, 154). And the dialogue resumes.

The worship of Krishna in the *Gita* is very much a matter of intention: the mode of worship is less important than the attitude of mind in which it is made. The *Gita* is frequently critical of Brahmanical sacrificial practice as an end in itself, but stresses that any form of sacrifice is acceptable to Krishna. Even worshippers of other gods than Krishna, who do not know Krishna, are accepted by him if their intention is pure (IX, 23). Although the perspective here is limited to known forms of religion, the Hindu may interpret this as applying to other world religions, and from it deduce a form of 'anonymous Hinduism'.

The vast range of teaching in the *Gita* cannot easily be summed up, but Krishna's words: 'Turn to me, thine only refuge, for I will deliver thee from all evils; have no care'—perhaps represent the goal of its teachings. To this we may add the testimony of Shankara:

> When doubts haunt me, when disappointment stares me in the face and when I see not one ray of light on the horizon, I turn to the *Gita*, and find a verse to comfort me, and I immediately begin to smile in the midst of overwhelming sorrow . . .

To Gandhi the *Gita* was his 'infallible guide of conduct', and his disciple Vinoba Bhave said:

> I live and move in the atmosphere of the *Gita*. The *Gita* is my life's breath . . . I swim in the sea of the *Gita* when I speak of it; but when I am alone, I dive to the depths of this ocean of nectar and there rest at ease.

WW/EJS

Bibliography

The *Gita* has been translated many times. The following are perhaps the most easily accessible versions.

F. Edgerton, *The Bhagavad Gita*, 2 vols., Harvard, 1952.

S. Radhakrishnan, *The Bhagavad Gita*, London, 1948.

R. C. Zaehner, *The Hindu Scriptures*, London, 1966.

R. C. Zaehner, *The Bhagavad Gita*, Oxford, 1969.

9

BHAKTI

THE *Bhagavad Gita*, as we have seen, contains a wide range of teaching and in fact synthesizes a variety of earlier attitudes and doctrines. But its main contribution to the history of religion in India is seen in two closely-linked doctrines, the doctrine of *nishkama karma* (desireless action) and the doctrine of *bhakti* (loving devotion). The second of these requires close attention. It is a common misapprehension in the West that Hindu teachings are to be judged by the extent to which they conform to the monistic ideal of *Advaita Vedanta*. Most living Hinduism, however, is characterized by *bhakti*, devotion to a personal deity.

The *Gita* is not the manifesto of the founder of a new religion. We do not know what were the origins of *bhakti* piety, but they are not to be found in the *Gita*, which clarifies and makes a normative statement of what was already an ancient doctrine. Perhaps *bhakti* was the normal reaction to the over-intellectualization and over-subtlety of some of the *Upanishads*—a form of theistic protest. In others of the *Upanishads* the principle of devotion is clearly stated. This is particularly true of the *Svetasvatara Upanishad*, which ends with the assurance that 'To the great-souled man who loyally and greatly loves his God, who loves his spiritual master even as his God, the matter of this discourse will shine with clearest light . . .' (VI, 23).

Bhakti in religion is the worship and devotion shown to a *bhagavan* (Lord: Krishna in the *Gita* is called *Shri Bhagavan*), but it is also the attitude which the devotee shows to a spiritual master, or *guru*, as the personal and immediate manifestation of the deity. In the *Gita* Krishna represents both Lord and *guru*. To follow the *bhakti marga* is to relegate works and even knowledge to a secondary place, and to accept salvation, *moksha*, from God as an act of free and undeserved grace. It is also to make the quest for salvation less of a profession in itself: in *bhakti* devotion one can continue to live in the world, while ceasing to be of the world, i.e. motivated by desire. Instead the sole motive should be the love of God, which alone leads to complete fulfilment and ultimately to the beatific vision. Intention is all-important: even those who worship other gods (than Krishna) with *bhakti* really worship Krishna (IX, 23); Krishna is recipient and Lord of all acts of sacrifice (IX, 24), whatever may be the station in life of the one who makes the offering (IX, 30). *Bhakti* is therefore egalitarian as other Hindu ways of salvation are not: '. . . whosoever makes Me his haven, base-born though he may be, yes, women too, and artisans, even serfs,—theirs it is to tread the highest Way' (IX, 32).

In the subsequent history of the *bhakti* movements, this tendency is well marked. *Bhakti* literature is to a large extent written in the vernacular languages, particularly Marathi, Hindi, Bengali and Tamil, and is of course predominantly devotional in its emphasis. It is thus available to all. There are what might be called *bhakti* philosophies, notably those of Ramanuja (Vaishnava) and the *Shaiva Siddhanta*, but the strength of the movements lies in their popular appeal.

Vaishnava *bhakti* centres in many cases on the figure of Krishna, partly as depicted in the *Bhagavad Gita*, but also as he appears in the *Bhagavata Purana*; Rama of the *Ramayana* is another popular *bhagavan*. In the Vaishnava schools, *bhakti* is a highly emotionally charged attitude; often there may be an allegorical eroticism involved, particularly when inspiration is drawn from the *Bhagavata Purana*. In this book the attitude of man to God is described as being that of the utter love and adoration of Krishna by the *gopis* (herdmaidens) of Vrindaban. Among Vaishnava *bhakti* poets of the mediaeval period may be mentioned Kabir, Tulsidas, Tukaram and Chaitanya, while modern representatives of this tradition include Ramakrishna and Rabindranath Tagore.

Shaiva *bhakti* takes its origins from the theistic *Svetasvatara Upanishad*, and the line then goes through the Shaiva *Agamas* to the Tamil devotional poets of the eighth and subsequent centuries, the best known of whom is Manikka Vachakar. In the literature of Shaivism, *bhakti* appears in general to have a stricter and more ascetic character than corresponding Vaishnava sources; in Shaivism there is less erotic imagery, due to the fact of the early independence of the Tantric sects, in which Shaiva eroticism is most fully developed.

To summarise *bhakti* theology is out of the question in this context, but the following points may be mentioned. (i) To the *bhakta*, God and the soul are separate entities, and remain so, even when a union between them has been brought about. Love demands separation—a sentiment expressed by Tukaram: 'Water cannot taste itself, nor trees taste their own fruit: the worshipper must be separate, thus alone pleasure arises from distinction.' (ii) God is completely gracious, desiring nothing but the wellbeing of man: 'My unique love, Thy grace overflowed Thine heart in order that I may partake of it, springing from within me' (Ramalinga Swami). (iii) By contrast, man is sinful and imperfect: 'I am unreal! My heart is unreal! My devotion is unreal! Sinner as I am, I can attain Thee if I but cry for Thee! O Sweet Lord! . . . Be gracious, that I may reach Thee!' (Manikka Vachakar). Sin in this sense is to be understood as the craving for sensual pleasures. (iv) Man is capable of showing devotion to God, and often does so by showing devotion to his *guru:* 'The *guru* is the skilful helmsman, Divine Grace the favourable wind; if with such means man does not strive to cross the ocean of life and death, he is indeed lost' (Chaitanya). (v) Of the many means of showing *bhakti* directly to God, the most widely recommended is the practice of *nama japa*, the constant repetition of the Divine Name. The devotee may also repeat his own personal *mantra*, a word or phrase communicated to him by the *guru*. The Divine Name, however, has the highest power. It is both means and end, it communicates ultimate salvation, it is superior to pilgrimages and other forms of worship, and it may be done at any time and in any place: 'Constant chanting of *Krishnanama* roots out all the evil influences of lust, anger, greed, infatuation and pride' (Chaitanya). The chanting of 'Hare Krishna, Hare Rama' in Western quasi-Hindu movements is a practice derived directly from the Chaitanya sect of *bhakti* devotion.

EJS

Bibliography

A. J. Appasamy, (Ed.), *Temple Bells: Readings from Hindu Religious Literature*, Calcutta, 1930.
G. A. Grierson, 'Bhakti-Marga,' in *E.R.E. II*, 1919, pp. 539–551.
N. Söderblom, *The Living God*, London, 1933.
H. H. Wilson, *Sketch of the Religious Sects of the Hindus*, London, 1861.
R. C. Zaehner, *Hinduism*, Oxford, 1966², pp. 125–146.

10

THE DOCTRINE OF AVATARS

AN *avatar* is literally a 'down coming' or a 'manifestation' of the god in a particular form, sometimes human, sometimes semi-human or even animal. Although there are avatars of various gods (Sita, for example, is said in some texts to be an avatar of the goddess of the earth) the doctrine is particularly associated with Vishnu. A theological exposition of the avatar doctrine occurs in the Bhagavad Gita where Vishnu, in the form of Krishna, explains the reason for his descent:

For protection of the virtuous
For destruction of the wicked
For the establishment of Right (*dharma*)
Age after age I come into being. (IV, 7–8)

Thus it is believed that there are many avatars or incarnations of God, for he manifests himself in the various ages of the world, whenever wickedness threatens to overthrow righteousness.

The doctrine of avatars was systematized and the number fixed at ten, although many more are listed in later literature and in modern Hinduism it is common to call any great person (e.g. Ramakrishna) an avatar. The first six of the traditional avatars require only a brief mention. When the earth was overwhelmed by a universal flood Vishnu appeared as a gigantic fish (*Matsya*) to warn Manu (the Indian Primeval man) of the immanent danger. When the flood actually came then Vishnu, in the form of the fish, came to Manu and towed his boat to the safety of the northern mountain. On the occasion of another flood Vishnu appeared as a tortoise (*Kurma*) to churn up the waters and thereby recover such treasures as the water of life and Lakshmi that lay submerged. As the boar (*Varaha*) Vishnu raised up the earth from the primeval waters and restored it to its rightful place. In his fourth and fifth appearances as the lionman (*Nara-simha*) and the dwarf (*Vamana*) respectively, the Supreme God thwarted the malevolent intentions of two powerful demons and as Rama with the axe (*Parashu-Rama*) he assumed human form as the son of a brahmin to destroy the kshatriyas when the world was in danger of being completely dominated by them.

The seventh and eighth avatars, Rama-chandra, the hero of the Ramayana, and Krishna whose exploits are recorded in the Mahabharata and the later Puranas, need to be examined in more detail. We will begin with Rama since he is said to have appeared first, although his deification is undoubtedly later than that of Krishna.

Rama was the favourite son and appointed heir of Dasharatha, king of Ayodhya. The king had previously made a promise to his second wife agreeing to grant her one wish. She requested that her own son be named as successor and that Rama be banished for a period of fourteen years. Rama refused to allow his father to break the vow but finally agreed on a compromise which permitted his step-brother to rule during his absence. Accompanied by Sita, his devoted wife, and by his brother Lakshmana Rama retreated to the forest where he waged a successful war on the demons. Ravana, master of the demon pack, took his revenge by carrying off Sita to his kingdom in Ceylon. When Rama learned of her fate he enlisted the support of Hanuman, the monkey king. Hanuman's army constructed a bridge of rocks across the straits and beseiged the capital of Ravana. After a series of skirmishes Rama defeated the demon king in single combat. Sita then proved her faithfulness to Rama in an ordeal by fire and they returned reunited to Ayodhya where Rama, his exile now ended, began his reign of ten thousand years after which he returned, amid great ceremony, to the abode of Vishnu.

It is possible that the story of the downfall of Ravana contains a kernel of historic truth since Ceylon was colonized by Indians of Aryan speech; but the task is usually attributed to Vijaya and not to Rama. With the deification of this popular epic hero it is not only Rama who is brought into an association with Vishnu; the monkey-faced Hanuman, so popular as to have his own cult, is also drawn into the Vaishnavite fold by being presented as the helper and companion of Vishnu 'in the flesh'. At this stage Rama is no more than a great heroic figure and an avatar of Vishnu. It was only later that he became an object of adoration in his own right; so much so, that two later Upanishads exalt him as the Supreme God and the author of the Hindi Ramayana adores him as the world's redeemer.

Even more important is the eighth avatar, the god Krishna, who is perhaps the oldest avatar and to many Vaishnavites the only full incarnation of Vishnu. In spite of being so prominent a figure in the Hindu pantheon his origins are shrouded in mystery. The word Krishna, which means 'black' or 'dark', occurs in the *Rig Veda* but not as the name of a god. The *Chandogya Upanishad* mentions a certain Krishna, the son of Devaki who was instructed by the sage Ghora, and by the fourth century B.C. Krishna had become the central figure of a widespread and influential cult. The main ingredients of the Krishna legend can be pieced together from the *Mahabharata* and the later *Puranas*.

Krishna was said to be the son of Vasudeva and Devaki of the Yadava tribe and the nephew of the tyrannical king Kamsa whose death at the hands of the eighth son of Vasudeva and Devaki had been predicted. To prevent this Kamsa slew all his nephews at birth but Krishna and his elder brother were saved and brought up as the sons of the cowherd Nanda. The brothers spent their youth slaying demons in the forest and enjoying amorous adventures with the daughters of the cowherds. Krishna eventually turned against Kamsa and after slaying him, took over the kingdom. After a further period of wanderings in which he slew many demons and assisted the Pandavas to regain their kingdom (the main theme of the Mahabharata) Krishna was faced with a terrible feud amongst his own followers during which he was slain by an arrow when a hunter mistook him for a deer. Many different and independent strands are all combined in the Krishna story. The adventures of the heroic Krishna are probably the oldest and may preserve elements of historic tradition.

The ninth avatar is said to be the Buddha and was included so that even heretical elements could be absorbed into Vaishnavism. The tenth and last avatar is Kalkin who is yet to make his appearance. The figure of Kalkin, which has never assumed an important place in Hinduism, bears traces of later Buddhism and may even contain elements of Zoroastrian and Christian eschatology.

The avatars are revelations of a personal God who cares for man. The birth, suffering and death each experienced shows the humanity, the life in the flesh, of these descents of deity. The purpose of their descent is to renew the true order or harmony of the universe when this is disturbed in the various ages. The avatars also stand as models of heroism and nobility (especially

Rama) which inspire the faithful, and as symbols of the passionate love relationship between man and God (especially Krishna in the later texts such as the *Vishnu* and *Bhagavata Puranas*). Christian influence upon this doctrine is extremely unlikely before the nineteenth century. Although the doctrine has always provided a focal point for the devotion of countless Hindus it has not been accepted by all, thus Shankara paid little attention to it, and it is denied by the Arya Samaj on the grounds that it did not appear in the Vedas.

WW/JRH

Bibliography

J. E. Carpenter, *Theism in Medieval India*, London, 1926.
J. Gonda, *Aspects of Early Viṣṇuism*, Utrecht, 1954.
V. Ions, *Indian Mythology*, London, 1967.
E. G. Parrinder, *Avatar and Incarnation*, London, 1970.

II

INTRODUCTION TO THE MIDDLE PERIOD

IT SEEMS BETTER to speak of the Middle Period in the development of Hinduism, because to call it Medieval would be misleading to Western readers. Some of the great systems of philosophy, as well as devotional movements, have their roots well before the Christian era and so are not medieval in our sense. If the early period is to be regarded as classical, with the Indus Valley culture, the Vedas and Upanishads, and the great Epics, then the Middle Period extends nearly two thousand years, right down to modern times. The classical period used to be called Brahminism, and the strangely different popular religion was regarded as later and called Hinduism. But the discovery of the Indus Valley cultures has revealed probable pre-Brahminical origins for much of later Hinduism, and the tenacity and long unchanging character of Hinduism is now revealed.

The six orthodox schools of philosophy were formulated in the Middle Period from their tentative beginnings, though the greatest philosophers, Shankara, Ramanuja and Madhva, come later in our own Middle Ages. Unorthodox systems, like Jainism and Buddhism, were long pre-Christian though they are beyond our present scope. The great religious movements of Vaishnavism, Shaivism and Shaktism may well go back to prehistory, but now they re-emerge and continue to hold great sway in India today. Yoga and Tantra may be equally ancient and are still potent.

The importance of the Middle Period is that it shows the development of philosophies ranging from non-theism to monism and dualism. Even more importantly this long span of time witnessed the virtual disappearance of nearly all the Vedic gods and developed the very different and passionate cults of Krishna, Rama, Shiva and Kali. EGP

12

ORTHODOX PHILOSOPHY (I)

GENERAL BELIEFS AND MINOR SCHOOLS

In the development of Hindu philosophy after the Vedas (including the Upanishads) distinctions were made between Orthodox and Unorthodox schools. The former were *astika* ('it is'), accepting the Vedas and their authority, while the latter were *nastika* ('it is not'), denying the authority of the Vedas for the validity of their own systems. Even the Unorthodox however, except the Charvakas, held certain basic beliefs in common with the Orthodox, and the latter were not all theistic.

Belief in *karma* and transmigration (*samsara*) is unquestioned, it is a fact not to be argued; actions bear fruit and if this is not exhausted in the present life it will be carried over into the future. *Karma* explains the inequalities of life and it runs through birth, death and rebirth. But all the systems agree that the round of existence can come to an end and liberation (*mukti*, *moksha*) can be attained. All the systems, except Buddhism, believe in a permanent self or soul (*atman*, *purusha*, or *jiva*), which is described in various ways but agreed to be eternal and untainted in its nature by the actions of the bodies to which it is attached in successive births. The final goal is complete peace, free from *karma* and its entail of constant birth and death. The general attitude of the philosophies is world-denying and pessimistic, with an emphasis upon the sorrows of life in a country with high disease and mortality rates, but they are optimistic in confidence in the indestructible soul and the final end of emancipation. These attitudes demand a high moral and ascetic standard, abstaining from pleasures and from taking life, and purifying body and mind in ways such as are illustrated by Yoga. This world-denying attitude was not confined to philosophers and holy men, but the great achievements of India in general culture, art, government, and so on, must have been inspired by world-affirming religions such as Vaishnavism and Shaivism, for which some philosophers provided intellectual justifications.

The Unorthodox, who reject the Vedas and build upon the authority of their own teachers, are principally Jains, Buddhists and Charvakas. The Jains, who claim great antiquity, reject belief in a God, creator or Brahman. They believe that passions produce a kind of *karmic* matter which clings to the soul (*jiva*), but by dispassion *karma* rapidly dissolves and when no more is created the soul goes to Nirvana at the top of the universe where it abides for ever with other liberated souls. Buddhism not only ignores God, though accepting lesser deities under the Buddhas, but denies that there is a permanent self (*an-atman*, *an-atta*). Nevertheless Buddhism holds to the theories of *karma* (Pali, *kamma*) and transmigration, and holds out the ultimate goal of Nirvana. The Charvakas, named after a legendary founder, were materialists and atheists whose works have not survived and their theories have to be reconstructed from criticisms of opponents. Their doctrines are also called *lokayata*, meaning that only this world (*loka*) exists. They did not believe in *karma*, a soul or a future life, though a sub-sect may have held that there was a soul which died with the body. Anyway this life is all and is only for enjoyment. Contemporary with these schools were also the Ajivikas, whose name may mean 'mode of life' (*jiva*), referring to their extreme asceticism. They were atheistic and deterministic, seeing the whole universe to be conditioned by an impersonal destiny. Their greatest leader was Gosala, but none of his or later writings have survived.

The Orthodox schools, or *Astika-mata*, of Hindu philosophy are six, known as the Six Systems or Viewpoints (*Sad-Darshana*). The six are: Nyaya, Vaisheshika, Mimamsa, Samkhya, Yoga, Vedanta. All these schools had basic Sutras, texts or aphorisms, in Sanskrit. These served as starting-points for their special doctrines, and all of them accepted the Vedas formally though they differed widely in their interpretations and often omitted central Vedic doctrines.

Nyaya means 'right', and so right reasoning or logic, being concerned with the validity of the arguments by which conclusions are reached. Its basic text is the *Nyaya Sutra*, attributed to Gotama or Gautama, of uncertain date between the second century B.C. and the second century A.D., though its doctrines may go back earlier and there has been a vast amount of literature down the centuries. Nyaya is an analytical philosophy concerned with the laws of thought, elaborating schemes of inference, and inventing many philosophical terms. Ignorance is regarded as the root of suffering and transmigration, and complete knowledge (*jñana*) brings liberation. There is little reference to God or a Lord in the *Nyaya Sutra*, where he is the highest of a class of beings. Later Nyaya became more theistic through Shaivite inspiration, and it is particularly favoured today in Bengal.

Vaisheshika is perhaps older than Nyaya, though the systems blended from the fifth century A.D. The name comes from 'particularity' (*vishesha*) and so it has been called Atomism because of its pluralistic concern with individuals and particulars. The *Vaisheshika Sutra* of Kanada dates from about the beginning of the Christian era. Vaisheshika considers that all things are composed of invisible and eternal atoms. There are many souls, different in status and condition, each of which suffers the consequences of *karma*. Even liberated souls have specific features. The *Vaisheshika Sutra* does not mention a God, but later on a Supreme Soul (*Param-atman*) was introduced to explain the combination of atoms and so he was a periodical creator.

Mimamsa, 'thought', examination or Exegesis, is the name generally used of the Purva Mimamsa, 'Earlier Exegesis' of the Vedic texts, in distinction from the more elaborate and religious Vedanta which is Uttara Mimamsa, 'Later Exegesis.' Vedanta differs from the Purva in many ways, and will be discussed later at greater length. Purva Mimamsa is not properly a system of philosophy but an interpretation of Vedic texts for sacrifices. The basic text is the *Mimamsa Sutra*, ascribed to Jaimini in the early Christian centuries. The Vedas are regarded as eternal, without reference to God, and they give injunctions for ritual and conduct. The Vedic gods retain their significance for ritual and the Vedic heaven, not Nirvana, is the goal of conduct. In later periods, however, the notion of ultimate release became influential. Jaimini did not so much deny God as ignore him, but some later Mimamsa teachers admitted the reality of the Supreme Being. Mimamsa held that all knowledge is true and the Vedas are eternally valid; both these theories influenced other schools, while Mimamsa itself was affected by later Nyaya.

EGP

Bibliography

A. L. Basham, *History and Doctrines of the Ajivikas*, London, 1951.
G. Bhattacharya, *Studies in Nyaya-Vaisesika Theism*, Calcutta, 1961.
M. Hiriyanna, *Essentials of Indian Philosophy*, London, 1951.
A. B. Keith, *Indian Logic and Atomism*, Oxford, 1921.
S. Radhakrishnan and C. A. Moore, *A Source Book in Indian Philosophy*, Princeton, 1967, (for selections from the texts of the chief schools and teachers).
N. Smart, *Doctrine and Argument in Indian Philosophy*, London, 1964.
N. V. Thadani, *The Mimamsa, Delhi*, 1952.

13

ORTHODOX PHILOSOPHY (II)

SAMKHYA-YOGA

SAMKHYA AND YOGA are closely connected from the first time of their appearance in literature. In the *Shvetashvatara Upanishad* (6, 13) Samkhya is virtually 'theory' or knowledge, and Yoga is 'practice'. The same meaning comes early in the *Bhagavad Gita* (2, 39 ff.), where Samkhya has revealed the true nature of the soul as eternal and Yoga is shown as the means of its realization. The *Gita* has a great deal of Samkhya terminology, though it is unlikely that there was a system of thought of that name when it was composed, and confusion is often made because Samkhya and Yoga in the *Gita* do not correspond exactly to the teachings in the texts of those two later systems. For example, the *Gita* is strongly theistic, whereas the Samkhya school was not at all so originally and Yoga only a little.

Samkhya means 'enumeration', perhaps because it enumerated categories of being though other schools did this also. Smart calls it Distinctionism. Zimmer argues that Samkhya and Yoga, like Buddhism and Jainism, came from the Indus Valley civilizations and like them were originally non-theistic.[1] The legendary founder of Samkhya was Kapila, from whom no works survive, but the oldest text is the *Samkhya-karika* of Ishvara-krishna, perhaps of the third century A.D.

Samkhya teaches two basic categories of Spirit and Matter, which are clearly distinct, Spirit being eternal and unchanging while Matter is also eternal but is in perpetual flux. Spirit is *purusha*, a word originally meaning 'person', and is not one since there are many Spirits, and so it is not like the single Brahman of the Upanishads which it ignores. Matter or Nature is *prakriti*, at first in a state of rest as the Unmanifest but evolving different elements under the impulse of *purusha*. In all there are twenty-five categories (*tattvas*) of which the first (or last) is Spirit, and the next comprise Matter and its evolutes. The *Samkhya-karika* (21 f.) says that the universe is formed from the union of Spirit and Matter, no doubt as male and female. Then from Matter issue the other categories. These are (after *purusha* and *prakriti*): Mind or the Great (*buddhi*, *mahat*), Ego, Reason (*manas*), the five senses (eye, ear, nose, tongue, skin), the five organs of action (speech, handling, walking, evacuation, reproduction), the five subtle elements which are the objects of the five senses, and the five gross elements (ether, air, fire, water, earth)[2].

There was no God in the Samkhya system, though Yoga added a twenty-sixth category in the Lord (see later). Yet Samkhya is not a purely naturalistic system since unconscious Nature depends upon the activation of conscious *purushas*, the informing and eternal souls, their union being compared to a lame man with good sight riding on the shoulders of a blind man with sure footing. *Purusha* is pure spirit and unchangeable, but in plurality, and there are countless selves both in bodily bondage and liberated. The true self is always free but liberation from the link with phenomena comes through knowledge, virtue and the practice of Yoga.

Prakriti is also composed of three Strands (*gunas*) which are present in all things in different proportions, thus accounting for the variety in the world. The *gunas*, like strands of a rope, are constituents or qualities. They are: *Sattva*, *Rajas* and *Tamas*; that is, Goodness or brightness, Passion or force, and Darkness or mass. These three play a considerable role in the *Gita*, where chapters 17–18 deal with them exhaustively. All the *gunas*, in the *Gita*, bind the embodied soul, though Goodness can help it towards final release by severing all worldly ties. Samkhya, like other Indian schools, held that the cosmos periodically dissolves and is re-formed, and the dissolution upsets the equilibrium of the *gunas*, which reappear in a new cycle. This process occurs without a divine creator, though the theory of the *gunas* was absorbed by theistic thinkers.

Yoga is closely associated with Samkhya, and as a philosophical system developed the two tended to coalesce although formally they are counted as two separate schools of the six orthodox systems. The basic text of Yoga is the *Yoga Sutra* (of which there are several English translations) attributed to Patanjali of the second century B.C., though it may be several centuries later in its present form.

Yoga differs from Samkhya on two major points. It emphasizes mystical or Yoga practices as a means for the attainment of liberation, whereas Samkhya, like the Upanishads, stresses knowledge and conviction of the truth. But more striking is Yoga's introduction of the Lord, Ishvara, as object of devotion. The *Yoga Sutra* (I, 23 f.) says: 'Or (concentration) is attained by devotion to Ishvara. Ishvara is a special kind of Purusha, which is untouched by affliction, Karma, fruits or hopes; in him the seed of omniscience is perfect; he is the Guru of the ancients, unlimited by time.'

This means that the Lord is eternal, but so are other *purushas*. He is different in never being affected by Nature or *karma*, and he is useful to the soul as a helper towards liberation. This is parallel to the first introduction of the Lord as an aid to devotion in the *Gita* (II, 61), but there is no trace in Yoga of the transcendental monotheism which the *Gita* later unfolded. For Yoga the Lord is an alternative, a methodical help, and the final goal is not union with him but isolation.

The methods of Yoga practice will be discussed later (under a separate heading of Yoga). It accepted the twenty-five categories of Samkhya, adding Ishvara as twenty-sixth. The dualism of Spirit and Matter came to be modified not only by the introduction of the Lord, but in the medieval period by identifications often made with a pair of the great deities. Since *purusha* means 'man' and *prakriti* was female they were easily assimilated to Shiva and Shakti, or other divine pairs in Tantric sects (see later on Tantra). So the cold non-theistic philosophical analysis of Samkhya came to be infused with the symbolism of popular religion.

EGP

Footnotes

[1] N. Smart, *Doctrine and Argument in Indian Philosophy*, pp. 76f., H. Zimmer, *Philosophies of India*, p. 60n.

[2] These categories can be represented by a diagram, see R. C. Zaehner, *The Bhagavad-Gita*, p. 140.

Bibliography

J. Davies, *The Sãnkhya Kãrikã of Ĩśwara Krishna*, London, 1894.
M. Eliade, *Yoga*, London, 1958.
C. Johnston, *The Yoga Sutras of Patanjali*, London, 1949[2].
E. H. Johnston, *Early Sãmkhya*, London, 1937.
J. H. Woods, *The Yoga-System of Patañjali*, Cambridge, Mass., 1966[3].
H. Zimmer, *Philosophies of India*, London, 1952.
Other books under Orthodox Philosophy I.

14

ORTHODOX PHILOSOPHY (III)

VEDANTA

VEDANTA IS USED in several senses. It is a name for the Upanishads, as the 'Veda's end' (*Gita* XV, 15). It is applied to those great systems of philosophy which are the 'end' or 'completion' of the Vedas. And in modern times Neo-Vedanta is a title adopted by pantheistic writers, of whom western examples are Aldous Huxley and Christopher Isherwood.

The Vedanta philosophy is also called Uttara Mimamsa, 'Later Exegesis' (see Mimamsa, under Orthodox Philosophy I, unit 12). The basic text is the *Vedanta Sutra* or *Brahma Sutra* (perhaps referred to in *Gita* XIII, 4), said to have been compiled by Badarayana and written down early in the Christian era. The *Vedanta Sutra* consists of 555 short verses, cryptic and ambiguous, which demand a commentary. The first two verses run: 'Desire to know Brahman; from which origin of this.' On these verses commentators wrote hundreds of pages, for they indicate the desire for true knowledge, the nature of Brahman, and the origins of the universe and souls.

Vedanta is divided into three main schools, with important differences. The great philospher of strict Non-dualism (*A-dvaita*) or Monism was Shankara, who lived about A.D. 788–820. A South Indian Brahmin, of the Shiva religion though he also composed hymns to Krishna, Shankara in his short life travelled widely, reformed religion, founded a monastic order, and wrote long commentaries on the *Vedanta Sutra*, the principal Upanishads and the *Bhagavad Gita*. Shankara took the existence of the Self (*atman*) as undoubted, both universal and infinite. It is identical with Brahman, which is existence-knowledge-bliss (*Sat-chit-ananda*, or *Sacchidananda*). The world exists but only for the perceiver, as the play (*lila*) of the divine and so it is *maya* (power, illusion, transience). Maya is like a rope which is mistaken for a snake; the snake is the illusion but the reality is Brahman. Brahman is indescribable and non-objective, and such negatives led Shankara's critics to call him a crypto-Buddhist, comparing his doctrine of the Absolute with the teaching of the ultimate Void in Mahayana Buddhism. For Shankara liberation from the phenomenal and illusory comes through knowledge and virtue. 'As long as the individual self does not free itself from ignorance in the form of duality . . . so long it remains individual . . . and does not rise to the knowledge of Atman which expresses itself in the form "I am Brahman"'. This is the complete development of the 'That thou art' of the Upanishads.

Shankara has been called the Aristotle or Aquinas of Hinduism and his great work was in presenting the teachings of the Upanishads in a consistent system. The title Shankaracharya, 'teacher' applied to him has been adopted by leading philosophers and monks of his school, and is sometimes misinterpreted today as indicating 'high priests' of Hinduism. Although it is common nowadays to present Shankara's monism as the 'perennial philosophy' of India, there are other teachers and schools which have been and remain as important and they are even more influential in religion.

Two centuries later Ramanuja (eleventh century) taught a modification of Upanishadic doctrine in 'qualified non-dualism' (*vishisht-advaita*) or 'difference non-difference' (*bhed-abheda*). Ramanuja was also a Brahmin of southern India who toured the north, established a monastery, and wrote on the *Vedanta Sutra*, Upanishads and *Gita*. His commentary on the latter is more perceptive of the monotheism and devotion of the *Gita* than was Shankara's commentary, and Ramanuja has been aptly compared to Plato. Ramanuja identified Brahman with the personal God Vishnu and this brought a religious warmth which coloured all his teaching. He held that God, souls and the world are all real, but the latter depend entirely on God and exist as his body. God is the soul of the body, controlling it as the immanent principle outside of which nothing exists. Souls and the universe are not a 'play', since man needs God but God also needs man. Ramanuja developed the words of the *Gita* (VII, 18) which said that the wise man was the very self of God, and so God cannot maintain himself without him. Liberation therefore is not identification with the divine in the sense of complete absorption, for while the soul will live in full communion with God that will demand an object and a God superior to man. The 'That thou art' shows a distinction remaining between 'that' and 'thou'.

Ramanuja's teaching gave philosophical justification to the devotional movements of Vaishnavism (see later section). Two major divisions arose among his followers. In the south was the 'cat-hold' (*marjara*) school, teaching passive acceptance of God's grace as a kitten is carried in a cat's mouth. In the north was the 'monkey-hold' (*markata*) school, teaching that man should cling to God by his own efforts as a monkey clings to its mother.

Thirdly came Madhva (1197–1276), also a South Indian Brahmin who wrote commentaries on the *Vedanta Sutra*, Upanishads and *Gita*. Madhva, through his Vaishnavite affiliations, completely opposed Shankara's monism and taught a frank dualism (*dvaita*). God, souls and the world are distinct, though the two latter depend upon God, who is Brahman or Vishnu. God is both above the world and immanent in it, and there are countless souls whose liberation from evil will bring them to perpetual adoration of God, while evil souls will remain infinitely remote from God. Madhva explained away all the Upanishadic passages that suggested monism as figurative; 'that thou art' really means 'not that'. A surprising feature of Madhva's system is the introduction of Vayu, a Vedic wind god, as a mediator between God and man, and of whom Madhva himself was later said to be an *avatar*. Some writers have suggested Christian influences upon him from the Indian Syrian churches, but this is questionable. Although Madhva's system gave full play to the subject-object relationship of divine and human, yet later devotional leaders often found his followers coldly intellectual and many preferred the more complex system of Ramanuja.

Differently from the other orthodox systems, the Vedanta thinkers and their schools are the true followers of Upanishadic teachings. Their leaders were the founders and inspirers of continuing philosophical and devotional schools.

EGP

Bibliography

J. A. B. van Buitenen, *Rāmānuja on the Bhagavadgītā*, 's-Gravenhage, 1968[2].
S. Radhakrishnan, *The Brahma Sūtra*, London, 1960.
S. S. Rao, *Vedānta-Sūtras with the Commentary of Srī Madhwacharya*, 1936[2].
A. M. Śāstri, *The Bhagavad-Gītā with the Commentary of Śrī Śankarāchārya*, Madras, 1961[5].
G. Thibaut, *The Vedānta-Sūtras with the Commentary by Śankarācārya*, Madras, 1962[2].
G. Thibaut, *The Vedānta-Sūtras, with the Commentary of Rāmānuja*, Madras, 1962[2].
Other books under Orthodox Philosophy I.

15

THE GODDESS AND OTHER DEITIES

THAT THERE WERE female fertility cults in the Indus Valley cultures is attested by the many figures of pregnant women that have survived. Crushed by the Aryan invasion, and hidden by the Vedas which have few and sketchy goddesses, the Great Mother emerged eventually to become a great, or, as Zimmer says, the greatest power in the Orient.[1] In the literature the goddesses began to appear as the Shakti, the 'power' or 'strength of their consorts. But already in the Great Epic the Mother figures under various names, and progresses in the Puranas and innumerable later texts.

The Mother Goddess is generally the wife of Shiva and is joined with him in much mythology. She has many names: Uma ('light'), Parvati ('daughter of the mountains'), Annapurna ('bestower of food'), Durga ('inaccessible'), Kali ('black'). More generally she is Devi ('the goddess') or Mahadevi ('Great Goddess'), or Mother. In southern India many village goddesses have the title Mata or Ammai, and are vaguely connected with the Great Mother.

Among the many writings the *Markandeya Purana* gives one of the most famous texts on 'the Wondrous Essence of the Goddess', described as an invincible warrior-maid who was formed from the combined powers of the gods, thus concentrating their primeval *shakti*. She fought a cosmic demon, Mahisha, who took the successive forms of buffalo, lion and elephant, and eventually killed him with her trident. More calmly in other myths the goddess sits with Shiva and their family amid the snows of Mount Kailasa, though it is in their union and conflict that life vibrates and persists. In some of the most popular pictures, seen in all the bazaars of Calcutta, Kali the black, with protruding tongue, garland of skulls, and hands holding weapons and severed heads, stands stark naked upon the prostrate body of—her beloved consort Shiva! Here she is

Death and the Destroyer, though it must be remembered that Shiva is destruction also for his devotees, and that creation will come again after destruction.

The philosopher Shankara (see Orthodox Philosophy iii, unit 14) wrote a famous hymn to Kali, as the one who fills all beings with energy. She gives abundance as the mother, but also death and renunciation, since her hands hold both delight and pain, death and immortality. Many later Shaktas (followers of Shakti) rebuked the dark goddess for sending evil, yet besought her grace and universal presence, as the mother who cares for her children. Like Shiva, Shakti is ambivalent, reflecting the joys and sorrows of life.

The mother cult has been strong in South India, and also in Bengal where it gave its name to Calcutta (Kali-ghat, 'steps of Kali', down to the Ganges). Here and in other Kali temples animal sacrifice is still performed, to the disgust of many Hindus of other cults. The chief image is a crude idol, yet people, especially women, come to pray to the goddess and hang votive gifts on the trees in the courtyard in thanks for help and healing in their families. Ramakrishna, the nineteenth century saint, was a priest in a temple of Kali and had visions of her as mother, and some of the poems of Rabindranath Tagore reflect the mother-love. (For Shakti cults see 'Tantra', unit 19).

Shiva and Parvati were parents of Ganesha or Ganapati, 'lord of the Ganas' who were demigods attendant upon Shiva. When the Great God in anger blasted his son's head, he replaced it in penitence with an elephant's head. Ganesha is the elephant-headed god, clearly a primitive nature deity but very popular all over India today. Riding a rat, he symbolizes good fortune and his favour is sought by Hindus of all sects for good luck. Surprisingly he is a patron of literature, processions of students chant the praise of the pink elephant, and books begin with his invocation. There is a *Ganesha Gita* which imitates the *Bhagavad Gita*.

The other son of Shiva and Parvati was the war-god Skanda, also called Karttikeya, and in the south Subrahmanya. He was probably a non-Aryan god and other southern deities are identified with him. Skanda appears in art in human form but with six faces and riding a peacock.

Hanuman the monkey-god, also non-Aryan, and Lakshmi the wife of Vishnu have been mentioned under Rama and Vaishnavism. Sarasvati was a sacred river in the *Rig Veda* and later became the wife of the creator Brahma. She is represented in human form, often with only two arms, with a lute and a book, and is patron of music and letters. In this function Sarasvati has survived, whereas Brahma has virtually disappeared since he is reputed to have only one temple today in the whole of India, at Pushkar in Rajasthan.

Most of the old Vedic gods have been forgotten. The celestial and moral Varuna had become a mere sea spirit by the time of the *Gita*, the great warrior Indra was humbled by Krishna and his attributes largely taken over by Shiva. The names of Vedic gods may still be mentioned in formulas of family ritual among the upper castes, but few people know any Sanskrit and the active religion of most Hindus centres round Vishnu and even more his *avatars*, Rama and Krishna, and round Shiva and Shakti and their attendants. In the villages there are many local gods, deified heroes and natural forces, and malignant powers like snakes and smallpox. There is a tendency among modern missionary Hindus to identify the local gods with the chief figures of the great pantheon: Vishnu, Shiva or Shakti.

EGP

Footnote

[1] H. Zimmer, *Myths and Symbols in Indian Art and Civilization*, 1946, pp. 189 ff.

Bibliography

A. Avalon, *Hymns to the Goddess*, London, 1913[2].
A. Daniélou, *Hindu Polytheism*, New York, 1964.
J. Dowson, *A Classical Dictionary of Hindu Mythology*, London, 1968.
L. S. S. O'Malley, *Popular Hinduism*, Cambridge, 1935.
R. Tagore, *Gitanjali*, London, 1913, etc.
H. Zimmer, *Myths and Symbols in Indian Art and Civilization*, New York, 1947.

16

VAISHNAVISM

THE WORSHIP OF VISHNU was only a minor feature of the *Rig Veda* though that document is fairly clear about his activity and this is consistent with later pictures; he strides across the worlds and is established in the highest heaven. But Vishnu worship received a great expansion though his association with the *avatars*, incorporating other myths, and especially concentrating on Rama and Krishna who were heroic or darker gods from other levels of life (see earlier articles). Vaishnavite religious communities appear from about the second century B.C., and Shaivite somewhat later, so that the cults of the two gods Vishnu and Shiva are sometimes called the two Indian religions (rather than 'sects' since they were not schisms from an established church), though Gonda has recently shown how much overlapping there has been between Vaishnavism and Shaivism.[1]

Some of the earliest Vaishnavas were the Pancha-ratras ('five nights'), a name said in the *Shatapatha Brahmana* (XIII, 6, 1) to have been applied to a sacrifice which Narayana (Vishnu) performed in order to become everything. The Pancharatras worshipped one God under the name of Vasudeva and gradually became absorbed into the growing Vishnu cults. Their doctrines of the 'entrances' of the God into human form fitted the *avatar* theory.

Vaishnavites generally were known as Bhagavatas (worshippers of Bhagavat, the Lord, Vishnu or Krishna especially), and it was from such circles that the Krishna teaching of the *Bhagavad Gita* developed. From about A.D. 1000 various teachers, and especially Ramanuja, inaugurated a mingling of Vishnu traditions which became known as the Shri-Vaishnavas (*Shri* meaning 'sacred' or 'holy', and used of male and female deities and saints).

After the *Gita*, and the Great Epic of which it forms part, Krishna mythology developed in many other writings which are exceedingly popular. The *Harivamsha* (family of Hari-Vishnu), perhaps before the fifth century A.D., was appended to the Epic and related the histories of the ancestors of Krishna, told of his own exploits, and looked to the end of the present world age, But it was in the Puranas ('ancient stories') and devotional poetry that Krishnaism received its greatest development.

The Puranas follow the epics in providing for the masses great collections of stories which have inspired devotion, drama and sculpture down the ages. There are said to be eighteen principal Puranas, though there are more, all from the Christian era in their present form in Sanskrit verse. They are supposed to deal with five topics, which some of them do not: creation, dissolution, gods, sages and kings. Vishnu and his *avatars* are the most important subjects, but other gods are prominent, especially Shiva.

The *Vishnu Purana*, about the fourth century, takes Vishnu as God and other deities as his energies. It gives details of the birth of Krishna that were not in the Epic, his mischievous childhood, life among cowherds, dancing with milkmaids (*gopis*), fighting demons, reigning as king and final death. The *Bhagavata Purana*, most popular of all, from about the ninth century, lists twenty-two *avatars* and gives tales of Krishna in its tenth and eleventh books. Favourite are the relationships of Krishna with the *gopis* at Brindaban (Vrindavan), which is the divine Brindaban Lila ('sport'). Krishna steals the clothes of the bathing *gopis*, plays the flute to them, and dances in a way that makes each think he is dancing with her alone. This circular (*rasa*) dance becomes important in Krishna cults, but the eroticism is given a spiritual meaning.

The *Bhagavata Purana* said that Krishna went off with one of the *gopis*, and in later writings she is named as Radha and regarded as an *avatar* of the goddess Lakshmi or Shri, the consort of Vishnu. In the twelfth century a Bengali poet, Jayadeva, composed in Sanskrit the *Gita Govinda*, 'Song of the Cowherd', in which the love, estrangement and reconciliation of Krishna and Radha are described. Later poets took up the theme: Vidyapati and Chandi Das in Bengal, and Princess Mira Bai in the west, all singing of the loves of Krishna and Radha in sensuous terms.

In the late fifteenth century Chaitanya, a Bengali Brahmin, went into trances, led processions of song and dance (kirtans), and acted episodes of Krishna and Radha, at times wearing female dress to impersonate Radha. He visited the traditional sites of the cult at Brindaban and after his death great temples were built there for the still popular festivals and pilgrimages so movingly described by Klostermaier.[2]

Not all Vaishnavas are so erotic or ecstatic. Some of the oldest Vaishnavas in South India were the Alvars, who composed Tamil hymns to Rama and Krishna. They referred to the *gopis* but not to Radha. Similarly the Madhvas, followers of the philosopher of that name (see Orthodox Philosophy iii, unit 13), accept the *Bhagavata Purana* but not Radha since she is not named there. But others, like the Vishnu-swamis, worship Radha along with Krishna.

Rama is also widely worshipped, and reformers like Kabir and the Sikhs, from the fifteenth century, rejected the *avatars*, especially Krishna but used the names Rama and Hari for God, along with other titles. Tulsi Das made a popular Hindi version of the Ramayana, the 'Holy Lake of the Acts of Rama', in which Rama appears with human and divine features.

Vishnu's consort, Lakshmi, is the *Shri* par excellence, and as goddess of fortune she is popular in homes, shops, offices and schools. Her festival, Divali or Deepavali, in October–November is a 'cluster of lights' for the new year. Lakshmi was said to be born with Vishnu in his various *avatars*, generally appearing from a lotus which is her symbol. Kama, the god of love, is said in some stories to have been born of Lakshmi.

Vishnu is a benevolent deity though in himself rather colourless and remote, worshipped by certain people of what is sometimes called the Great, Sanskritic and philosophical, tradition. He only plays a small part in the Little tradition of the masses, but the stroke of genius which associated Vishnu with the *avatars*, especially Krishna and Rama, ensured the growing popularity of this side of Vaishnavism. It became the religion of one God, replacing the impersonal Absolute among philosophers like Ramanuja and Madhva, and providing in the Krishna-Radha cults a focus for the loving devotion of countless Hindus.

EGP

Footnotes

[1] J. Gonda, *Viṣṇuism and Śivaism.*
[2] K. Klostermaier, *Hindu and Christian in Vrindaban.*

Bibliography

F. R. Allchin, *Tulsī Dās, The Petition to Rām*, London, 1966.
W. G. Archer, *The Loves of Krishna*, London, 1957.
A. Daniélou, *Hindu Polytheism*, New York, 1963.
J. Gonda, *Viṣṇuism and Śivaism*, London, 1970.
K. Klostermaier, *Hindu and Christian in Vrindaban*, London, 1969.
E. G. Parrinder, *Avatar and Incarnation*, London, 1970.

17

SHAIVISM

THE CULTS OF SHIVA run alongside, and sometimes overlap, those of Vishnu, though for countless Hindus today Shiva is the chief or only God. From the time that the doctrine of the *Trimurti*, 'three-formed', appeared in the *Harivamsha* (see Vaishnavism, unit 15), it was easy to reconcile rival gods, though for the Shaivites the three-faced Brahma-Vishnu-Rudra were aspects of the one Shiva, while for the Vaishnavites they were manifestations of Vishnu. Sometimes the two gods Vishnu and Shiva are combined in the names and imagery of Hari and Hara, their respective titles. There was a tendency on the one hand to 'inclusivism', and on the other to 'passive intolerance', and although religious persecution did not reach the depths that it attained in European organizations, yet it was often acute, leading to insults and communal riots.[1]

The cult of Shiva may be very ancient, if it goes back in some forms to the cross-legged figure with mask and horns, perhaps with erect phallus, and surrounded by animals, which appears on a few seals from the Indus Valley. This has been called a Proto-Shiva, and in later religion Shiva is the Great Yogi, Lord of Beasts, and god of fertility. (See also Yoga, unit 20). Shiva is unknown to the Vedas, but the storm god Rudra, who is later identified with him, has some of his attributes, being dark and fearful and dwelling in the mountains. In the *Shvetashvatara Upanishad* Shiva ('auspicious') is first of all an attribute of the one God Rudra, and then his personal name. Here for the first time the impersonal Brahman is identified with a God of attributes, creator and immanent as well as transcendent. In the last verse of this Upanishad occurs the first mention of *bhakti*, 'love' for God. This powerfully influenced the *Bhagavad Gita*, though the latter work concentrated upon Krishna as God.

In the Great Epic, *Mahabharata*, Shiva is not so prominent

as Vishnu, though when he appears he tends to overshadow Vishnu. Here and in the Puranas (see Vaishnavism, unit 15) many stories illustrate the ambivalent character of Shiva, that make him both repulsive and fascinating. He is a fierce deity, addicted to cremation grounds, wearing skulls and snakes, and with the matted locks of an ascetic. He carries a trident, as his followers do still. Shiva has a 'third eye' to burn the unwary to ashes; he is Death and Time destroying everything; his neck is blue from poison which he drank to save the gods. On the other hand Shiva is 'Lord of the Dance', *Nata-raja*, as depicted in many bronzes, and in the *Tandavȧ*, 'frantic', dance he shatters the world with his drunken attendants. Shiva is regularly represented by the *linga*, and often united with the *yoni*, male and female organs. Yet he is also perpetually chaste, and when his consort Parvati sought to become his wife she had to undergo fierce austerities. With their children, Ganesha and Karttikeya (see next section), they sit on the peaks of the Himalayas while the bull Nandi, Shiva's attendant in all temples, gazes lovingly at him.

In the *Kurma Purana*, which formally is given to the praise of Vishnu in his Tortoise (*Kurma*) Avatar, there is a long section devoted to Shiva called the *Ishvara Gita*, Song of the Lord, which follows the *Bhagavad Gita* in many ways. But here Vishnu and Shiva sit together on a throne, and in place of the fearful vision of the *Gita* Shiva performs his famous dance, and appears to his devotees as the supreme God. Some later Shaivite texts speak of *avatars* of Shiva, but these are pale copies of Vaishnavism, and *avatars* are unnecessary to Shaivism where God appears to his devotees personally as divine Guru ('teacher').

The union of the transcendental deity with the revealed Lord was largely the work of Shaiva Siddhanta, 'the doctrine of Shiva', in southern India, first of all in Sanskrit and then in Tamil texts which have remained popular in worship. For Shaiva Siddhanta the Lord of Cattle (*Pashu-pati*) is bound to the souls who are his beloved cattle. He is different from them, and the monism of the philosophers is denied since worship demands subject and object. The soul needs the free grace of God to deliver it from the sin and evil in which he is enslaved by egotism. Manikka Vachakar, in the tenth century, sang passionate verses of the grace which came down to earth and of the love greater than a mother's. Yet this is different from the *bhakti* and erotic cults of Vaishnavism, and it is surprising to find that these cults of Shiva present the clearest monotheism, the deepest sense of sin, and the purest divine and human love. (For other rituals, see 'Tantra', unit 18).

There are other schools of Shaivism. In Kashmir the Trika, 'triad', was so called from its three principal scriptures. Differently from Shaiva Siddhanta this Trika Shaivism was monistic, agreeing with the philosopher Shankara (see Orthodox Philosophy iii, unit 13) in the unreality of the visible world which only exists for the soul that does not realize its true nature. Salvation is dependent upon enlightenment, sudden in the manner of a conversion, but different from love.

More important still today are the Lingayats or Virashaivas ('heroic'), said to have been founded in the twelfth century A.D. Their doctrines are a 'qualified non-dualism' (see Orthodox Philosophy iii, unit 14), but their practices are more distinctive. All members of the sect carry the only permissible symbol of Shiva to them, the *linga*, in a container round their necks or held in the hand during worship. They are opposed to images in general, originally rejected the authority of the Vedas and the brahmins, opposed sacrifice and pilgrimage, and gave equality to all, even women. Their dead are usually buried instead of being cremated, and this and other practices may suggest Islamic influences. The Lingayats are militant propagandists for Hinduism today, especially in the south, seeking to convert again those who have taken up other religions, and they have drawn somewhat nearer to orthodoxy. For the ordinary people Shiva himself may be a God formally acknowledged but worshipped in rituals by the upper classes according to the Vedas and other texts, yet like Vishnu he is also identified with local and village gods and is prominent in the cults of Shakti and Tantra (see following sections).

EGP

Footnote

[1] J. Gonda, *Viṣṇuism and Śivaism*, pp. 92 ff.

Bibliography

A. Daniélou, *Hindu Polytheism*, New York, 1964.
M. Dhavamony, *Love of God according to Śaiva Śiddhānta*, Oxford, 1971.
P. E. Dumont, *L'Īśvaragītā*, Paris, 1933.
J. N. Farquhar, *Modern Religious Movements in India*, London, 1915.
J. Gonda, *Viṣṇuism and Śivaism*, London, 1970.
J. H. Piet, *Śaiva Siddhānta Philosophy*, Madras, 1952.
R. C. Zaehner, *Hinduism*, Oxford, 1962.

18

THE SHAIVA SIDDHANTA

IT IS OFTEN not realized in the West that there exists in the south of India an independent religious and philosophical tradition, with literature written not in Sanskrit but in Tamil. Authoritative accounts and translations of these trends in Hindu thought are few, owing to the extreme difficulty of the Tamil language. The most outstanding of the south Indian schools is that known as Shaiva Siddhanta.

South Indian Shaivism is in its present form a composite faith, made up of Vedic and pre-Vedic elements, and although the authority of the Vedic scriptures is recognized, these are interpreted through the medium of an extensive literary tradition, beginning with a series of documents called the Agamas (28 in number) and going on to a body of Tamil literature, mainly in the form of hymns. This tradition is expressly anti-Vedantic, and whereas the Vedantic tradition insists that supreme reality is to be found within man, the Shaiva tradition sees God within the created world.

The first element in south Indian Shaiva literature is a collection of Tamil devotional writings dating from the 10th century, and called *Tiru Murai* (holy scripture). The best known portion of this is the *Tiru Vachakam* (holy word) of Manikka Vachakar, which contains poetry of great depth and beauty. Then come a number of philosophical treatises, such as the thirteenth-century *Shiva-gnana-bodham* of Meykander, on which the Shaiva Siddhanta system is built.

The theology of the Shaiva Siddhanta centres around three terms: *Pati* (God = Shiva), *Pashu* (flock = soul) and *Pasha* (fetter, also called *mala*, dirt). It teaches that there is ultimately one God, Shiva, and that the souls of men are held in bondage by the fetters of *pasha*, from which they may be freed by the love of Shiva. The system is neither monistic nor dualistic: it teaches that there are a number of eternal substances, all of which are real, but all of which owe their existence to Shiva. God, souls and the empirical world are all therefore completely real, and have existed from all eternity, since realities can never be created or destroyed.

Shiva (*pati*) is the incomparable one, who holds in being the whole universe. The other gods exist only by the express will of Shiva, and even then in a lower class. The other two gods of the great triad, Brahma and Vishnu, operate under the control and at the command of Shiva. He has five modes of operation—as creator, sustainer, concealer, saviour and destroyer—and his nature is absolute knowledge and intelligence. Other beings may have a measure of intelligence, but only Shiva is boundless intelligence. Similarly, he is absolute bliss, and without him, souls cannot experience even a measure of bliss.

The doctrine of *pati* is different from the Vedanta doctrine of *brahman* in that Shiva is said to be both immanent and transcendent: there is no opposition between his nature as *nirguna* and as *saguna*. He is immanent in the world as *shakti* (originally his consort, called in mythology Uma, Parvati, Kali, etc.), which represents his energy, will and creative power, and related to Shiva as a ray of sunlight is related to the sun. The world which the *shakti* of Shiva creates exists in relation to him as a pot of boiling water is related to the fire. In the Universe (boiling water) there is fire (Shiva), and the boiling water cannot exist except by the action of the fire; nevertheless the two are not identical, and the existence of the fire is in no way determined by the need to boil water!

Matter (*pasha*) contains three elements, distinguished from one another by their different effects. These are called *anavamala*, *karmamala* and *mayamala*. *Anavamala* is the pollution inherent from the beginning in matter, like salt in sea-water, and holds the soul in the deepest darkness. *Karmamala* consists of the actions of the soul, in so far as they are turned in the direction of matter. As in other Indian philosophical systems, the good and bad deeds which make up *karma* bring their own retribution, which has to be worked out either in this present life or in future incarnations. *Mayamala* in Shaiva Siddhanta does not mean 'illusion' as in Vedanta, but rather the formless, non-intelligent energy out of which the material world can derive—the clay out of which Shiva forms the world through the action of his *shakti*.

The soul (*pashu*) is one of a fixed and eternal number of such souls. Each one is bound in various ways to matter, and takes on form and qualities from that to which it is most closely assimilated. So the soul can be entirely gross if assimilated to matter, entirely divine if assimilated to God.

Shaiva Siddhanta has an elaborate path of salvation, taking the form of a ladder of spiritual evolution, as the soul is more and more freed from matter and grows closer to God. The lower 'means of grace' are centred on personal discipline, ritual observances and yoga. At a higher level it is necessary for the individual to find a *satguru* (true teacher), who has himself attained a high rung on the ladder, and who makes use of a variety of methods in order to free the disciple once and for all, and release him from the round of rebirth. By the grace of Shiva (the Tamil word *arul*, grace, corresponds closely to the Christian *charis*) the soul is finally enlightened. It is, however, interesting to note that this enlightenment is not a complete absorption into God (another case of deliberate contrast with the Vedanta of Shankara): in the state of release the soul keeps its individuality, and it is therefore proper to speak of 'personal salvation'.

Since one of the strengths of south Indian Shaivism is in its devotional poetry, we may end by quoting an example:

When thou didst make me, Thou didst know my all:
But I knew not of Thee. 'Twas not till light
From Thee brought understanding of Thy ways
That I could know. But now where'er I sit,
Or walk, or stand, Thou art for ever near.
Can I forget Thee? Thou art mine, and I
Am only Thine. E'en with these eyes I see,
And with the heart perceive, that Thou art come
To me as lightning from the lowering sky.

EJS

Bibliography

V. A. Devasenapathy, *Of Human Bondage and Divine Grace*, Annamalai University, 1963.

M. Dhavamony, *Love of God according to Śaiva Siddhānta*, Oxford, 1971.

F. Kingsbury and G. E. Phillips, *Hymns of the Tamil Saivite Saints*, London, 1921.

T. M. P. Mahadevan, *The Idea of God in Saiva-Siddhanta*, Annamalai University, 1955.

G. U. Pope, *The Tiruvācagam*, Oxford, 1900.

H. W. Schomerus, *Der Çaiva-Siddhānta*, Leipzig, 1912.

Fr. Zacharias, O. C. D., *An Outline of Hinduism*, Alwaye, 1956, pp. 328–341.

19

TANTRA

TANTRA, 'RULE', 'RITUAL', is the name given to certain occult teachings and practices which are non-Vedic and are probably linked with primitive male and female cults. Some of the practices overlap with forms of Yoga (see Yoga, unit 20), particularly in magical repetitions and the use of symbols, and in physiology. Others are especially expressive of female cults.

In Tantra the development of psychic powers is sought by special yogic practices, depending upon physiological identifications. There are said to be six wheels (*chakras*), concentrations of psychic power, at different points along the chief vein (*sushumna*) of the body which runs up the spinal column. In the lowest wheel, at the base of the trunk, is the 'serpent power' (*kundalini*) which is normally quiescent but can be awakened by Yoga. Being aroused the serpent power goes up the great vein, passing through the six wheels of power, and unites itself with the great centre of psychic energy (*sahasrara*) which is at the top of the vein inside the skull and is generally symbolized as a lotus. The awakened serpent power is supposed to give supernatural knowledge and magical faculties, and many of the claims to Yogic and Tantric marvels are justified from this dubious physiology. Complete union of the serpent power with the psychic centre in the skull is thought to bring liberation.

Many Tantric texts are in the form of dialogues between Shiva and his spouse, Shakti or Durga, and deal with five subjects: the creation, the destruction of the world, worship of the gods, attainment of objects and superhuman powers, and modes of union with the supreme spirit. The Tantric sects do not deny the usefulness of normal rituals for ordinary worshippers of the gods, but claim that their own adepts need special initiations and more occult ceremonies. Magical diagrams (*mandalas*, *yantras*) are drawn on the ground, highly coloured, and serve to represent the gods and their abodes, and the psychic energies which are supposed to derive therefrom when effective incantations are made. The most powerful *yantra* is the *Shri-Yantra*, which has four entrances, with male and female symbols and sanctuaries of the gods.

The Shaktas (worshippers of the Shaktis, see 'Goddess', unit 15) are divided into two main groups, the 'right-handed' (*Dakshina-charis*) whose worship is respectable and open, and the 'left-handed' (*Vama-charis*) whose practices are secret and suspect. The name 'left-hand' is also said to have been adopted because the goddess sits on the left side of her consort, and because Tantric rites break normal Hindu taboos. The 'left-hand' worshippers meet at night, in a temple, a house, or a cemetery, and after ordinary worship of the deities they proceed to practise the Five M's (*Makaras*). These are: *Madya*, alcoholic drink; *Mamsa*, eating meat; *Matsya*, eating fish; *Mudra*, symbolical gestures with the hands, as in dances; *Maithuna*, sexual intercourse. The five M's broke the taboos of ordinary Hinduism, but were intended to do so deliberately in order to produce greater spiritual power. In some Tantric groups the rites were only performed symbolically, in others husbands enacted the rituals with their wives, and yet others were indiscriminate. It is difficult to tell how much of this survives today, though it is said to occur occasionally in private, but since these Tantric rituals are 'left-hand' they are secret and there may be more rumour than actuality.[1]

Tantric ideas are represented in the erotic sculptures of some Hindu temples, and famous places such as the so-called Black Pagoda, the sun temple at Konarak, indicate from their sculptures the popularity of sexual mysticism in medieval India which may have come down from aboriginal cults. It might appear remarkable that Tantric worship flourished in Buddhism, though this is explicable from its absorption of a great deal of popular religion. The Buddhas and Bodhisattvas were regarded as male energies which had female counterparts, like Tara, and from their union spiritual potencies emerged. Magical powers from them were sought in the Thunderbolt-Vehicle, *Vajra-yana*. Not only were sacred texts (*mantras*) uttered, and magical diagrams (*yantras*) drawn, but the Tantric devotee would identify himself and his partner with Buddha and Tara, breaking all taboos, even to murder. This was strictly controlled, however, open only to initiates, and has disappeared.

EGP

Footnote

[1] See G. M. Carstairs, 'Patterns of Religious Observance in Three Villages of Rajasthan', in *Aspects of Religion in Indian Society*, ed. L. P. Vidyarthi, Meerut, 1961, pp. 67, 90.

Bibliography

A. Avalon, *Shakti and Shākta*, Madras, 1929. *The Serpent Power* Madras, 1931. *Principles of Tantra*, Madras, 1955[2].
S. B. Dasgupta, *An Introduction to Tantrik Buddhism*, Calcutta, 1950.
J. Marquès-Rivière, *Tantrik Yoga*, London, 1940.
P. S. Rawson, *Tantra*, Arts Council, London, 1971.

20

YOGA

Yoga as a philosophical system is discussed under 'Orthodox Philosophy, ii', unit 13. Here some of its methods will be considered. Yoga is a Sanskrit word, related to Latin *jugum* and English *yoke*. It has many meanings and in the *Bhagavad Gita* each of the eighteen chapters is given the title of one Yoga or another. Basic to Yoga, as to yoke, is the double meaning of 'discipline' in being yoked, and 'union' in yoking together.

Yoga is characteristically Indian and its first appearance may be in the cross-legged figure on some of the Indus Valley seals (see 'Shaivism', unit 17). This is often called a Proto-Shiva, for in later religion Shiva is the Great yogi. Yoga begins to emerge in the fusion of Aryan with other beliefs and practices, in the later of the classical Upanishads (*Shvetashvatara* VI, 13). Thereafter the term is used of many kinds of religious exercise and any ascetic may be called a yogi or yogin.

The *Yoga Sutras* of Patanjali (2, 29 f.) set out Eight Stages of Yoga, not unlike the Eightfold Path of Buddhism though less practical. These are: Abstention or self-control, Observance, Posture, Breath-control, Sense-restraint, Mental-steadiness, Contemplation or meditation, Concentration or deep meditation. The Eight Stages are then expounded more fully (2, 30–3, 3). Abstention (*yama*) entailed five moral rules, the Great Vow, like the Buddhist five rules: non-violence, truth, honesty, chastity, avoidance of greed. Observance (*niyama*) demanded full observance of the rules and devotion to the Lord. Posture (*asana*) is defined as that which is steady and easy, but later there were many variations, such as the Lotus Posture (*padmasana*) in which gods and sages are often shown, with legs crossed and feet placed soles upwards on opposite thighs. Breath-control (*pranayama*) is said in the Sutra to be external and internal, long and short; but later emphasis was placed upon breathing in, breathing out, holding the breath, and also to breathing up one nostril and down the other. Many rhythms have been practised, one of the commonest being 1, 4, 2, for intervals of breathing in, holding and breathing out. Some advanced Yogis have claimed to be able to hold their breath for long periods, or suspend it altogether, hence practices of burying alive or claims to control the heart-beats.

Sense-restraint (*pratyahara*) aims at abstracting the sense organs so that they take no account of their surroundings and come to full mastery of the senses.

Mental Steadiness (*dharana*) comes from fixing attention on a single object, such as the end of the nose, the navel, a symbol or an image. Contemplation (*dhyana*) is filling the mind with the object of attention. Concentration (*samadhi*) comes when the mind is only conscious of the object, unconscious of itself, and the whole personality is dissolved for a time.

This eightfold method of Yoga is called Royal Yoga (*raja-yoga*) and is the basic form for meditation, being concerned principally with mental discipline though emphasizing also physical posture and control. This is very similar to the Meditation-Yoga (*dhyana-yoga*) taught in the *Gita* and the *Shvetashvatara Upanishad*, but it is notable that the *Gita* (6, 10 f.) speaks of sitting in solitude, does not mention breath-control here, and gives the Lord as the object of control which will lead to his Nirvana.

There are other varieties of Yoga, some of which may be ancient and others later developments. *Mantra-Yoga*, Yoga of Texts or Spells, emphasizes the repetition of magical syllables or words as a means of achieving abstraction of consciousness and arriving at supernormal states. *Laya-Yoga*, Yoga of Dissolution, has often been propagated in the West, aiming at the disappearance or absorption of the self, and it may have practices akin to Tantra (see Tantra).

Hatha-Yoga, the Yoga of Force, is generally regarded as parallel to Royal Yoga, concentrating upon physical exercises, often very difficult and acrobatic. The tortuous postures and harsh discipline are well explained by Theos Bernard[1]. *Hatha-Yoga* seeks to attain Single-pointedness (*ekagrata*) by discipline, concentration and fixation upon symbols. Some forms of it included sexual union as a means to liberation (see Tantra).

Such Yoga practices have often led to claims that supernatural powers (*siddhis*) are obtained: levitation, fire-walking, burial alive, becoming invisible, flying great distances, and knowing the moment of death. These are some of the most notorious, and photographed, sights of India and also those most likely to bring Yoga into disrepute. Bernard curtly dismisses such claims as 'no miracles', 'nothing supernatural', at the end of his course. Some of the greatest yogis, like mystics in other religions, have taught that pretence to abnormal physical powers is only a lower stage of development, liable to falsification, and to be passed over in the search for ultimate concentration and liberation.

That many popular yogis follow their hard and unusual paths primarily for gaining supernormal powers rather than immediate salvation is highly probable. Whether they can attain powers inexplicable by modern science remains to be examined, and there is room for biological and psychological study of Yogic practice, down to the value or otherwise of breathing rhythms and holding the breath. The physiological interpretations of Indian Yoga (see 'Tantra', unit 19) appear quite fanciful, but there is little question of the great powers of endurance of many yogis. Living an ascetic life, enduring extremes of cold and heat with little or no clothing, controlling the breath and perhaps the heart for long periods, and living to an advanced age with full possession of the faculties, these are powers common to many yogis and beyond the reach of the ordinary undisciplined man. For the normal person there is great value in meditation, with bodily stillness, mental concentration, and general peace, and the appeal of Yoga to the West is evidence of the need that it fills in many lives. The modern philosopher Aurobindo taught an Integral Yoga, seeking to combine the best of physical and spiritual worlds, with full play to work, study and meditation, with the aim of rising to the Life Divine on earth in Superman united with the Supermind.

EGP

Footnote

[1] Theos Bernard, *Hatha Yoga* (1950).

Bibliography

K. T. Behanan, *Yoga, a Scientific Evaluation*, New York, 1937.
T. Bernard, *Hatha Yoga*, London, 1950.
M. Eliade, *Yoga, Immortality and Freedom*, London, 1958.
Aurobindo Ghose, *Synthesis of Yoga*, New York, 1950.
Rishabhchand, *The Integral Yoga of Sri Aurobindo*, Pondicherry, 1953.
E. Wood, *Yoga*, London, 1959.

21

INTRODUCTION TO THE MODERN PERIOD

THE STUDY OF EARLY and classical Hinduism does not call for, and seldom arouses, an interest in the details of Indian history. To be sure, there are landmarks—the Aryan invasions, the life of the Buddha, the campaigns of Alexander the Great, and so on—which help to locate the main features of the story; but one seldom feels that the historical landmark is indispensable. Certainly it was in no way indispensable to the Hindu of classical times. The entire story of the beginnings and early development of Hinduism was viewed in the broadest possible way as part of a pattern of world history which was in no sense unique, and which there could be little point in recording with precision. Hence the historical data which the modern student of Indian religion happens to possess, are at best approximate. We cannot, for instance, 'date' the *Bhagavad Gita* or the *Brahma Sutra* more closely than within a time-span of four to six hundred years. Matters improve somewhat in the period which the West calls 'the Middle Ages', thanks largely to Islamic chroniclers. But it is not until the entry of India into the field of (again from the Western point of view) world history that Hinduism becomes in any sense 'historical', and the study of political, social and other branches of history becomes imperative for our understanding of Hinduism itself.

Historical periods are seldom so clear-cut as the student would want them to be, and in this present case, it may seem unjust to divide up Indian religion by means of Western fences; but since one means by which the Western student may begin to understand modern Hinduism is by observing Hindu reactions to his own intrusive culture, the procedure is perhaps not unjustified. In fact there are good grounds for saying that the major new factors influencing Indian religious thought in the modern period are (i) Hindu reactions of various kinds to the impact of Western culture and religion, (ii) the emergence, from the late nineteenth century, of the Indian national movement, and (iii) the effort to build an expressly secular state out of one of the most 'religious' of the nations of the world. For the purposes of historical study, we may take the modern period to have begun in the years around 1830, and to fall into five fairly distinct phases.

1. Between *c.* 1830 and *c.* 1875, India began to feel the full impact of the West. Before 1830, British—and earlier, Portuguese, French and other—influence had been felt largely in commerce and politics. In the area of religion, the British East India Company believed in leaving well alone. Before 1813 no Christian missionary had been allowed into the Company's territories, and the Company even found itself in the rather odd position of administering a large number of Hindu temples. But in 1813 and 1833 successive revisions of the Company's Charter allowed free access to Christian missionaries, and in 1830 the opening of Alexander Duff's first school in Calcutta meant the beginning of a serious assault on the minds, as well as the purses and political allegiances, of Hindus. In 1835 the influence of Lord Macaulay led to the adoption of English-language Western higher education as a deliberate policy.

This first phase was, then, characterized by the initial impact on Hindu India of English-language education and (often in intimate association with it) Christianity. The period was roughly bisected by what is variously called the Indian Mutiny or the First Indian War of Independence in 1857–58, which led to the direct assumption of power over India by the British Crown and the final end of the already moribund Mughal Empire (the last Mughal Emperor, Bahadur Shah II, being sent into exile in Burma). A fairly typical expression of the religious life of the time was Ram Mohan Roy's *Brahma Samaj*, with its uneasy oscillations between various types of Eastern and Western thought (unit 24).

2. The second phase, from *c.* 1875 to 1914, was on the one hand a time of flourishing British imperial sentiment, but on the other witnessed the emergence, and indeed the adolescence, of the Indian national movement. At first constitutional, by the turn of the century the movement was beginning to turn radical, largely under the influence of expressly anti-Western religious and political leaders. The national movement early entered into an instinctive alliance with what soon came to be seen as a

genuine renaissance of Hinduism led by men of the highest calibre. In fact, it is particularly noteworthy how many political leaders of this period exercised great religious authority.

3. Then came the First World War, which had the effect of weakening the already precarious prestige and authority of the British in general, and Western missionaries in particular. Although many of the leaders of the national movement were (or soon would be) in prison, the stage was being set for the final struggle for political supremacy in India—a struggle in which religion was to continue to play a large part.

4. The fourth phase probably began with General Dyer's Amritsar massacre of 1919—the event which more than anything else turned M. K. Gandhi from a constitutional reformer into a non-violent revolutionary. It ended with what has been described as 'the end of the Vasco da Gama epoch' on Independence in 1947. This phase is Gandhi's phase, although the name of Nehru should be kept alongside that of Gandhi as witness to a tension between a fundamentally religious and a radically secular approach to the problems of India's future. During these years, Indian nationalism was fully grown and fully self-conscious, taking its direction from the personality of Gandhi, but subject to pressures from conservative Hindu opinion at the one extreme, and from secularists at the other.

5. On Independence and the partition of India and Pakistan in 1947, India's future seemed assured. But the assassination of Gandhi in the following year; the need to balance national and regional interests; the language problem; religious pluralism; international involvements (not least with China)—these and other factors made it clear that the hard struggle for nationhood was only just beginning. The role of religion in this recent development is a matter not only of Hindu, but also of Muslim, Christian, Sikh, Parsi, Buddhist and Jain concern.

Significantly, however, it is in this last phase that Indian thought has begun once more to arouse popular interest in the West—unfortunately, in a West almost entirely ignorant of the course of Indian thought and Indian history, distant or recent. It is not suggested that history is the only key to the understanding of recent Hindu thought and practice; but modern Hinduism is 'historical' as ancient Hinduism was not, and in the units which follow, the link between belief and background will constantly be borne in mind.

EJS

Bibliography

V. Chirol, *India*, London, 1926.
M. Edwardes, *The Last Years of British India*, Mentor ed. 1967.
J. N. Farquhar, *Modern Religious Movements in India*, London, 1915.
C. H. Philips (ed.), *The Evolution of India and Pakistan*, 1858–1947, 2 vols., London, 1962.
D. S. Sarma, *Studies in the Renaissance of Hinduism*, Benares, 1944.
P. Spear, *India, Pakistan and the West*, Oxford, 1967[4].
P. Spear, *A History of India*, Vol. 2, Harmondsworth, 1965.

22

THE IMPACT OF ISLAM

ALTHOUGH THE DECISIVE influence on Hinduism in the modern period has been that of Western religious and secular thought, it should not be forgotten that the India to which Western merchants and soldiers first came in the seventeenth and eighteenth centuries was an India under Muslim rule. And in some ways, Hinduism at the opening of the modern period—i.e. in the early nineteenth century—had already been modified by the contacts to which the Muslim conquest had given rise. This was, however, an uneven process: although Muslim rule extended nominally over the greater part of India, the influence of Islam as a religion was greatest in the north and north-west; in the south, such influence was comparatively slight.

From the orthodox Muslim point of view, there could be no compromise with the religious practices of Hinduism, and the early years of Muslim conquest in the north (beginning in the late twelfth century) were marked by the virtual destruction of large areas of Hindu influence. The temples, with their vast collections of images of gods and goddesses, were particularly vulnerable to Muslim iconoclasm (it being one of the basic tenets of Islam that no image of Deity is to be made, let alone worshipped). The monasteries, Hindu and Buddhist alike, also suffered. Conversions to Islam were wholesale, particularly in the north-west—leading ultimately to the establishment of the Muslim state of Pakistan. To be sure, individual Muslim rulers might proceed somewhat more gently than was the rule—for instance, the Mughal emperor Akbar the Great (1542–1605), who produced an eclectic cult compounded of various religious elements, and who married Hindu princesses—but on the whole the history of Hindu-Muslim contacts has been one of official and deeply-felt antagonism. Time and an ingrained habit of compromise led Hindus eventually to tolerate Muslim rule, as they were later to tolerate the British; nevertheless, hostility would from time to time break to the surface.

The only Hindu people in India ever seriously to oppose Muslim rule by the methods of guerilla warfare were the Marathas, and it was a seventeenth century Maratha chieftain, Shivaji, who was to become in the nineteenth century a symbol of Hindu resistance to foreign oppression. This may perhaps be said to be an indirect result of Muslim influence, but one in which political motives predominated.

Other areas of indirect influence included the structure of the caste system, which in some areas took on firmer outlines during the Muslim period, and the practice of reverence for the cow. Muslims had no particular reason not to slaughter cattle or to abstain from eating beef, but both practices were regarded with horror by Hindus. Muslim attitudes certainly helped to make the cow into a comprehensive symbol of Indian Hindu nationalism—a character which it has retained to this day.

However, there is one area of religious belief in which Muslim influence, though difficult in some cases to evaluate, was certainly felt. This was the area of theistic belief. Closely linked with this was the rejection in some quarters of image-worship as a worthy means of doing honour to God. Theism—the worship of one personal Supreme Being—was latent in classical Hinduism from a very early date. Among the many gods of the Vedic and post-Vedic pantheon, it was possible for one to take on the attributes of all others, and to be worshipped exclusively. Vishnu and Rudra-Shiva in particular were honoured in this way. So the Muslim teaching of the oneness of God in some cases fell on ground that had already been prepared.

Kabir (*c.* 1440–1518) was a weaver of Benares, whose own brand of poetical theistic mysticism places him squarely on the Hindu-Muslim frontier. He in fact rejected many of the outward signs of Hindu faith, including caste, but remained in other ways a devout Vaishnava. He called himself 'both the child of Allah and of Ram (Rama)', and his teaching centred on a doctrine of the divine Word (*Shabda*): 'I am a lover of the Word which has taught me the unseen.' Kabir's genius was for the writing of poetry, and some of his sayings have passed into the Holy Book (*Guru Granth Sahib*) of the Sikhs. Guru Nanak, the founder of Sikhism, was a disciple of Kabir, and taught the essential unity of God, whom he called *Sat Kartar* (True Creator) and *Sat Nam* (True Name), and emphasized the necessity of worshipping God in love. Yet Nanak stood in a rather closer relationship to traditional Hinduism than did Kabir. A sect of followers of Kabir, the *Kabirpanthis*, still refuse to visit Hindu temples, and worship in their own buildings, without the use of images.

It may have been in the sixteenth century that the attempt was first made to incorporate Allah into the Hindu pantheon, under the name of Satya-Narayana, or Satyapir (*pir* is a Muslim saint). And certainly the devotional poetry of the later *bhakti* saints of Hinduism, although offered to God under a Hindu name (e.g. Ram), contains little to offend either the Muslim or the Christian. Out of the many examples that might be quoted, we may take these lines from the Maratha poet Tukaram (1606–1649:) 'I am Thy servant, Thou my Lord; Grant that this difference of high and low, Set between me and Thee, May never vanish.' 'Pray no more for utter oneness with God.' 'In joy Thou watchest over all things, Indwellest all things, Yet art apart, above, beyond.'

Both the worship of God in theistic forms and the rejection of image-worship are relatively common in modern Hinduism. The best example of the two combined would be Ram Mohan Roy, who was educated on the Muslim pattern. In his case, however, there was in later years some Christian influence. Significantly, though, Christian missionaries thought him a Unitarian. This type of theism, in which Islamic influence is clearly seen, has become less common in recent years, partly due to the polarization of Hindu and Muslim opinion.

EJS

Bibliography

Archer, J. C., *The Sikhs in Relation to Hindus, Moslems, Christians and Ahmadiyyas*, Princeton, 1946.
J. S. Hoyland, *An Indian Peasant Mystic: Translations from Tukaram*, London, 1932.
S. M. Ikram and P. Spear (eds.), *The Cultural Heritage of Pakistan*, Karachi, 1955.
F. E. Keay, *Kabir and his Followers*, London, 1931.
H. McLeod, *Guru Nanak and the Sikh Religion*, Oxford, 1968.
W. Cantwell Smith, *Modern Islam in India*, London, 1946.
M. T. Titus, *Islam in India and Pakistan*, Calcutta, 1959.
G. H. Westcott, *Kabir and the Kabir Panth*, Cawnpore, 1907.

23

THE IMPACT OF THE CHRISTIAN WEST

THERE ARE TWO EXTREMES to be avoided in writing of the impact upon Hinduism of the Christian West. The first is the view common at the turn of the century but uncommon today, which would ascribe to the Christian West everything of social, ethical and religious value in modern Hinduism; the second is the view very common indeed at the present time, that everything connected (however indirectly) with Western colonialism must *ipso facto* be evil. Politically motivated blanket judgments, whatever their source, are to be shunned, however. In order to understand modern Hinduism, it is above all necessary to see how Hindu thought reacted and adapted to currents of thought prevalent in Western circles. Perhaps it is as yet too early to estimate accurately the extent of the actual, as distinct from the supposed, influence upon India of the West. In the meantime, however, we may speak of certain areas of influence, and remind the student of the words of Rabindranath Tagore, that '. . . if it be true that the spirit of the West has come upon our fields in the guise of a storm, it is nevertheless scattering living seeds that are immortal'.

Broadly speaking, there were two important sources of influence on Hindu thought: Western science and Protestant Christianity (on the whole, Roman Catholicism was less influential in the earlier part of the period). Bal Gangadhar Tialk said in 1906 that 'If our religion is threatened with any hostile criticism, it comes from these two.' Hostile criticism there certainly was: but there was more. There was also a long and intricate process of cultural osmosis in which Hinduism met and absorbed Western impulses, and in return began to influence the West also. This process is difficult to systematize, but the following points may be made.

1. The most important area of impact was in Western education,

whether administered by missionary agencies (the first in the field), the government or by Indians themselves. Following upon the work of Alexander Duff and the advocacy of Lord Macaulay in the 1830's, English-language higher education spread rapidly in the remainder of the nineteenth century. Its influence was all-pervasive in the upper classes, and gradually created new types of Hindu, some passionately nationalistic, others semi-secularized, called by orthodox Hindus 'men without a *dharma*'. The use of the English language itself modified much Hindu thought, often in subtle ways (not least in the use of the word 'Hinduism'). The schools and colleges taught Western science, geography, economics, history, literature and of course Christianity. Old attitudes came to be seen as untenable, although traditional patterns of behaviour remained. In politics, liberal ideals were inculcated, and the growth of the national movement was facilitated. In religion, Western education as such created few Christians (the Christian mission had more success among the lower classes), but it did a great deal to change the shape of Hinduism. It is important to recognize that this was not a result of the teaching of a doctrine or dogma, but of a universal ideology containing many Christian ideas and ideals. It was the very fact that this came through secular education rather than through the open work of Christian missions that led to its widespread acceptance. To become a Christian, since it involved breaking caste, was never possible to more than a minute fraction of Hindu society; but one could become educated without committing treason against India and the Hindu religion.

2. However, the direct impact of Christian missions should not be underestimated. This was greater in the lower reaches of society than among high-caste Hindus, but the work of missionaries called forth a decided response, sometimes positive, sometimes negative. A Christian Church was created; and Hinduism itself was stirred to reaction. Without the presence of Christianity, much of the Hindu renaissance cannot be fully understood. And if imitation be the sincerest form of flattery, then Hindus certainly appreciated Christian missionary methods. At times, some missionaries sincerely believed that Hinduism was crumbling under the impact of Christian teaching; but what was happening was that Hinduism was changing shape. Always adaptable, it proved capable of absorbing much Christian teaching, including the person of Jesus Christ, without ceasing to be Hinduism.

3. More easily catalogued are the effects of Western philanthropy and social reform—sometimes mediated by missionaries, sometimes not. The abolition of widow-burning (*sati*), the suppression of the professional stranglers (*thags*), the reform of marriage laws, and in particular the Hindu law prohibiting widow remarriage—were all brought about as a result of combined missionary and government action, often backed up in later years by informed Indian opinion.

4. Finally should be mentioned the indirect influence exercised by a century of rule by the British Crown in the areas of travel and communications, language, law and administration, industry and commerce.

It goes without saying that not everything the British did in India is to the West's credit. For instance, far too many individual Westerners in India failed completely to understand the nature of the society they were so keenly absorbed in altering. Some missionaries—though not as many as popularly supposed—were bitterly opposed to Hinduism in every shape and form. But the whole Western episode in Indian history deserves to be studied and understood (not merely condemned) by anyone who would understand the nature and character of religion in modern India.

EJS

Bibliography

C. F. Andrews, *The Renaissance in India*, London, 1912.
G. D. Bearce, *British Attitudes towards India*, 1784–1858, London, 1961.
C. A. Bodelsen, *Studies in Mid-Victorian Imperialism*, Copenhagen and London, 1924.
V. Chirol, *Indian Unrest*, London, 1910.
J. Cumming (ed.), *Political India* 1832–1932, London, 1932.
B. T. McCully, *English Education and the Origins of Indian Nationalism*, New York, 1940.
L. S. S. O'Malley, *Modern India and the West*, London, 1941.
K. T. Paul, *The British Connection with India*, London, 1927.
E. J. Sharpe, *Not to Destroy but to Fulfil*, Lund, 1965.

24

RAM MOHAN ROY AND THE BRAHMA SAMAJ

RAM MOHAN ROY has been called '. . . the pioneer of all living advance, religious, social and educational, in the Hindu community during the nineteenth century'. He was born in 1772 or 1774 of a Kulin Brahmin family long active in the Muslim government of Bengal, but followers of the school of Chaitanya. At the age of twelve he was sent to study at Patna, then a Muslim centre of civil service training, where he made the acquaintance of Sufi teachings, and probably also the works of Muslim rationalists. There was instilled into him a dislike of image-worship, which opened a breach between himself and his family. 'When about the age of sixteen,' he wrote, 'I composed a manuscript calling in question the validity of the idolatrous system of the Hindus. This, together with my known sentiments on that subject, having produced a coolness between me and my immediate kindred, I proceeded on my travels. . .' Although the breach was not permanent, Roy was living in Benares at the time of his father's death in 1803. Shortly after, he entered the service of the East India Company, from which he retired in 1814, settling in Calcutta. By this time he was a convinced theist. He had studied the Upanishads, and was sure that they taught pure theism, uncontaminated by idolatry of any kind.

Roy's first attempt at organizing a society for the propagation of his principles was made in 1815; this was, however, shortlived. In the meantime he had encountered for the first time the teachings of the Christian missionaries, in which he recognized his own theistic position. In 1820 he published a book called *The Precepts of Jesus, the Guide to Peace and Happiness*, a venture which unfortunately brought him neither peace nor happiness: his version of Christianity was taken entirely from the Gospels, and was attacked, particularly by the Serampore

Baptists (Carey, Marshman, Ward) as being a distortion of the Christian Gospel of justification by faith. This controversy was to drag on for a number of years.

Roy was by this time an active social reformer. He threw the whole weight of his authority behind the efforts of the newly-arrived Scottish missionary Alexander Duff to create a Western-style education system in Calcutta, and he was also concerned to improve the lot of women. He campaigned for the abolition of child-marriage and *sati* (suttee)—the latter concern probably intensified when his own sister-in-law burned to death on her husband's funeral pyre.

On August 20, 1828, the first meeting took place in Calcutta of Roy's new society, the *Brahma Sabha* (the name of which was soon changed to *Brahma Samaj*, or Brahma Society). It met every Sunday evening for worship. Services began with the chanting in Sanskrit of passages from the Upanishads (by Brahmins in a separate room); these were then translated into Bengali, a sermon was delivered in Bengali, and hymns were sung in Sanskrit and Bengali. The society was gathered on a strictly *ad hoc* basis, and was without formal constitution or creeds. In this way Roy believed that he was restoring the purity of ancient Hindu worship. The movement, though it gradually grew more eclectic, remained formally Hindu, at least as long as Roy remained in charge.

This was not for long. In November 1830, Roy sailed for England, partly to study Christianity, and partly to give evidence before a Government committee. In England and France he made a tremendous impression on society, but his health proved unequal to the strain, and he died and was buried in Bristol in 1833 (his body was later removed to Arno's Vale Cemetery in London).

Ram Mohan Roy was the first Hindu in modern times to apply the latent eclecticism of India to Western, as well as to Eastern, religious thought. In his cast of mind he was essentially Hindu, despite his disagreement with certain important social and ritual principles of Hinduism (as well as his rejection of image-worship, he repudiated the doctrine of *karma* and *samsara*, and wished—in theory—to see the caste system modified). He was influenced by Islam and Christianity without becoming a Muslim or a Christian, and it was almost certainly Western influence which made him a social reformer, though he desired to find a Hindu motivation for it. K. T. Paul (an Indian Christian) wrote of him: 'If Britain had not been there, he would probably have been a prophet in the succession of Kabir and Nanak, establishing a new sect of Vaishnavism coloured by the theism of Islam and the devotional life rendered richer by the experiences voiced by the Sufis. As it was, these influences prevailed with Ram Mohan Roy to the end of his life.'

After Roy's death, control of the Brahma Samaj passed to the Tagore family, particularly Debendranath Tagore (father of the poet Rabindranath), under whom the society became more explicitly Hindu. Belief in the inerrancy of the Veda was however given up, and the Upanishads became their main standard of faith. A third phase was entered with the accession of Keshab Chander Sen to a position of authority in the society. Sen was more deeply influenced by Christianity than either Roy or Tagore had been, and in time the movement divided into reformed (under Sen) and conservative (under Tagore) sections. A further split followed in the late 1870's. These developments seriously weakened the movement; nevertheless it has always been more influential, particularly among intellectuals, than its numbers might indicate.

EJS

Bibliography

S. D. Collett, *Life and Letters of Raja Rammohun Roy*, Calcutta, 1962[3].

G. S. Leonard, *A History of the Brahmo Samaj*, Calcutta, 1934.

K. Nag and D. Burman (eds.), *The English Works of Raja Rammohun Roy*, 3 vols., Calcutta, 1945–1951.

P. K. Sen, *Biography of a New Faith*, 2 vols., Calcutta, 1950.

I. Singh, *Rammohun Roy*, New York, 1958.

25

DAYANAND SARASVATI AND THE ARYA SAMAJ

IF THE BRAHMA SAMAJ served to some extent as a meeting-ground of Eastern and Western ideologies, the Arya Samaj, founded by Swami Dayanand Sarasvati in 1875, serves as its antithesis in its uncompromising rejection of every foreign impulse. It has been said that 'The Arya Samaj cared nothing for the foreigner, neither for his conversion nor for his opinion' (Lajpat Rai), but this is a slight exaggeration. The Arya Samaj was certainly a Hindu reform movement first and foremost, but its rejection of the West and of Christianity was explicit, as indeed was its rejection of Islam. From its first beginnings the movement sought to purge Hinduism of every accretion, whatever its source, and to return to an ideal Hindu past—the past of the divinely inspired Vedas.

Dayanand was born in 1824 of a Shaivite Brahmin family in Gujerat. The story of his conversion (or enlightenment) has often been told. Its outlines are as follows. At the age of 14 he was taking part in a temple vigil, and was the only one of the devotees awake. A mouse entered, explored the image of the deity, found it harmless and began to eat the sacrificial food. Dayanand was at first horrified, but then came to the conclusion that the image was not what it was supposed to be, i.e. the visible presence of the deity. He was told, not unreasonably that the image only *represented* God, but this he could not accept, and from that moment he was firmly opposed to image-worship. This his family regarded as apostasy, and tried to cool his reforming ardour by marrying him off; but he left home and became a *sadhu*. For fifteen years he wandered in search of knowledge, and learned Yoga. Eventually he found a *guru*, Virjananda Sarasvati, who obtained from him a pledge to reform Hinduism from the falsehoods contained in the Puranas—the mythological treatises which provide such an important part of the content of popular Hinduism.

From this point his public life began—starting in controversy and continuing in controversy. In his zeal for the purification of Hinduism, Dayanand was a thoroughgoing iconoclast, and entered repeatedly into disputation with representatives of Brahmanical orthodoxy. This culminated in a great disputation at Kashi, presided over by the Maharaja of Benares, at which Dayanand lost the day, and his following. The disputation turned on the status of the Puranas—whether they belonged in the Hindu canon at all, and whether the attitudes they teach (including such points as incarnation and image-worship) were genuine parts of Hindu belief and practice. In rejecting incarnation, it may have been that Dayananad was rejecting the authority of the *Bhagavad Gita* also, though this is not certain. It is, however, certain that he rejected the institution of caste, maintaining that all men are brothers.

After the Kashi *débacle*, Dayanand went first to Calcutta, where he met members of the Brahma Samaj, but was not able to reach agreement with them; from there he seems to have gone to Allahabad and then Bombay, where the Arya Samaj was started in 1875. He lived for eight more years, occupied in constant travelling and preaching, mainly in the north of India; he died on October 30, 1883.

Dayanand's aim he stated as follows: 'That alone I hold to be acceptable which is worthy of being believed by all men in all ages. I do not entertain the least idea of founding new religion or sect. My sole aim is to believe in truth and help others to believe in it, to reject falsehood and to help others in doing the same.' He believed that there was but one God, who had to be worshipped without images. Where Hindu scriptures appear to teach polytheism, this is merely the surface meaning: all names of gods are in fact names of one God. All truth is contained in the Vedas, and where other scriptures contradict these, they are to be abandoned. But he was thoroughly orthodox in his belief in *karma* and transmigration and his belief that salvation consists in release from transmigration. Another aspect of his belief centred on the symbol of the cow (unit 37), which he held to be of the utmost sacredness; in 1882 he formed the *Gaurakshini Sabha* (Association for Cow Protection)—an early example of the semi-political use of the symbol.

The first three points of the creed of the Arya Samaj are as follows: '(1) God is the primary cause of all true knowledge, and of everything known by its name. (2) God is All-Truth, All-

Knowledge, All-Beatitude, Incorporeal, Almighty, Just, Merciful, Unbegotten, Infinite, Unchangeable, without a beginning, Incomparable, the Support and the Lord of All, All-pervading, Omniscient, Imperishable, Immortal, Exempt from fear, Eternal, Holy, and the Cause of the Universe. To Him alone worship is due. (3) The Vedas are the books of true knowledge, and it is the paramount duty of every Arya to read or hear them read, to teach and preach them to others.' As well as their purely revivalist work among Hindus, members of the Samaj concentrated on education—helped considerably by their insistence that the reading of the Vedas should be open to members of all castes—and on youth work, in the Young Men's Arya Association. A Women's Arya Samaj was also started. By 1911, despite a split fairly soon after Dayanand's death, it was estimated that the Samaj had almost a quarter of a million members, most of them in the north of India. Unlike the Brahma Samaj, the Arya Samaj has continued to be a vigorous organization.

In the Arya Samaj we see what is virtually a prototype of Hindu reaction against external religious influence, coupled with a sincere desire to purify Hinduism from what are taken to be false teachings. Its political relevance was clear from the first, and it was no coincidence that some notable nationalist leaders of the earlier part of this century were Aryas. Its doctrine owed nothing to the West, though many of its methods were taken over from Christian missions.

EJS

Bibliography

J. N. Farquhar, *Modern Religious Movements in India*, London, 1915, pp. 101–129.
L. Rai, *The Arya Samaj*, London, 1915.

26

SHRI RAMAKRISHNA

SHRI RAMAKRISHNA PARAMAHAMSA (1834–1886) was born Gadadhar Chatterji, of a poor but orthodox Brahmin family in Bengal. Unsophisticated and in the formal sense uneducated, the almost unqualified reverence with which he is regarded in India today—some even going so far as to call him an incarnation of God—is proof of the influence of the holy life on the Hindu religious mind. Of his teachings, that of the equality of all religions (never seriously canvassed before his time) is now axiomatic to all, or almost all, Hindus.

Ramakrishna began his religious life as a young man, as a *pujari* (household priest) in private service. In 1855 he took up a position at a new temple of the goddess Kali at Dakshineshvara, Calcutta. There he soon showed an extraordinary degree of devotion to Kali, whom he came to regard as his mother and the mother of the universe; devotion passed into ecstasy, and to the end of his life he was able to enter into the state of *samadhi* at will—and sometimes in spite of his will. Marriage changed nothing, and he pursued his quest for a personal vision of Kali with even greater intensity, neglecting his duties to do so. He learned from various ascetics the doctrines and practices of Vedanta and Yoga, and made the acquaintance of the Tantric scriptures. From this time on, his religious life passed through a series of stages, in each of which he attempted to enter into a new dimension of experience. First came the attempt to realize the love of Krishna, imagining himself to be Radha, and even, so it is said, dressing himself in women's clothes. Later came attempts to identify himself in imagination with the outcastes (by performing menial tasks), and later still he 'became' in imagination first a Muslim and then a Christian—in each case in order to enter into what he took to be the Muslim and Christian experience of God. From 1871 he was joined by his young wife, not as a wife but as a disciple.

Ramakrishna's public ministry began in the late 1870's. He was never an itinerant preacher, however: as his reputation for sanctity spread, he was sought out by an increasing number of disciples, who often travelled great distances simply to hear him talk. Until his death in 1886 it seems that he talked incessantly, in a colloquial and often coarse Bengali. From these years comes the material which, gathered by a faithful follower, was later published as *The Gospel of Sri Ramakrishna*.

The cornerstone of his teaching was the omnipresence of God. In essence God is impersonal (the teaching of Advaita Vedanta), and yet God may be manifested in any accepted form of deity, male or female, and in any person. However, it is clear that he recognized the presence of the divine most clearly in the female principle, or *shakti*. Of deities, Kali, the great mother, was the most real to him; and it is said that he would worship the divine even in the person of a prostitute. His wife Narada Devi incarnated this same principle, though not in any special sense.

As God is in every person, without distinction or exception, so, according to Ramakrishna, God is in every religion, and can be found through any and every religion. Had he not proved it by living as a Muslim and a Christian? Actually, of course, what Ramakrishna had done was temporarily to clothe his own intensely personal religious experience in the language and symbolism of Islam and Christianity respectively. This did not make him either a Muslim or a Christian, and the question is far more complicated than Ramakrishna or his followers would allow. It should also be noted that while Ramakrishna could say, 'Every man should follow his own religion. A Christian should follow Christianity, a Muslim should follow Islam, and so on'—he could add 'For the Hindus the ancient path, the path of the Aryan Rishis, is the best'.

This idea of the equality of all religions is one which the student of modern Hinduism encounters on every hand. Again in Ramakrishna's words, 'A truly religious man should think that other religions also are paths leading to the truth.' Few Hindus would quarrel with this judgement; in fact it has become virtually a dogma, which one denies at one's peril. But its roots should be clearly seen. If a religion is a purely provisional expression of man's search for one ineffable and impersonal Reality, an attempt to clothe in symbols and words the intrinsically inexpressible, then every such attempt, in so far as it leads the seeker closer to this one Reality, must have similar value to every other such attempt. The goal is beyond words and symbols; hence every set of words and symbols must be as good—or as inadequate—as every other set. However, those religions, like Judaism, Christianity and Islam, which can speak of the will of God and the revelation of the will of God (God conceived as personal), are unable to use this language or accept Ramakrishna's simple doctrine on this point.

Ramakrishna died on March 15, 1886. He had written no books, founded no sect, no society. That his name is revered today is due entirely to the body of faithful disciples he left after him, chief among them Narendra Nath Datta (Swami Vivekananda). He it was who was instrumental in founding the Ramakrishna Mission, which today has branches all over India, and in many other parts of the world. A Ramakrishna Mission centre, such as that in Bombay (its headquarters are in Calcutta), comprises a hospital, hostel, library and *ashram*. At the centre of the *ashram* is a meditation hall, the murals of which depict the religious leaders of mankind, including Jesus, Muhammad, the Buddha, Zoroaster and many more. Presiding over them all is the figure of Ramakrishna himself, surrounded by the instruments of reverence and worship. It was said of him, 'We offer to Him worship *bordering* on divine worship.' Probably for the faithful, the qualification could be omitted.

EJS

Bibliography

Nalini Devdas, *Sri Ramakrishna*, Bangalore, 1966.

Swami Gambhirananda, *History of the Ramakrishna Math and Mission*, Calcutta, 1957.

F. Max Müller, *Ramakrishna: his Life and Sayings*, London, 1899.

Swami Saradananda, *Sri Ramakrishna, the Great Master*, 2nd ed., Hollywood, 1952.

The Gospel of Sri Ramakrishna, Madras, 1957[3].

27

SWAMI VIVEKANANDA

IT WAS IN THE PERSON of Swami Vivekananda (Narendra Nath Datta, 1863–1902) that Hinduism first came to the serious notice of the West on the West's own ground. At the World's Parliament of Religions, held in Chicago in 1893, Vivekananda 'represented' Hinduism to such good effect that he is today celebrated as Hinduism's first 'missionary to the West'. Although the title is a trifle misleading, the foundation of Vedanta societies and other Hindu organizations in America and Europe certainly dates back to Vivekananda; in India, his initiative in founding, shortly after his triumphal return from America, the Ramakrishna Mission, was of the utmost significance for the twentieth century pattern of Hindu thought and practice.

Datta (the title Vivekananda was taken when he became a *sannyasin*) was educated at the Scottish Church College in Calcutta, and in his early years absorbed a good deal of Western secular thought. He spent some time on the fringes of the Brahma Samaj, but the decisive influence on his life was that of Ramakrishna. From being, as a friend put it, 'a rampant Vedantist-cum-Hegelian-cum-Revolutionary' he became a fervent disciple of the Bengali prophet. However, he never showed the slightest tendency to become a religious recluse, and the need for social action on genuinely Hindu foundations was prominent in his thought from the first. After the death of Ramakrishna, he spent some time in retirement and travel, from which he emerged in 1892. At this time the World's Parliament was being organized, and friends in Madras collected enough money to send him as a delegate.

In America, as well as appearing at the Parliament, and prompting one New York paper to write that 'after hearing him we feel how foolish it is to send missionaries to this learned nation', he took close note of many features of Western life.

Some he admired—for instance the willpower of the many immigrants then flocking into the United States. But the overall materialism of Western society distressed him. It seems that it is to Vivekananda we owe the myth of the spiritual East and the materialist West (as though there were no spirituality in the West and no materialism in the East)—based directly on his American experiences. On his return to his motherland he was hailed as a herald of the new age for India; his 'four years of glorious work for the Motherland and her ancient religion', writes D. S. Sarma, made every Indian feel an inch taller, and made 'the present Hindu Renaissance self-conscious and adolescent'. Immediately he set about organizing the Ramakrishna Mission, with its headquarters at Belur, near Calcutta.

Vivekananda had only five more years to live, but those years were filled with speaking engagements. Like his master, he was an indefatigable talker, and although he claimed only to be reproducing Ramakrishna's thought, he added to it certain important dimensions.

The basis of Vivekananda's thought was, indeed, identical to that of Ramakrishna. He was for the most part an orthodox Vedantin, and one who believed that while all religions are true and good, every man should remain in the religion in which he had been brought up. Hindus especially, he maintained, have no need to seek elsewhere for the spiritual basis of practical life in the world. Least of all should they seek in the West.

His teaching nevertheless owed more than he would perhaps admit to Western impulses. Two aspects in particular have Western, rather than Hindu, roots: first the emphasis on social action, and secondly the generally evolutionary framework of what he called *Comprehensive Vedanta*. In each case, however, the justification he provided in Hindu terms. Social action he motivated by saying that every Self (*atman*) is one with every other Self: 'Why should I love everyone? Because they and I are one . . . There is this oneness, this solidarity of the whole universe. From the lowest worm that crawls under our feet to the highest beings that ever lived—all have various bodies, but one Soul. . .' (*Works*, II, 414 f.) The enlightened man should even renounce salvation (*moksha*, *mukti*) for the sake of others: 'Do you think, so long as one *Jiva* endures in bondage, you will have any liberation? So long as he is not liberated—it may take several lifetimes—you will have to be born to help him, to make him realise Brahman. . .' (*Works*, VI, p. 235). There are strong resemblances here to the Buddhist doctrine of the *Bodhisattva*.

Vivekananda could not conceive of the existence of contradictory schools of thought within Hinduism. All alternative views are, in his opinion, complementary. Past doctrinal disputes he ignores completely, maintaining that the three major schools of Vedanta—*Dvaita*, *Vishishtadvaita* and *Advaita*—are steps on a ladder of spiritual evolution, which reaches its crown and climax in the *Advaita* vision of the oneness of *Brahman* and the Soul. 'The same God whom the ignorant man saw outside nature [*Dvaita*], the same whom the little-knowing man saw as interpenetrating the universe [*Vishishtadvaita*] and the same whom the sage realises as his own Self, as the whole universe itself [*Advaita*]—all are the One and the same Being, the same entity seen from different standpoints. . .' (*Works*, III, 422 f.)

Vivekananda's comprehensive vision was of the utmost importance for the future of Hindu thought, and few later Hindu thinkers have been uninfluenced by him, But he was also a symbol of the Hindu Renaissance, revered now not only for what he taught (which is frequently repetitive and sometimes superficial), but for what he was—an instrument of revival, religious and national:

'What our country now wants are muscles of iron and nerves of steel, gigantic wills which nothing can resist . . . That is what we want, and that can only be created, established and strengthened by understanding and realising the ideal of the *Advaita*, the ideal of the oneness of all. Faith, faith, faith in yourselves; faith, faith in God—this is the secret of greatness.' (*Works*, III, p. 190).

EJS

Bibliography

Nalini Devdas, *Svami Vivekananda*, Bangalore, 1968.

The Complete Works of Swami Vivekananda, 7 vols., Calcutta, 1960.

The Life of Swami Vivekananda, by his Eastern and Western Disciples, Calcutta, 1960.

28

SHRI AUROBINDO

Of all the religious thinkers of modern India, none is more widely admired than Aurobindo Ghose (Shri Aurobindo, 1872–1950). Called by Radhakrishnan 'the greatest intellect of our age', he devoted forty years of his life to the exposition of the inner meaning of the classical Hindu tradition. From his famous *ashram* at Pondicherry he exercised, largely through his writings, a vast spiritual influence. In the twenty years since his death, this influence has, if anything, increased; particular interest has been shown in the resemblances between his thought and that of the Jesuit Pierre Teilhard de Chardin. However, in the early years of his career there was no sign of the visionary in his makeup, and his life as a whole provides one of the most interesting examples of the interaction between India and the West in the field of religious thought.

Aurobindo was educated in England, at St. Paul's School and King's College, Cambridge. He appeared to have adapted well to European culture, and his scholarship was brilliant (he took a First in Classics). But he was growing more concerned at the turn events were taking in India, and in 1893 he returned home, a militant nationalist. At first he identified himself with the recently-formed Indian National Congress, but gradually became disenchanted with its slowness, and turned to political journalism in the attempt to spur his people into more effective action. At this time the national movement was largely the prerogative of a middle-class elite; Aurobindo's goal was to engage the mass of the people. This he did by interpreting accepted Hindu doctrine in political categories. 'Nationalism is not a mere political programme; Nationalism is a religion that has come from God. . .'

In Bengal, where the greater part of Aurobindo's political work was done, the Shaiva and Shakta elements in Hinduism had long been prominent, while the Vaishnava movement had been powerfully represented by the school of Chaitanya. Shaktism in particular could be made into a powerful political weapon, as the motherland was personified as divine. Both Bengal and India as a whole were symbolized as Kali or Durga, struggling to escape from the oppression of the *maya* of the 'foreign devils', *daityas* and *asuras*. Thus in Aurobindo's words, '. . . the motherland in all her beauty and grandeur represents the goddess of our worship', and at the Durga Puja festival, the patriot is able to sense a depth of meaning inaccessible to the outsider. At the Durga Puja the patriot feels that 'his is a civilization which alone has accomplished the unity of man in God with God in man'. Here we have the roots of his most famous book, *The Life Divine*. Vaishnava elements, too, held a depth of nationalist meaning. Krishna, it was said, was active, though hidden, in the movement. 'Nationalism is an *avatar* and cannot be slain. Nationalism is a divinely-appointed *shakti* of the Eternal and must do its God-given work before it returns to the bosom of the Universal Energy from which it came.'

In 1908 Aurobindo was imprisoned by the British. While in jail, he received a revelation of Krishna, who told him: 'I am in the nation and its uprising and I am Vasudeva, I am Narayana, and what I will, shall be, not what others will . . . Something has been shown to you in this year of seclusion, something about which you had your doubts, and it is the truth of the Hindu religion . . . I am raising up this nation to send forth my word.'

Shortly after his release, Aurobindo abandoned politics altogether, entered an ashram, and his career entered an entirely new phase. One of his first actions was to start a magazine, the *Arya*, which aimed at '. . . a systematic study of the highest problems of existence, and the formation of a vast synthesis of knowledge'. His best-known books began life as articles in the *Arya*.

The philosophy which Aurobindo elaborated during his years of seclusion is of extreme complexity, and no more than a hint at its nature can be given here. A key is however provided by the doctrine of evolution, in which Aurobindo saw a link between East and West. As well as being steeped in Vedanta, he had read many Western evolutionary thinkers, for instance Bergson and Nietzsche. Man, he held, is ideally continually growing in consciousness, and man's growth corresponds to the creative impulse of the Supreme Existence, though to some extent in reverse. There is, he taught, a metaphysical 'ladder' with eight rungs: Existence, Consciousness-Force, Bliss, Supermind, Mind, Psyche, Life and Matter. The first three correspond exactly to the Vedanta triad of *sat*, *chit*, *ananda;* Supermind provides the transition from the unity of the Divine to the multiplicity of human life; Mind is the instrument of clarification and reason; Psyche, Life and Matter comprise the world as we know it. The whole purpose of man is to ascend the ladder as far as Supermind (attained by Aurobindo himself in 1926). There he perceives intuitively the oneness of things, understanding and at the same time transcending the multiplicity of existence. *Karma* exists in order to assist this process of growth, and as such is the instrument of the Divine Spirit. The means of growth is *Integral Yoga*—the comprehensive discipline of body, mind and spirit. Eventually, as the number of those who have attained knowledge of the nature of Reality grows, there will develop 'gnostic' communities, characterized by sympathy and understanding. This will be the nucleus of the new humanity, the revelation of the life divine in man.

'His main contribution,' writes Herbert Jai Singh, 'besides awakening Hinduism to a sense of dignity with regard to its rich traditions, is prophetic in constructing the vision of a super-humanity wherein the discords and strifes of today will be done away with, a new race of men will arise who will have mastered the art of living in union with God and men.'

EJS

Bibliography

Sri Aurobindo, *The Life Divine*, Pondicherry, 1947, *Speeches*, Pondicherry, 1952.

H. Chaudhuri and F. Spiegelberg (eds.), *The Integal Philosophy of Sri Aurobindo*, London, 1960.

G. H. Langley, *Sri Aurobindo*, London, no date.

H. and U. Mukherjee, *Sri Aurobindo's Political Thought* 1893–1908, Calcutta, 1958.

H. Jai Singh, *Sri Aurobindo: his Life and Religious Thought*, Bangalore, 1962.

V. P. Varma, *The Political Philosophy of Sri Aurobindo*, London, 1960.

29

RABINDRANATH TAGORE

EARLIER THIS CENTURY, Rabindranath Tagore (1861–1941) was perhaps the Indian writer and thinker who was best known in the West, not least since he had been awarded the Nobel Prize for literature in 1913. Now, however, he is less well known; he is little read, and tends to be dismissed as a romantic and rather over-ripe oriental minor poet. This is a great injustice to Tagore, for in him we have one of the most outstanding as well as the most accessible, Hindu thinkers of modern times. We may, if we will, call him an aesthete, but this must not obscure the fact that he was also a considerable scholar, an educationalist, and a master of words who exercised a formative influence on modern Bengali literature. Politically, he held independent views, involving him in controversy with Gandhi, whose motives he suspected slightly.

Tagore was the son of the Brahma Samaj leader Debendranath Tagore. He grew up in the atmosphere of the Brahma Samaj, from which he derived his love of the Upanishads—though his criticism of certain aspects of Hindu society was much more radical than any opinion of his father's. Among the other influences which helped mould his religious and social thought may be mentioned the *bhakti* poets, particularly Kabir, whom he translated into English; Chaitanya; Tulsi Das; and the Baüls (a Bengali antinomian movement rather reminiscent of the 'hippies' of the present day). As a result, Tagore's version of Hinduism appears to the observer to be more than usually eclectic, and indeed in some respects to be hardly Hindu at all. He deliberately abandoned the doctrines of *karma*, *maya* and *moksha*; he rejected the monist formula *tat tvam asi* ('thou art that'), and ascetic practices; he did not believe in incarnations; he broke completely with the caste system, which he called an 'incongruous anachronism' and a 'gigantic system of cold-blooded repression'; and he developed a view of the world which was highly positive, in the sharpest possible contrast to the Vedantic view. The view of the world as illusion, and the human reaction which saw the world as something to be shunned and abandoned in the quest for ultimate reality, he rejected completely. In Tagore's teaching, it was *in* the world that God had chosen to reveal himself, and therefore to run away from the world would be to run away from God.

But it cannot be emphasized too highly that Tagore was neither a systematic nor an analytical thinker. In his own words, 'I am a singer myself, and am ever attracted by the strains that come from the House of Songs'. In other words, whatever he taught, he taught largely through the medium of poetic imagery, and there is frequent impressionism and imprecision in his work. He had no interest in the history of ideas, and did not care where his impulses came from.

It has been said of Tagore that he was the first Indian poet to introduce 'a democratic conception of God' into religious verse. He was neither strongly *dvaita* nor *advaita* in the traditional sense; he speaks, it is true, of God as 'Lord of my life' and 'King', but also calls him 'Brother' and 'Friend'. To Tagore, the Divine is the Supreme Man, and the relationship between man and God should be that between lovers. The roots of this view are of course to be found in the *bhakti* movement, but it may be that some of Tagore's language is derived from Christian usage. Nothing is more characteristic of Tagore than his emphasis on the reality of Divine love, and it is not surprising that some Christians have mistakenly claimed him as an anonymous Christian.

There is also a sense in which Tagore was a practical man. His idealistic views, and his concern for humanity, led him to travel widely, calling for an end to war and oppression—characteristics which he associated particularly with the phenomenon of nationalism. The theme of his most important book (apart from his poetry), *Nationalism* (1918) is the opposition between the negative phenomenon of nationalism and the positive phenomenon of humanity. Nationalism—'organised selfishness'—had been imported by the West into India, to India's eternal loss. 'The naked passion of the self-love of Nations,' he wrote, 'in its drunken delirium of greed, is dancing to the clash of steel and the howling verses of vengeance'. Thus he denied, despite the character of the age, that India's problems were political; in his view, the main problem was social, to be served not by political debate and agitation but by education.

Tagore's main contribution in this area was the founding in 1901 of his college Shantiniketan (the Abode of Peace) at Bolpur near Calcutta. His Nobel prize-money was spent on this college, the site of which had been bought originally as an *ashram* by his father. The college was to be open to men and women alike—a practical application of his statement that '. . . in the future civilisation also, the women . . . will have their place . . .' Shantiniketan has no temple, emphasizing the equal role of all religions in the quest for peace; for a number of years one of Tagore's closest colleagues there was a Christian, a former missionary, C. F. Andrews. Prayer and meditation take place largely in the open air: a deliberate return to ancient Vedic practice, though of course in a much refined form.

Tagore's main personal characteristic was outward simplicity, although this was combined with a high degree of intellectual sophistication. It is perhaps invidious to single out one passage from his writings to illustrate this; nevertheless the following lines, addressed to his countrymen, epitomize practically everything he stood for—in religion, aesthetics, education and politics:

'Be not ashamed, my brothers, to stand before the proud and the powerful
With your white robe of simpleness.
Let your crown be of humility, your freedom the freedom of the soul.
Build God's throne daily upon the ample barrenness of your poverty.
And know that what is huge is not great and pride is not everlasting.'

EJS

Bibliography

S. Estborn, *The Religion of Tagore*, Madras, 1949.
K. R. Kripalani, *Tagore*, New York, 1962.
S. Radhakrishnan (ed.), *Rabindranath Tagore*, New Delhi, 1961.
R. Tagore, *Gitanjali*, London, 1913. *One Hundred Poems of Kabir*, London, 1915. *Nationalism*, London, 1917. *The Religion of Man*, London, 1931.
E. Thompson, *Rabindranath Tagore, Poet and Dramatist*, Oxford, 1926.

30

MOHANDAS KARAMCHAND (MAHATMA) GANDHI

FOR ALL ITS IDEALS, before the First World War the Indian national movement was extremely fragmented, and drew its inspiration from a great variety of sources. It had run into political trouble, thanks to the activities of its extremists, and was in danger of foundering. That the period between the war saw the re-emergence of the national movement on a genuinely national level was due almost entirely to the work of one man, M. K. Gandhi (1862–1948), also called 'Mahatma' and familiarly 'Bapu'. Gandhi, apart from being able to command the kind of allegiance given in India to a man of proven asceticism, also proved capable of gathering up most of the threads of the movement. Libraries have been written about his work as a political leader. What is not so clear is the nature of his religion. It is known that he united in himself Hindu, Jain and Christian elements; but their relative weight is disputed. Christians and Hindus both claim him; but although he was deeply influenced by some aspects of Christianity—in particular the Sermon on the Mount—in his teaching he remained Hindu, and died with the name of Ram on his lips.

Gandhi was born in 1869 of a Gujerati Kshatriya family. His early education was irregular, and he was married at the age of 13. In 1888 he was sent to England to study law, and in 1893 went to South Africa to look after the legal interests of an Indian firm. There he soon became aware of the disabilities suffered by Indian workers, virtual slaves of the indenture system; for twenty years he fought for their rights, with a measure of success. He was not at this stage a pacifist, and in the Boer War he served in the Indian Ambulance Corps. Influences on him from this period included Thoreau, Tolstoy and Ruskin; he bought a farm near Durban, where he set up a prototype community dedicated to the life of simplicity.

In 1906 his campaign began. The Transvaal Government had published an ordinance requiring the registration and finger-printing of all Indians; as the slogan of the resistance movement Gandhi coined the term *satyagraha* (soul-force or truth-force). Coupled with this in practice were the terms *ahimsa* (non-violence) and *sarvodaya* (the universal well-being of each and every member of humanity). On these three pillars Gandhi's thought and political programme were based.

The ordinance was repealed in 1914 (after Gandhi had spent some time in gaol), and in the following year he returned to India, where he was at once plunged into the thick of the national movement. At first he was a collaborationist, accusing Indians of wanting to talk rather than work, and concentrating on improving the lot of the untouchables, whom he renamed Harijans (sons of Hari=Vishnu=God). At that time he still hoped that freedom could be obtained gradually and peacefully. His change of attitude dated from the Amritsar massacre of 1919, when a crowd was fired on by British soldiers, and many were killed. It has been said that 'No matter where he went, the echoes of General Dyer's fusillade pursued him.'

In 1920 Congress adopted Gandhi's programme of non-cooperation and from that point on he was the symbol around which the whole of India could rally. His struggle was a moral and religious struggle; he insisted that India would have to conquer herself before she could be truly free; and by his discipline of himself (including his fasts) he set the example. He called India to return to her pre-industrial past, at least in spirit—to work at the spinning-wheel and wear only homespun clothing. He wished to see a purified India, a moral India and a free India.

The relationship between politics and religion in Gandhi's life is a complex one, and while some still view him as a saint, others speak of 'Machiavellianism redeemed' and 'bringing God into politics'. Gandhi's politics were unambiguous; his religion, non-dogmatic and subjective, was an agnostic theism. Certainly he believed in God (his background was Vaishnava) and in the worth of prayer and devotion, but he believed still more strongly in truth and in living an ethical and moral life. His belief in the doctrine of *ahimsa* has already been mentioned; to this, on the Hindu side, may be added his reverence for the cow, and his support for the caste system—though in a purified form, from which untouchability had been removed. But he showed on many occasions his love for the Sermon on the

Mount. In 1927 he said: 'I do not expect the India of my dream to develop one religion, i.e. to be wholly Hindu or wholly Christian, or wholly Mussalman (Muslim); but I want it to be wholly tolerant, with its religions working side by side with one another.' For reasons such as these he aroused the opposition of orthodox Hindus, who suspected him of religious treason, of being in league with the British and of trifling with the Muslims. In fact he was ultimately assassinated by a representative of right-wing Hindu orthodoxy.

Gandhi has few direct disciples in India today. The *ashram* which he founded at Sevagram is not quite the centre of action and reconciliation Gandhi wished it to be, partly because reverence for Gandhi himself has replaced concern for social action as its motive force. There is really no movement which can without more ado be characterized as 'Gandhism', either in politics or in religion. The hopes of modern India tend to be pinned to the very industrialism which Gandhi himself suspected so profoundly. Gandhi is revered as a great man, a saint, a symbol; his ideas are seldom followed. Of those who have drawn the consequences of his witness, and are attempting, or have attempted, to carry on his work, the names of Vinoba Bhave and Annasaheb Sahasrabuddhe should be mentioned—in each case men who are attempting to persuade landowners to return some part of their land to the peasants.

EJS

Bibliography

L. Fischer, *Gandhi: his life and Message for the World*, Mentor pb. 1954.
M. K. Gandhi, *The Story of my Experiments with Truth*, (many editions) *Satyagraha in South Africa*, 2nd ed. Ahmedabad, 1950. *The Collected Works of Mahatma Gandhi*, Delhi 1958 ff. (in progress).
H. S. L. Polak and others, *Life of Gandhi*, London, 1949.
J. S. Sharma, *Mahatma Gandhi: a Descriptive Bibliography*, Delhi, 1955.
D. G. Tendulkar, *Mahatma*, 8 vols., Bombay, 1952 ff.

31

SARVEPALLI RADHAKRISHNAN

THE MEN MOST PROMINENT in the twentieth-century renaissance of Hinduism have frequently owed their influence to a combination of two things in their lives: the status of an active reformer and the status of a holy man. Gandhi is the outstanding example of this. Radhakrishnan, however, is strictly speaking neither of these things. He is neither a radical reformer nor a *sannyasin*. He is a philosopher, technically a Vedantin, an ex-university professor (for some years Spalding Professor at Oxford) who has drunk deeply at the wells of Western scholarship while remaining a Hindu. He has been involved in politics —first as Indian Ambassador to Moscow, then as Vice-President and finally as President of India. It has been said of him that he approximates to the Platonic ideal of the philosopher-king. But he appears always to have sat loose to politics; principally he has always been a scholar.

Radhakrishnan was born in 1888, and was educated in Christian missionary institutions, foremost among them Madras Christian College (1905–1909). In his young days he was deeply influenced by the precept and example of Swami Vivekananda, which made him proud to be a Hindu. He was also hurt by the attitude of some Christian missionaries of the old school, who were rather apt to decry everything Hindu. 'My religious sense,' he later wrote, 'did not allow me to speak a rash or a profane word of anything which the soul of a man holds or has held sacred.'

Radhakrishnan's first teacher of philosophy was the Scottish missionary professor A. G. Hogg, and it may well have been Hogg's book *Karma and Redemption* (1904–1905 in article form), in which the ethical basis of Vedanta was subjected to criticism, which prompted Radhakrishnan to write his first work of Hindu apologetics, *Ethics of the Vedanta* (1908). Already he had formulated his basic concern (in which one hears echoes of

Vivekananda), that 'Religion must express itself in reasonable thought, fruitful action, and right social institutions'. This is a high ideal, but it is scarcely that of classical Hindu teaching, for which such matters as 'fruitful action' and 'right social institutions' have always been peripheral. However, this was one of the ways in which Hinduism was changing—by finding in the classical tradition support for the world-affirming view of life which was being presented to India by the impact of the West. Such was Radhakrishnan's concern; he became an apologist, and an apologist he has remained.

There is, however, one feature of Radhakrishnan's early development which is worthy of mention, particularly for the sake of the Western student. It is his almost total lack of understanding of, and feeling for, Christian theological categories. He seems always to have been unable to take very seriously a view of life which differs radically from his own. He writes repeatedly about Christianity, but is content with what seems to him to be Christianity—a turn of-the-century liberal moralism based on the ethical example of Jesus—and not with Christianity as Christians see and understand it. Inevitably this gives a slightly hollow ring to his statement that the meeting of East and West may pave the way for unity 'if mutual appreciation takes the place of cold criticism and patronizing judgment'.

Radhakrishnan's view of the nature of religion is expressed in many places in his writings, of which this may serve as an example: 'Religion is essentially a concern of the inner life. Its end is to secure spiritual certainty which lifts life above meaningless existence or dull despair. It must be judged by its own standard, whether it gives security to values, meaning to life, confidence to adventure. . .' The concern of philosophy is practically identical with this, and Radhakrishnan's philosophy is a practical philosophy of a Vedantist type modified by contacts with the West. As an idealist he is much concerned with unity, wholeness and comprehensiveness—all three of these characteristics which he finds *par excellence* in the Hindu way of life. He makes much of the unitary character of Hinduism, and its acceptance of unity in diversity. 'Hinduism is . . . not a definite dogmatic creed, but a vast, complex, but subtly unified mass of spiritual thought and realization'. Understandably, he tends to play down historical conflicts within Hinduism —a point which the historian of religion may well hold against him.

However, there is something typically Hindu about Radhakrishnan's overall interpretation of religion. Ever since Ramakrishna, the dogma of the transcendental unity of religions has been widely accepted by Hindus. The monistic doctrines of Vedanta, in which all phenomena merely demonstrate aspects of the one Reality, lends support to this attitude. Difference of background, emphasis and interpretation are, it seems, only temporary misunderstandings which will eventually disappear in the light of full knowledge. Again, the historian of religion has difficulty in accepting this view, which fails to do justice to the uniqueness of separate religious traditions. As an interpreter of philosophy, Radhakrishnan deserves serious attention; as an exponent of a theory of 'comparative religion' (his own phrase), his views must be treated with caution.

It should also be noted, finally, that Radhakrishnan, on his own ground, reinterprets classical Vedanta to the extent of insisting on the dependent reality of the world, and life in the world. He does not say exactly how the empirical world is related to the Absolute, but he argues that the Vedantin is not exempt from concern with the world just because he happens not to be able to identify it with ultimate Reality.

In his insistence that the *sanatana dharma* can provide the foundation of tolerance and peace that the world needs, Radhakrishnan has proved himself to be a thinker of more than Indian significance.

EJS

Bibliography

H. Kraemer, *Religion and the Christian Faith*, London, 1956, pp. 99–136.
D. G. Moses, *Religious Truth and the Relation between Religions*, Madras, 1950, pp. 97–122.
S. Radhakrishnan, *The Hindu View of Life*, London, 1927. *East and West in Religion*, London, 1933. *Eastern Religions and Western Thought*, London, 1940[2]. *The Bhagavad Gita*, London, 1948. *The Principal Upaniṣads*, London, 1953. *The Brahma Sutra*, London, 1960.
P. Schilpp (ed.), *The Philosophy of Radhakrishnan*, New York, 1952.

32

WORSHIP IN THE TEMPLE

WORSHIP IN THE ARYAN INDIA of Vedic times took place in the open air, and not in enclosed sanctuaries. It is not impossible that the practice of worship in temples was adopted from the Indus peoples. The earliest temples were probably of wood, and have not survived; the most ancient surviving Hindu temples date from the early Middle Period, and are often hewn out of the living rock. By classical times there had developed an elaborate parallelism between the life of the gods and the life of earthly kings, and the Hindu temple of this period has to be viewed on the analogy of the king's court. Just as there were many kings, so there were many gods, each with his home, his courtiers, consorts and attendants of various kinds. Ultimately the gods were believed to live in the mountains, and so each temple could be thought of as a replica of an individual god's mountain home; the very shape of the temple was reminiscent of a mountain, with its tower and galleries and central holy place in which the deity dwelt. Around the tower and walls it became usual to depict the teeming life of the spirit-world.

The gods were originally believed to share most human characteristics, except mortality, though developed to a higher degree. Philosophically it might be held that they were bound up, like men, in the wheel of *karma*, but in the popular mind, they needed the sustenance which regular sacrifice provided. Given certain rules of conduct from man's side, they were benevolent, and might be visited at certain times by anyone seeking audience (again like a king). The god, dwelling in the holiest place at the heart of his temple-palace, was surrounded by his family and servants, and the daily and seasonal cycles of the temple cult represented the personal service given to the god by his subjects. Manuals exist giving precise details of these operations; for instance, in Vaishnava morning worship there were sixteen (including washing feet, rinsing mouth, bathing, dressing, perfuming and feeding). While these things were going on, hymns would be sung, bells rung, incense burned and music played. Once over, the god would be ready to receive worshippers, who would come to do *puja* (worship), i.e. to pay their respects and make their requests, and in return to share the god's banquet, water (*tirtha*) and food (*prasada*). The god also received food and refreshment during the day, and evening worship ends with his being laid to rest for the night.

This is the daily cycle. The great seasonal cycle involves celebrations appropriate to the times of year, with on occasions the deity moving out in solemn procession in his car. Frequently small shrines are erected at which he may rest when on a progress of this kind.

Implicit in these practices is the belief that the image of deity actually is a living personal god (one may contrast, however, the attitudes of Ramakrishna [unit 26] and Dayananda Sarasvati [unit 25] to image-worship). It is believed that a god may take any form he pleases: 'The Manifestation worshipable is that form of the Lord, in which the Lord is pleased without any kind of limitation as to times, places, or persons, to be present and manifest Himself to all, in temples and homes.' (Govindacharya.) 'We should believe in the Divine Presence infilling the Images of the Deity.' (Ramakrishna.)

The practices of the *puja* (which the student should not confuse with the congregational worship of a church, mosque or synagogue) are capable of a high degree of spiritualization. Each part of the temple may be given a symbolical and spiritual meaning—the central shrine symbolizing the heart of the worshipper, the tower the upward flight of the spirit, and so on, and since every god and every image of god may be taken to represent a function or attribute of the Supreme, the individual's inward worship in a temple may be of quite a different character from the classical 'royal' pattern, centering on meditation rather than the significance of sacrifice. It is entirely in line with this that a Ramakrishna Mission centre should have a meditation hall which in its general form is reminiscent of a temple, though with the figure of Ramakrishna himself serving as the focus of the worshipper's thoughts (as *guru*, not deity).

The common people's attitude to the temple remains, however, substantially unchanged. Although all the actual worship is conducted by *pujaris* (who may or may not be Brahmins), the visitor may 'endow' the reading of prayers or *mantras*. His (or her) own role is often limited to the giving of gifts of flowers or money, and his main ritual action may be to circumambulate the central shrine, keeping it always on his right shoulder. Whether his temple be a great 'cathedral' sanctuary, or merely a shabby box belonging to a local mother-goddess, his attitude will be substantially the same, because here he is in touch with a focus of the sacred. Other such foci are rivers, lakes, waters, *ashramas* where the holy men dwell, and cow-pens. It may seem a far cry from the temple to the cow-pen, but in the perspective of the sacred, both have their given place; indeed a cow-pen may on occasion be a poor man's temple.

There is no obligation for any Hindu to participate in temple worship, and in modern times there have been a number of movements which have called in question both its efficacy and its necessity. But again on the popular level, even an outwardly secularized Hindu will enter a temple in order to do *puja* on his way to work. The Hindu has full freedom of thought and interpretation; but the custom of *puja* still has a deep hold on him.

EJS

Bibliography

C. G. Diehl, *Instrument and Purpose*, Lund, 1956.
S. Kramrisch, *The Hindu Temple*, Calcutta, 1946.
K. W. Morgan (ed.), *The Religion of the Hindus*, New York, 1953, pp. 185–188.

33

WORSHIP IN THE HOME

IN THE PREVIOUS UNIT we saw that the Supreme, revealed in the gods and goddesses of Hinduism, is believed to be able to manifest himself in any form or any place he pleases, 'in temples and homes'. And for the orthodox Hindu, worship (*puja*) centres on the home, and on the religious duties prescribed for him there by his caste *dharma*. These duties vary according to his caste, the duties of a Brahmin being the most detailed and onerous; the duties of a Shudra, at the other extreme, are in theory limited to service of other, higher castes. In a higher-caste home a room or part of a room is set apart for *puja*. It contains either a shrine, with an image of the family's chosen deity, together with other symbols of the sacred and vessels and instruments of worship (bowls, lamps, etc.), or, in poorer families, pictures of deities (which may be bought in all the bazaars for a few coppers). The Christian is sometimes surprised to find the image of Jesus—usually a Sacred Heart image—in the company of Krishna, Lakshmi and Ganesha on the walls. In some homes worship may centre on an abstract diagram, made up of squares, circles and triangles, called a *mandala* or *yantra*. The theory of these is highly complex, but is based on the fact that each geometrical shape symbolizes an element, and the design as a whole represents the universe.

Household worship makes use of fire for purification (a symbol of the sun), water, also for purification, food-offerings, incense, flowers and coloured powders—the latter for ornamentation. It is carried out at certain fixed times: sunrise, midday and sunset. When worshipping, the orthodox Hindu will be dressed in the traditional way, wearing the sacred thread (worn over the left shoulder and hanging to the right hip; it is made of cotton for Brahmins, hemp for Kshatriyas and wool for Vaishyas) and caste or sect marks (*tilaka*) on the forehead and sometimes the arms and other parts of the body.

Apart from the obligation to worship on a minimum of these three occasions, the orthodox have five areas of obligation—to worship the gods (by fire), the *Rishis* or Brahman (by recitation of the Veda), the ancestors (by water), all beings (by scattering food outside the door), and men (by exercising hospitality). In addition there are stringent food regulations, particularly for Brahmins. Probably today there are relatively few Hindus who perform all the duties of their caste, but there are meritorious acts, capable of being performed at any time, which to some extent take their place. The commonest of these is *japa*, the constant repetition of the name of a god or a *mantra*, which forms an important part of *bhakti* devotion. *Japa* may of course be undertaken anywhere, at any time.

Among more specific household rituals, the most important is *śrāddha* (not to be confused with *śraddhā*, faith), or the offerings made by all Hindu adult males to their forefathers, reaching back three generations. It consists of water offerings, and the offering of rice balls, together with prayers, and is carried out annually on the anniversary of the death of the ancestor in question. The justification of this rite is Vedic, and it presupposes quite a different view of man's destiny to that contained in the doctrines of *karma* and transmigration—i.e. the continued existence of the fathers in 'heaven'.

It is quite natural for the Hindu of today to speak in addition of 'sacraments' (although this word is of course Christian). In the *Laws of Manu* these are said for a Brahmin to be twelve in number: 1. Ceremony on conception. 2. Ceremony on first indication of conception of a living male. 3. Parting the mother's hair. 4. Touching the infant's tongue with honey and butter at birth. 5. Naming. 6. Taking the child to see the sun. 7. Feeding with rice (5th–8th month). 8. Tonsure (3rd year). 9. Investiture with sacred thread. 10. Further tonsure (16th–24th year). 11. Return home after course of study. 12. Marriage. Today, however, Hindu sacraments are generally taken to be four in number: birth, initiation, marriage and death. All are carried out, at least in part, in the home, although it is regarded as highly auspicious for a Hindu to die on the bank of a sacred river, and following death the corpse is carried to a sacred spot (of which the most famous is the Burning Ghat in Benares) to be cremated. In the past, measures were taken to prevent the ghost of the deceased returning to its former home, but today the only trace of such belief is the presence at the home of a team of hired drummers, who will beat their drums furiously to drive away evil spirits. However, the nearest relatives are regarded as ritually impure for a time following a death, and offerings are made to assist the deceased in his journey to the beyond during this time, after which the regular *shraddha* ceremonies are taken up.

The orthodox Hindu home, then, is regulated throughout by the precepts of the *Dharmashastras*, one of which *Āpastamba Dharmasutra* (7.20) sums up the fundamental attitude involved in these words:

> 'One should not observe the ordained duties with a worldly end in view, for, in the end, they bear no fruit. Just as when a mango is planted for the fruit, shade and fragrance also result, even so the ordained duty that is performed is attended by material gains. To the words of the hypocrite, the criminal, the heretic, and the juvenile, one should react with neither hate nor deception. In all realms, one should conform to the conduct which enjoys the consistent sanction of the noble ones, those who are well disciplined, elders, self-possessed, free from avarice and vanity. Thus one gains both worlds.'

EJS

Bibliography

V. M. Apte, *Social and Religious Life in the Grikya Sutras*, Bombay, 1954.

K. W. Morgan (ed.), *The Religion of the Hindus*, New York, 1953, pp. 176–184.

R. B. Pandey, *Hindu Samskaras: a Socio-Religious Study of the Hindu Sacraments*, Benares, 1949.

34

FESTIVALS AND PILGRIMAGES

THE HINDU CALENDAR has a large number of festivals, some of which are clearly seasonal, and others of which are connected with the legendary history of a god or goddess. The most typical and most popular of the former is Diwali, a festival of lights observed in October–November; among the latter may be mentioned the birthdays of the gods, especially Rama and Krishna. (A schematic outline of the Hindu calendar, with some major festivals, is given separately in unit 48.)

Holy times, together with holy places and to some extent also holy persons, give the devout occasion to increase their merit ('good *karma*') by going on pilgrimage (Skr. *pravrajya*)—a pilgrim (Lat. *peregrinus*, stranger or wanderer) being either one who abandons—temporarily—his or her normal pursuits in order to seek the spiritual and moral benefits obtainable in some particularly holy place, or one whose whole life is given over to such wandering.

The Indian sub-continent has a vast number of sacred sites, and devout Hindus will visit these as often as circumstances permit. However, there is no qualitative difference between his worship at the local shrine and his visit to a particularly important holy place. Pilgrimage raises worship to a higher level, and confers special benefits, but it is not different in kind from other forms of worship.

Among the holiest of goals for Hindu pilgrimage are the seven great rivers, especially the Ganges. And of the cities on the rivers, the best-known is Benares (Varanasi), with its many temples and its crowds of pilgrims. Every mile of the Ganges is sacred, but none more so than Gangotri, Kedarnath and Badrinath, at the sources of the river's three main branches, the Bhagirathi, the Mandakini and the Alakananda. The great Ganges pilgrimage begins at Hardwar, 'Hari's Gate', and passes through Rishikesh, the town of ascetics, to the three sanctuaries.

The entire pilgrimage, performed in May, June and July, covers over 600 miles. Where there are difficulties to be surmounted, this only adds to the merit acquired by the pilgrim, as well as serving as a mortification for the body. The best-known extra austerity is that which requires the pilgrim to measure his length along the entire road.

Other celebrated pilgrim cities of India include Mathura and Vrindaban, connected in legend with the boyhood and youth of Krishna, and Dwaraka, where he left the world. Often there is a pilgrim route round such a city, the following of which in its entirety (*parikrama*) brings especial merit. At individual shrines, it is common to circumambulate, keeping the shrine on one's right (*pradakshina*).

Strictly speaking, a pilgrimage may be undertaken at any auspicious time, but there is a close connection in practice between festivals and pilgrimages. The more important festivals —for instance those at Hardwar, Allahabad, Ujjain and Nasik —draw vast crowds, and it has been claimed that the *Kumbh Mela*, held near Allahabad every twelve years, attracts larger crowds than are to be found at any other religious festival anywhere in the world. Another vastly popular local festival which attracts crowds of pilgrims is the Jagannatha car festival at Puri, where an image of Krishna, mounted on a huge car (whence our word 'juggernaut') is dragged through the streets by hundreds of worshippers.

Some holy places—for instance Hardwar and Benares—are associated in the popular mind with the cult of the dead, and pilgrimages may be undertaken for the express purpose of consigning the ashes of a dead relative (cremated elsewhere) to the sacred waters of the Ganges. An odd development this century has been the sending of such ashes by post, with instructions to a local Brahmin to perform the last rites.

Since it is commonly accepted among Hindus that all religions are merely alternative paths to the same goal, it is not uncommon to find Hindus making pilgrimage to Buddhist, Jain, Christian and other holy places—in precisely the same spirit in which they will offer reverence to a Franciscan friar as readily as to a Hindu *sannyasin*. Buddhist pilgrimage centres in particular are, or have been, numerous in India, the most important of them being Bodh Gaya, the site of the Buddha's enlightenment.

We may sum up in the words of Swaprasad Bhattacharyya (in Morgan (ed.), *The Religion of the Hindus*, p. 188): 'As he worships before the Lord at Banaras, or Balaji the Lord at Tirupati, or the Great Mother at Conjeeveram, the pilgrim comes to see that all are equal before the Lord, in whatever form or place the deity may be worshipped. As the pilgrims from all over India mix together and worship at the great, ancient sites, they come to know and cherish the fundamental unity of this land of Bharata [India], made sacred in so many places by the presence of the Lord.'

EJS

Bibliography

Anon., *The Mountain of the Lord: Pilgrimage to Gangotri*, Bangalore, no date.
K. Klostermaier, *Hindu and Christian in Vrindaban*, London, 1969.
M. M. Underhill, *The Hindu Religious Year*, London, 1921.
L. P. Vidyarthi, *The Sacred Complex in Hindu Gaya*, Bombay, 1961.

35

ASTROLOGY

THE ROLE PLAYED by the complex science of astrology (*jataka*) in present-day Hindu belief and practice is extremely difficult to determine with any precision. That most Hindus have an active or at least implicit belief in astrology is something which most observers have noted; the problems arise when one comes to decide what is the relationship between these beliefs and other areas of Hindu thought.

The twin sciences of astronomy and astrology seem originally to have reached India from Mesopotamia by way of Greece, and to have served a twofold purpose. On the one hand, it was necessary to compute with some accuracy the times of seasonal sacrifices and other rituals; on the other, since the stars and planets were themselves believed to be deities, their movements and alignments were thought to affect the world of men. Astronomy was therefore a matter of straightforward (though complicated) observation and calculation, leading to the science of chronology. Astrology was an 'applied science'. In the classical Indian texts, the two together were called *jyotisha*, and classified as one of the six *Vedangas*, or subsidiary subjects to be studied by every student of the Veda (the others being phonetics, grammar, etymology, prosody and the ritual code).

However, belief in the power of stars and planets to influence the life of man can be shown to have existed in India from very early times. There are references in the *Atharva Veda* to constellations which influence human events, and texts in the same collection which are designed to ward off evil influences coming from the same source. The *Rig Veda* appears to presuppose some of the same ideas.

There are nine planets in Hindu astrology—the Sun, the Moon, Mercury, Venus, Mars, Jupiter, Saturn, Rahu and Ketu (the two last being the ascending and descending nodes of the moon's orbit). Some of these are instrinsically favourable, others malevolent; Saturn, Rahu and Ketu are particularly inauspicious (the two latter because they were believed to cause eclipses). Often Hindu temples will still have a special shrine dedicated to the nine planets, at which worship is offered before a marriage, a birth, or any other important event in the household.

The details of Hindu astrology are of incredible complexity, since the constellations, *nakshatras*, are believed to affect the lives of individuals in countless ways. The moon is believed to pass through 27 or 28 'mansions', and the sun through 12 'signs', *rashis*, which carry the following names: Mesha (Aries), Vrishabha (Taurus), Mithuna (Gemini), Karkata (Cancer), Simha (Leo), Kanya (Virgo), Tula (Libra), Vrishchika (Scorpio), Dhanus (Sagittarius), Makara (Capricornus), Kumbha (Aquarius) and Mina (Pisces). The life of the individual is determined by the precise positions of the planets and constellations at the moment of birth (head-appearance), and hence it is of the utmost importance that the exact time of birth should be known. Once this has been settled, then the relative influence of the twelve signs can be calculated in their application to twelve areas of a person's life: health; wealth and prosperity; brothers and sisters; parents and friends; children and learning; enemies; wife; length of life; good fortune and piety; works and career; income; expenditure.

The most obvious area in which this information affects the life of the individual is on marriage. The orthodox Hindu family will take great pains, when a marriage is to be arranged, to ensure that the astrological horoscopes of the prospective partners are fully compatible.

A further area of astrology which has retained its importance throughout Hindu history is in relation to auspicious and inauspicious times and seasons. In northern India, for instance, there are certain times at which no journey should be begun, no new enterprise started and no ceremony performed. These are Tuesday from 7.30 to 9. a.m., Friday from 9 to 10.30 a.m., Sunday from 10.30 a.m. to noon, Wednesday from noon to 1.30 p.m., Saturday from 1.30 to 3 p.m., Monday from 3 to 4.30 p.m. and Thursday from 4.30 to 6 p.m. It has also been pointed out that the meeting of an Indian board of company directors in Calcutta or Bombay may well appear to be thoroughly Western in its style—until the time comes to fix the date of the next meeting. Then the almanacs come out, and the members begin to calculate auspicious and inauspicious dates and times.

As we have said, there are certain difficulties in reconciling astrological belief with other items of the Hindu world-view, for instance the doctrine of *karma*; but when it is recalled that on the way to rebirth, the soul is believed to pass through various celestial houses, the possibility of a connection between the two is not unreasonable. Pragmatically, too, even if the future should be shaped by *karma*, it might be of advantage to be able to tap sources of information about the course of future events.

Thus astrologers have always been a present feature of public and private life in India. Some have been charlatans, but many more have been serious practitioners of what is regarded without question as a science. It might be argued that since astrology presupposes a geocentric view of the universe, the advent of modern science will inevitably mean the ultimate decline and death of astrology. This has, of course, already happened in the West, and it is happening in India—but only very gradually. Astrology is still recognized as a subject of academic study in several Indian universities, and there are many private astrological institutions, some of which are supported by public funds. Even a thoroughgoing secularist like the late Pandit Nehru, although he disliked the thought of members of his cabinet employing private astrologers, did little to interfere with them. So it is clear that although the secularized fraction of India may have begun to ignore the astrological tradition, it still retains its hold at the instinctive level.

EJS

Bibliography

V. M. Apte, in *The Cultural Heritage of India* I, Calcutta, 1958, pp. 289–292.
M. R. Bhat, *Fundamentals of Astrology*, Delhi, 1967.
B. V. Raman, *A Manual of Hindu Astrology*, Bombay, 1953[5].
A. Wayman, 'Astrology, India', in *Encyclopaedia Britannica* I, 1970 ed., pp. 641B–642.

36

THE IMAGE OF THE DIVINE MOTHER

THE IMAGE OF THE MOTHER—the earth symbolized in female form and with female attributes—is one of the most potent in the history of religion, and occupies an important place in the history of Hinduism. Already in the Indus Valley Civilization it seems that reverence was paid to terracotta figures of women, with prominent breasts and hips, dressed in girdles and elaborate pannier headdresses. Their facial features, on the other hand, were seldom other than rudimentary. Similar figures are known from peasant cultures throughout India. The Indo-Europeans (the other major element in early Hinduism) also knew of a sky-father, *Dyaus Pitar*, and an earth mother, *Prithivi Matar*, who are mentioned in the *Rig Veda*. Throughout the history of Indian religion, then, there is a tradition of worship of deity in male and female form, and it is in the female form that many Hindus have preferred to worship. Although goddesses represented, for instance, certain rivers and the dawn, it is the earth-goddess with whom we are chiefly concerned here.

The earth gives life; and all forms of life were believed to be derived from the earth. Plant, animal and human fertility were all gifts which it was in the power of the Mother to give. Prayers would be addressed to her, and gifts offered to her in order to ensure fertility. But the earth had another side. Her gifts might be withheld, and as long as men buried their dead (apparently the Indus practice) she would also receive the dead to herself, and destroy the body in decomposition. Hence the Mother was thoroughly ambivalent: gracious and yet severe.

Images of the Mother in Hindu iconography tend always to have this twofold character: on the one hand strikingly beautiful; on the other sinister and sometimes terrifyingly ugly. Durga and Kali in particular are often depicted as hags, while even the lovely Parvati, consort of Shiva, may sit calmly on the field of cremation threading human heads on to a string.

The image of the Mother becomes still more potent in the teachings of Tantrism or Shaktism. The Tantras or *Shakta Agamas* are Hindu scriptures which teach the worship of spiritual power (*shakti*) in the form of the Divine Mother (*Devi*). In terms of Samkhya theory, Shiva is *purusha* (soul) and Shakti is *prakriti* (matter or energy); it is Shakti who creates through the three *gunas*, *sattva* (goodness), *rajas* (passion) and *tamas* (darkness). Thus the world is a manifestation of the energy of the Divine Mother.

Tantrism, or Shaktism (that form of worship based on the Tantras) has exercised considerable influence on Hindu thought, though it is not much studied. A form of *bhakti* closely linked with Yoga, its practices aim, among other things, at the harnessing of spiritual forces within man, and it was once said that 'many a man who calls himself a Saiva or a Vaishnava is secretly a Sakta, and a brother of the left hand'. This may or may not have been true in the past; today it is certainly not true. The expression, 'brother of the left hand', incidentally, refers to 'left-handed Tantra', an esoteric form of Hindu practice in which devotees indulge in three 'forbidden things', i.e. wine, meat and sexual intercourse, with a view to transcending them (see unit 19).

Some parts of India have always had a higher proportion of Shaktas than others. Bengal was a particular stronghold of Shaktism, having one of the most important temples of Kali in the country (and also being the site of Ramakrishna's work, whose religion was a form of Shaktism. Towards the turn of the present century, Calcutta was the capital of British India, and was one of the leading centres of the national movement. Here a curious development took place in the image of the Mother: the interpretation of the national movement as a *Shakti* of God, and at the same time the interpretation of both Bengal and India as tangible forms of the Divine Mother. Thus one nationalist leader, Bankim Chandra Chatterjee, interpreted the history of India (or Bengal) in three stages: as *Jagatohatri* riding a lion (India past); as *Kali*, dark because ignorant of herself, trampling her own God under her feet (India present); and as *Durga*, supported by the goddesses of wisdom and wealth (India future). Aurobindo Ghose (Unit 28) also helped to make of every act of worship a nationalist demonstration by claiming, for instance, that the *Durga Puja* festival in honour of the Mother was a 'national festival' and could only be understood by the 'patriot'; nationalism itself he called a *Shakti* of the Eternal. The furore caused by the Partition of Bengal in 1905 can perhaps better be understood against this background.

We have quoted this episode as an example of the reinterpretation of time-honoured symbols. For most Hindus, however, the Mother in her local manifestation is still the most ancient and closest of deities. In the South of India, the name by which she is known locally may not be in the textbooks of Hinduism; but every villager knows that although the great gods, Vishnu and Shiva, have their uses, the greatest power—power over life and fertility and death—is wielded by the Mother. As Shashthi she is the universal mother and protector of all children, worshipped by women in Hindu households. As Shitala she may send smallpox, and is feared accordingly. As Uma she dwells in the mountains; as Sarasvati in the rivers; as Kali on the cremation ground—her names and aspects are, it seems, innumerable, and her attributes embrace the life of man from cradle to grave, and beyond. To those Hindus who fail to see why Deity should be regarded as exclusively masculine in character, the Divine Mother is an all-pervasive symbol.

EJS

Bibliography

J. G. Woodroffe, *Shakti and Shakta*, Madras, 1959[5]. *The World as Power*, Madras, 1957[2].

37

THE COW

REVERENCE FOR THE COW plays a striking role in Hindu mythology and in the day-to-day practices of Hinduism. The roots of this attitude are certainly very ancient, being based on the symbolism of the divine bounty of the earth; in this way the cow is an alternative symbol of the earth (see unit 36) as the 'mother' of gods and men. The mother-goddess Aditi is called 'the Cow, the sinless' in the *Rig Veda* (VIII, 90, 15), and this hymn continues: 'Weak-minded men have as a cow adopted me who came hither from the gods, a goddess, who . . . standeth near at hand with all devotions.' Further evidence of cow-worship in the earliest of the Hindu scriptures is found in the *Atharva Veda*, where the cow is said to sum up in herself the whole of creation: 'The cow accepted the sacrifice; the cow sustained the sun; within the cow entered the rice-dish and the priest. The cow they call immortality; the cow they worship as death; the cow becomes this all—gods, men, Asuras, Fathers, seers. Whoso knoweth this, he may accept the cow. . .' (X, 10, 25–27).

The myth of the earth taking the form of a cow receives its first detailed expression in the *Vishnu Purana* (ch. 13). There, Prithu, the monarch of all, approached the earth in order to make her yield plants; the earth refused, assumed the form of a cow and ran away, but was finally caught and persuaded to nourish the earth with her milk. Then Prithu milked the earth-cow into his own hand, and there grew up all manner of corn and vegetables for man's food.

Although in Vedic times there was no express prohibition of cow-killing or the eating of beef, by the time of the *Mahabharata* it was stated categorically that the killing of a cow was the greatest of all crimes: 'All that kill, eat, and permit the slaughter of cows, rot in hell for as many years as there are hairs on the body of the cow so slain' (XIII, 74, 4). The *Laws of Manu*, the greatest of the Hindu codes of law, are less extreme, laying down that the slaying of cows is a 'minor offence' (XI, 60), and that provided that the killer lives in a cow-house, bathes in urine, and follows the cows all day, standing when they stand and sitting when they sit, he may expiate his crime in three months (X, 109–117).

The cow, by reason of her sacredness, is also a practical means toward the expiation of other sins. Again according to Manu, 'He who unhesitatingly abandons life for the sake of Brahmanas or cows, is freed from the guilt of the murder of a Brahmana. . .' (XI, 80). Also, birth at an inauspicious time can be remedied by passing the infant beneath the body of a cow—a symbolical rebirth from the source of holiness. The *panchagavya*, or five products of the cow—milk, curds, clarified butter (*ghi*), dung and urine—are all used in purificatory rituals.

Of the many reasons for the tenacity of the cow-cult within Hinduism, special mention must be made of the association of Krishna with the cow; the legend of Krishna's youth, as told mainly in the *Bhagavata Purana*, depicts him as a cow-herd devoted to their care. Other reasons have to do with the Muslim invasions (the Muslims having no compunction about the slaughtering of cattle), and with the development of the doctrine of *ahimsa* (harmlessness, non-violence), which enjoined on the devotee reverence for all forms of life. A more modern development, though one with ancient roots, has been the symbolic identification of the cow with India as a nation—a localization of the original identification of the cow with the earth. In this sense, the cow is a political, as well as a religious, symbol.

At present, the cow plays a variety of roles in the religious life of Hindu India. In some temples, a cow is brought in every morning, placed with her back to the image of the deity and solemnly milked. In Hindu rituals, every part of the cow (as well as the *panchagavya*) is of significance: the feet symbolize the four Vedas, or alternatively, Dharma, the god of righteousness —concerning whom it is said that in the golden age, the cow of righteousness had four feet on the earth, in the silver age, three feet, in the bronze age two feet, and in the present iron age only one foot. The tip of her horns symbolize the gods; her face, the moon; her shoulders and stomach, Agni, the god of fire, and the sun; the end of her tail, the holy waters; the roots of her hairs, the holy ascetics; and so on.

It is still widely believed among Hindus that the cow is able to act as a pathfinder in the world beyond the grave, and that it is highly auspicious to be able to die clutching a cow's tail. For lower castes, a cow-shed sometimes fills the function of a temple—the focus of sacredness—in their daily lives.

Not surprisingly, then, the cow is a potent and evocative symbol of the Hindu way of life, and any attack on the cow may turn a normally calm Hindu into a raging fanatic. For almost a century now, orthodox Hindu political and semi-political parties have taken cow-protection as one of their test cases, promising to prohibit cow-slaughter as a mark of their orthodoxy. But as every visitor to India knows, the 'sacred cow' is not as a rule particularly well looked after (modern secularist writers sometimes talk about 'India's sacred skeletons'). In 1961 it was estimated that there were upwards of 175 million cattle in India—often terribly neglected, particularly in the cities, by virtue of their very sacredness. Not only is cow-slaughter and the consumption of beef forbidden in many areas, but controlled breeding and veterinary care is virtually impossible. And yet we must remember Gandhi's words—the authentic voice of Hindu devotion: '"Cow Protection" to me is one of the most wonderful phenomena in all human evolution; for it takes the human being beyond his species . . . Man through the cow is enjoined to realize his identity with all that lives . . . "Cow Protection" is the gift of Hinduism to the world; and Hinduism will live as long as there are Hindus to protect the cow.'

EJS

Bibliography

W. Crooke, *The Popular Religion and Folk-Lore of Northern India*, London, 1896, Vol. II, pp. 226–235.

'The Veneration of the Cow in India,' in *Folk-Lore*, 1912, pp. 275–306.

Encyclopaedia of Religion and Ethics, Vol. IV, pp. 224–226.

T. Margul, 'Present-day Worship of the Cow in India,' in *Numen*, 1968, pp. 63–80.

38

ETHICS AND MORALITY

IN CLASSICAL TIMES, Hindu ideas concerning ethics and morality centred entirely on two concepts, *karma* and *dharma*. The former denoted the totality of actions, good or bad, which were able to affect the individual's future destiny. The belief in rebirth, or *samsara*, provided the framework within which this idea was worked out in each instance: good *karma* would ensure a favourable rebirth: bad *karma* an unfavourable one. There was, however, no one immutable law for all men and all women, by the observation of which good *karma* could be ensured. Rather, there were many laws, many *dharmas*, according to the station in life of the person concerned. Here the framework was that of the caste system.

The comprehensive system of personal ethics which this represents had developed over a long period of time. The earliest Hindu scriptures (particularly the *Rig Veda*) contain the concept of *rita*, or cosmic law, guarded by the great gods Mitra and Varuna, to which man had to adapt himself. This involved man knowing his place *vis-à-vis* the gods, and maintaining his relationship with them by means of prayer and sacrifice. Thus it is appropriate to speak of Varuna as Lord of the moral order; in the hymns dedicated to Varuna man comes as a suppliant and a sinner, begging forgiveness for his transgressions, which might be moral but might equally well be ritual in nature.

Rita represented not only the moral order and the natural order, but also the social order. As such, it was something over which priests (Brahmins) had a great deal of control, since they controlled the sacrifice by which the gods were propitiated; the warriors (Kshatriyas) enforced it. This aspect was summed up in the structure of the four classes (*varnas*), each of which had its appropriate role in the maintenance of the whole. Ethical and moral behaviour, then, means essentially responsible action within the framework of one's own *varna*. But the overall concept of *rita* was nevertheless losing its hold; Varuna declined in importance. As a plurality of gods came to dominate the Hindu tradition, so a plurality of ethical principles, *dharmas*, dominated Hindu morals.

These principles are stated in great detail in the *dharmashastras*, of which the best known is the *Laws of Manu*. Each class had its own place within the totality, and its own appropriate modes of behaviour. But by this time (around, or just before, the Christian era) the idea of rebirth had achieved unquestioned status in Hindu thinking. Hence faithful performance of one's own *dharma* (the *dharma* of one's own group) was held to bring good *karma*, and hence a good rebirth. The *dharma* of a Brahmin was of course more detailed and more onerous than that of a Shudra. But as the *Bhagavad Gita* was to emphasize, it is not permissible to attempt to fulfil someone else's *dharma*: it is better to perform one's own *dharma* badly than another's well.

Within this framework there were in reality two types of ethics. One was directed to the man living in the world, and laid down four permissible types of behaviour—*artha* (the acquisition of wealth), *kama* (the enjoyment of the pleasures of life), *dharma* (here understood mainly as a life of ritual piety) and *moksha* (release from the round of rebirth). But to direct oneself to the fourth of these aims involved the devaluation of the other three. In every case the type of ethics involved was highly individual: clearly, on the *karma* hypothesis one could do nothing to alleviate another's misfortune or suffering. If the true aim of human life was to reach *moksha*, then it was necessary to concentrate on one's own salvation. The interim ethic of the first three aims lifted the individual gradually out of the mass of ignorance; the absolute ethic of *moksha* urged him to abandon the world (including other people) altogether. Thus classical Hinduism focused its ethical concern entirely on the individual's quest for salvation. It urged on him the positive virtues of detachment, compassion and renunciation, but it was mainly concerned with avoiding anything which would hold him fettered in the world of senses and phenomena. The maintenance of purity was all-important: the seeker after salvation was prohibited from killing, stealing, committing adultery, lying and consuming intoxicants.

For the ordinary Hindu, a further focus of ethics was the family. The great Epics depicted what was in many ways the ideal: children were shown as dutiful to parents, parents as attached to their children; wives and husbands in relations of mutual respect; love and harmony as present everywhere. Hence the Epics served—and to a great extent still serve—as paradigms of ideal behaviour for the common man with his family. A recent observer has summed up that 'The code of morality of the ordinary Hindu is much the same as that of most civilized nations, though it is nowhere reduced to a code.'

The most recent period in Indian history has seen extensive influence from the West, with its typical emphasis on social ethics—an ideal somewhat different from that of *varnashramadharma*, or ethics within the family and caste. Hinduism has accepted this social ideal, but has found some difficulty in reconciling this with its traditional ethical attitudes. In fact the traditional attitudes have been, if not suppressed, at least reinterpreted. The 'modern' Hindu believes in progress rather than in cycles of time: as J. N. Farquhar wrote many years ago, '. . . men's hearts are now set on India's future, and they constantly see golden visions'. He also believes in alleviating suffering, rather than in merely ascribing it to *karma*. He may be very critical of the past rigidities of the caste system, with its separate *dharmas*, and may well emphasize general social justice. He has learned much from the example of Vivekananda and especially from Gandhi about the importance of *sarvodaya* (the common good).

In the past, Western observers have been highly critical of the individualistic basis of Hindu ethics, and such criticism is not altogether unjustified. But Hinduism is highly adaptable, and there is no more adequate example of this quality than in its capacity for accepting the need for social ethics on the widest possible basis, and for re-examining its traditional doctrines accordingly. It should be noted, finally, that we have as yet no adequate study of these recent developments in Hindu thought, and no single book can therefore be recommended for further reading.

EJS

Bibliography

A. G. Hogg, *Karma and Redemption*, 1st ed. 1909, new ed. Madras: Christian Literature Society, 1970.
E. W. Hopkins, *Ethics of India*, London: Oxford U.P., 1924.
J. Jolly, 'Ethics and Morality (Hindu)', in Hastings' *Encyclopaedia of Religion and Ethics* v, 1921, pp. 496–498.
J. Mackenzie, *Hindu Ethics*, London: Oxford U.P., 1922.
E. W. Scott, *Social Ethics in Modern Hinduism*, Calcutta: Y.M.C.A., 1953.
S. C. Thakur, *Christian and Hindu Ethics*, London: Allen and Unwin, 1969.
R. C. Zaehner, *Hinduism*, London: Oxford U.P., 1966, pp. 102 ff.

39

SEX AND MARRIAGE

MENTION HAS ALREADY been made (unit 36) of the symbolism of the Divine Mother and the principle of fertility in Hinduism, and also of a type of devotion known as Tantrism or Shaktism, in which the *shakti* (consort) of a deity is regarded as the divine energy revealed in every act of creation. This metaphysical doctrine led to—or perhaps in part rationalized—certain practices, particularly among adherents of so-called 'left-handed' Tantrism (unit 19). In brief, sexual intercourse was used as one means of God-realization. Intercourse is depicted in medieval temple sculpture, and in the past temple prostitutes formed part of the staff of some Indian temples (although it should be emphasized that the practice has long been illegal). Ideally, the act was symbolical of the relationship between the soul and God, though it had more esoteric aims, involving self-transcendence and the release of occult powers. On an entirely symbolical level, Hindu mysticism (in common with other types of mysticism elsewhere) may make use of erotic and quasi-erotic language to express the state of separation, and the desire for union, between man and God. The best-known expression of this in the texts is the record in the *Bhagavata Purana* of the relationship of the youthful Krishna and the *gopis* (herdmaidens) of Vrindaban.

Otherwise, desire (*kama*) is treated in a somewhat ambivalent manner in the Hindu tradition: although it is regarded as one of the four legitimate aims of life (*kama*, *artha*, *dharma*, *moksha*), it can be the enemy of spiritual attainment, particularly when indulged in for its own sake. It can be spiritualized, however. The celebrated *Kama Sutra* (which has been called '. . . a sex manual so dull and technical that Kinsey, by comparison, reads like a thriller') is really a manual of aesthetics and enjoyment meant to be read within the total context of Hindu life.

The legitimacy of *kama* belongs in the context of the four

stages (*ashramas*) of Hindu life, of which the second stage, that of a married householder (*grihastha*), is that in which *kama* and *artha* find their fulfilment. However, the four stages and the four aims have traditionally been taken to apply only to men, and only to men of the highest castes. The position of the partner, woman, in Hindu society has always been ambiguous: on the one hand venerated as a symbol of the divine, and on the other treated as an inferior being. 'Her father protects her in childhood, her husband protects her in youth, and her sons protect her in old age; a woman is never fit for independence' (*Manu* IX, 3).

The role of women in marriage has traditionally been one of submission, obedience and service, on the pattern of Sita's submission to, and love for, Rama in the *Ramayana*. Marriage was contracted before puberty, and was, as far as the woman was concerned, unrepeatable. The remarriage of widows was prohibited, even when the husband died before the marriage could be consummated, and it was regarded as the ultimate proof of love and devotion if the widow immolated herself on her husband's funeral pyre. This practice (*sati*, suttee) was abolished by law in 1829, although isolated instances have occurred since. The only alternative to *sati* in many cases was a life of perpetual seclusion in the *zenana*, or women's house. The last century has, however, seen a number of reforms which have radically altered the position of women in Hindu society, and the sombre picture presented in the texts (and in the older literature) is no longer completely applicable. The fact that India has a woman Prime Minister should not be overlooked.

Turning to the marriage itself, a Hindu wedding is a great social occasion—often involving a family in great expense. The ceremonies, which are highly symbolical,[1] are crowned by a feast to which as many people as possible are invited, after which the newly-weds as a rule go to live with the family of the bridegroom. The institution of the 'joint family' is of great antiquity, and the ties between the generations which are maintained in this way are of considerable importance. The marriage itself will in the majority of cases have been arranged by the relatives of the couple, full account having been taken of caste, subcaste, kinship and horoscope. The 'matrimonial' columns of Indian papers contain regular advertisements for marriage partners, most specifying caste and subcaste, and requiring horoscopes. However, some do not. Under the pressure of modern ideas, marriage is becoming somewhat freer, at least in the cities. Inter-caste marriages do take place, but since the obstacles are so immense, these are few. Otherwise the Hindu tends to look askance on the Western practice of free choice of partners, and points to the high level of divorce in the West as proof of the superiority of the Hindu way. In India, it might be said that marriage is looked upon as the beginning, and not as the optional climax, of human love. It being the object of marriage to produce offspring (especially sons to perform the *shraddha* ceremonies), the average Hindu, particularly in the villages, is not favourably disposed to methods of voluntary birth control, which may seem to threaten the future of the family.

During the marriage ceremony, these words may be addressed to the bride by the bridegroom:

> With utmost love to each other . . . may we walk together and take our resolves together. May we make our minds united, of the same vows and the same thoughts. I am the words and you are the melody; I am the melody and you are the words. I am the heaven, and you are the earth. I am the seed, you are the bearer. I am the thought, you are the word; I am the melody, you are the words . . .

EJS

Footnote

[1] Described briefly by Bhattacharyya, in Morgan (ed.), *The Religion of the Hindus*, p. 182.

Bibliography

Pamela E. Devafaj, 'The Family in India,' in Anantakrishnan *et al.* (eds.), *India Today*, Bangalore, 1967, pp. 57–70.
P. D. Devanandan and M. M. Thomas (eds.), *The Changing Pattern of Family in India*, Bangalore, 1966.
J. N. Farquhar, *The Crown of Hinduism*, London, 1913, chapter 2.
C. B. Mamoria, *Population and Family Planning in India*, Allahabad, 1963[2].
Taya Zinkin, *India Changes!* London, 1958, chapters 4–6.

40

CASTE

A HINDU IS A HINDU not because he accepts certain doctrines or philosophies, but because he is a member of a caste. Hence it is strictly speaking impossible to become a Hindu, other than by being born into a caste.

The origins of the caste system are somewhat obscure. The Sanskrit word for caste is *varna*, 'colour', and it is widely believed that this originally had to do with the skin-colour of the invading Aryans as opposed to that of the indigenous Dravidians, thus making the caste system into a sort of primitive colour bar. However, this is by no means certain. Three of the four castes were Aryan to begin with, only the fourth being non-Aryan. And since the Aryan social organization was roughly divided into three functions (authority, power, production), it seems that here we have the roots of the system. The 'colour' element may have had to do with the distinctive marks worn by members of the different groups (not to be confused with later sect marks). The word 'caste' is derived from the Portuguese word *casta*, 'breed', and the commonest Indian word is *jāti*, 'birth'.

The four original castes were: (1) *Brahmana* (commonly anglicized to 'Brahmin'), the priestly caste. (2) *Kshatriya* or *Rajanya*, the warrior and ruling caste. (3) *Vaishya*, the caste of farmers and craftsmen. These are the three 'twice-born' castes, since each has an initiation ceremony corresponding to a second birth. (4) *Shudra*, the caste of servants and slaves. According to *Manu* (1, 88–91):

> To Brahmanas he assigned teaching and studying (the Veda), sacrificing for their own benefit and for others, giving and accepting (of alms). The Kshtriya he commanded to protect the people, to bestow sacrifices, to study (the Veda), and to abstain from attaching himself to sensual pleasures; the Vaishya to tend cattle, to bestow gifts, to offer sacrifices, to

> study (the Veda), to trade, to lend money, and to cultivate land. One occupation only the Lord prescribed to the Shudra, to serve meekly even these other three castes.

Although *Manu* also says that 'there is no fifth caste' (x, 4), in time the remainder of the population, technically outside the system altogether and therefore called 'outcastes', came to be classified as *panchamas*, 'the fifth estate'.

By the time of *Manu*, the caste system was clear in all its essentials. The Brahmins were the great central body around which all other classes revolve like satellites: invested with divine dignity by virtue of their function as sacrificers, and bound together by stringent rules. Other castes, too, had codes of rules, *dharma*, by the observation of which their members remained 'Hindus in good standing'. A link was made with the doctrine of *karma* since a man's caste was a guide to his past *karma*, and his observance of *varnashramadharma* (the totality of caste law) was his main source of *karma* for the future. Caste law regulated such things as marriage, dietary matters, table fellowship, and above all occupation. During subsequent centuries, as Hindu society itself diversified, the castes also diversified into groups of sub-castes, each characterized by occupation and status. Early this century, it was calculated that there were some 3000 castes, and that the Brahmins were divided into 1800 sub-castes! Today, a caste may well combine features of an extended family, a fraternity, a sect and a trade union.

The caste system has certainly been the one factor preserving Hindu culture and religion through the centuries. It has protected the lives of individuals and placed them in a larger context. However, it should not be thought that it has been utterly rigid. In the course of time, the origins of some castes have been forgotten or obscured, and often a simplified three-fold division into Brahmins, other castes, and outcastes has resulted. The two extremes of the priests and the so-called 'untouchables' have been the effective poles of the system; in between, the details have become blurred. But while the status and role of the Brahmin has persisted unchanged, or virtually unchanged, the status of the outcaste has altered radically in recent years. Originally the touch or even shadow of the out-caste was enough to pollute a Brahmin, and he was forbidden to live in contact with other castes, to use their wells or to enter their temples. Sometimes, indeed, they were regarded as being in league with the powers of darkness, and therefore to be propitiated. In the villages, a good deal of this may survive, but legislation has recently abolished the category of untouchability (opposed, however, by the orthodox in some instances) and they no longer suffer from the same disabilities as in the past. In the public life of the cities, little account is now taken of formal caste differences, though in private, traditional distinctions are maintained. Untouchability was in Gandhi's view the great blot on Hindu society; he coined the term *Harijans* (children of God) to describe untouchables, and set in motion reforming forces which had previously been the prerogative of mainly non-Hindus.

Gandhi did not wish to see the caste system abolished altogether. Other reformers, both religious and secular, are less conservative, and wish to see its total disappearance. Tagore, for instance, said that 'The regeneration of the Indian people ... directly and perhaps solely depends upon the removal of the condition of caste'. The system is changing, certainly; but its disappearance is not likely within the forseeable future.

It should be noted, finally, that it is possible for the Hindu to renounce caste by becoming a *sannyasin*, or holy man. Having abandoned the world in his quest for release, he abandons caste also. It is also possible, by transgressing caste law, to lose caste temporarily or permanently. Temporary loss of caste is easily remedied; permanent loss is entailed, for instance, on Christian baptism—a price which few Hindus have been willing to pay.

EJS

Bibliography

F. G. Bailey, *Caste and the Economic Frontier*, Manchester, 1957.
E. A. H. Blunt, *The Caste System of Northern India*, London, 1931.
J. N. Farquhar, *The Crown of Hinduism*, London, 1913, pp. 153–210.
J. H. Hutton, *Caste in India*, London, 1946.
L. S. S. O'Malley, *Indian Caste Customs*, Cambridge, 1932.

41

THE SECULARIZATION OF HINDUISM

SINCE INDEPENDENCE, India has been a secular state in the sense that there is no established state religion, and full freedom of religious belief and practice is guaranteed to all adherents of all religions; but India is very far indeed from being a secular state in the sense of being an irreligious state. Rather, the problem is one of religious plurality within a secular framework, the conflict of disparate religious ideals, values and motivations with the pressing needs of modern society. The modern world has made its impact on India; how does Hinduism react?

We must be careful here not to impose Western intellectual patterns on what is an essentially non-Western phenomenon. The so-called secularization of Christianity in the West does not without more ado provide a pattern by which we can judge the secularization of Hinduism. Hindu secularization is different from Christian secularization, just as Hindu atheism is different from Christian atheism.

In their encounters with the modern world, three things tend to happen to religions. First there is a marked increase in formal unbelief—wholesale rejection of the entire structure of belief in the supernatural, and its replacement by equally firm trust in the processes and methods of this world, particularly as epitomized by 'science'. Second, there is an attempt by 'progressive' elements within the religion in question to adapt to the demands of the new age, and to strive for a new relevance. And thirdly, there is reaction against both these trends on the part of out-an-out traditionalists.

1. Typical of the first trend is the view of Jawaharlal Nehru, that 'We have got to get rid of that narrowing religious outlook, that obsession with the supernatural and metaphysical speculations, that loosening of the mind's discipline in religious ceremonial and mystical emotionalism, which come in the way of our understanding ourselves and the world.'[1] This is a point of view

taken by an increasingly vocal section of the Indian intelligentsia, sometimes under the influence of Marxism, but more often simply on the basis of Western materialism. Writers and speakers who adopt this standpoint are usually utterly intolerant of the whole basis of Indian traditional thought, though their strongest language is reserved for the world-negating metaphysic of Hinduism, the law of *karma*, cow-worship and the caste system.

2. The attitude underlying the attempt to adapt is typified by Radhakrishnan: 'Leaders of Hindu thought and practice are convinced that the times require, not a surrender of the basic principles of Hinduism, but the restatement of them with special reference to the needs of a more complex and mobile social order.'[2] The difficulties are caused when one comes to try to decide exactly what these 'basic principles of Hinduism' really are. Are these the sacrificial practices and doctrines of the Vedas, the philosophical monism of Vedanta, the mythology of the Epics, the 'perennial philosophy' of the Self, the doctrine of religious equality, the pattern of *karma* and *samsara*, or a combination of all of these? Restatements of Hinduism have been legion in modern times; we have seen some of them; but what elements are typical?

Radhakrishnan's own position is that of Advaita Vedanta, one of the doctrines of which concerns the 'unreality' of the world. His main effort at restatement, apart from his advocacy of religious coexistence, concerns the *mayavada*, which he maintains does not mean that life in the world is unreal. He insists that '. . . no theory has ever asserted that life is a dream and all experienced events are illusions'.[3] He does not identify the world with ultimate reality, but he clearly regards it as having a derived or provisional reality, which makes it eminently fit for the exercise of creative effort. A similar motivation clearly underlay the work of Vivekananda, Aurobindo, Gandhi and Bhave—to mention only four names. All have attempted to restate the Hindu view of life in terms applicable to India's place in the modern world.

3. However, the loudest and most insistent Hindu voices are often not those of the adaptors, but those of the conservative parties; not of universalists, prepared to allow all religions place in the world, but of Hindu particularists.

The right-wing parties—the *Mahasabha*, the *Rashtriya Swayamsevak Sangh* (*RSS*) and the *Jana Sangh* being the most important—envisage Indian unity as Hindu unity, usually on the basis of the Hindi language and the image of an unrealistic and idealized Sanskrit-speaking Vedic India. Their attitude to religious tolerance is strikingly ambivalent. The 1962 Election Manifesto of the Hindu *Mahasabha* called for curbs on Christian missionaries, a legal ban on the entry of all new missionaries, and the banning of conversion from Hinduism. Similarly a leader of the *RSS* stated that non-Hindus should have full freedom of worship 'so long as they do not seek to destroy or undermine the faith and symbolism of the national society'. He apostrophized the 'Vedantic vision' of the unity and equal value of all religions, and then added: 'All groups who share in this vision and discipline can become equal compatriots but none else. Traitors cannot be assimilated into the national fellowship until they change in spirit.'[4]

Of the specific issues within this essentially political debate, that of cow-slaughter is one of the most explosive: the right-wing parties undertake to forbid cow-slaughter, and castigate opponents for ambivalence on this point. Language and caste are also vital areas of passionate controversy.

In the secularization debate, one thing is clear, that in the process of coming to terms with the modern world, emphasis is being laid less on doctrinal aspects of religion, and more on burning social issues within India, If India is ever to be a unified nation, some form of coexistence, not merely between liberal and conservative Hindus, but also between Hindu, Christian, Jew, Muslim and other religious communities must be found. It is also undeniable that on the level of the intelligentsia and the meritocracy, social service is now taken very much for granted, while old text-book doctrines are being more and more swallowed up in the cauldron of modern life. As P. D. Devanandan has written, 'the essential secularistic basis for the Gandhian view of life has become a fundamental of faith in contemporary Hinduism'.[5] This does not mean that the old doctrines are dead, but they are widely ignored. What remains in many cases is a husk of traditional observance—a husk which many Hindus find hard to fill with meaning.

And yet Hinduism is capable of unlimited freedom of intellectual interpretation. The process of secularization marks the increasingly serious questioning of tradition in the name of progress. As such it is both inevitable and inexorable. As yet, it is marked only among certain classes of intellectual. If it ever succeeds in penetrating to the mass of the people, it will be time to speak of the full secularization of Hinduism. Until then, we can only wait and watch.

EJS

Footnotes

[1] Nehru, *The Discovery of India*, Bombay 1961, pp. 552 f.

[2] Radhakrishnan, *The Hindu View of Life*, p. 92.

[3] *The Hindu View of Life*, p. 50.

[4] M. A. Venkata Rao, in M. S. Golwalkar, *Bunch of Thoughts*, Bangalore, 1966, pp. xxix f.

[5] Devanandan, *Preparation for Dialogue*, Bangalore, 1959, p. 75

Bibliography

M. A. Jhangiani, *Jana Sangh and Swatantra*, Bombay, 1967.

A. D. Moddie, *The Brahmanical Culture and Modernity*, New York, 1968.

M. Pattabhiram (ed.), *General Elections in India* 1967, Bombay, 1967.

A. B. Shah and C. R. M. Rao (eds.), *Tradition and Modernity in India*, Bombay, 1965.

A. B. Shah, *Challenges to Secularism*, Bombay, 1968.

This is a continuing debate, which is giving rise to a continual stream of publications, particularly articles in such leading periodicals as *Political Science Review*, *Seminar* and *Religion and Society*.

PART TWO

THE TEACHING OF HINDUISM

42

THE PRESENT AND FUTURE OF RELIGIOUS EDUCATION

THE PRESENT LEGAL POSITION is well enough known. This section will confine itself to a discussion of attitudes and methods so that a discussion of the place of world religions, especially Hinduism, in religious education can be put into its wider context.

During the sixties a number of attitudes to religious education emerged. Among a minority small in numbers but made up of many well known people including some educationists, there is the view that religious education should be abolished. They tend to regard the subject as an attempt to indoctrinate children and often see teachers of R.E. as the fifth column of the church. Belief is a personal matter, instruction should be confined to home and church, it has no place in state schools. That many of the opponents of R.E. do their cause no good by ignoring the changes which have and are taking place in the subject, preferring to create an 'aunt-sally' which most specialists have already knocked down should comfort no one of tender conscience. There is a case to be made even against the new approach.

Sensitive to this and to the boredom which many teenagers have expressed there has also been a movement towards an open-ended form of R.E. in which moral education plays a prominent part. The work of the Farmington Trust, the relatively new journal *Moral Education* and the Campaign for Moral Education together with the Report of the Social Morality Council *Moral and Religious Education* all point in this direction, though *Teenage Religion* by Harold Loukes published in 1961 had anticipated them. Some would like to see moral education as a subject in its own right and an alternative to religious education. Meanwhile it should be noticed that an important result of this trend has been the reduction of that element in religious education which is concerned with the

Beyond or the transcendent. Whatever name one wishes to choose, the fact remains that the swing towards a discussion of personal ethics and social problems has deprived students of the obligation or right to face ultimate questions and seek answers. Superficiality in education is all too easily achieved, science can be the naming of parts, reading can be taught by teachers careless of what the literate should be encouraged to read, environmental studies can be nothing more than 'going walk about'. Harold Loukes did include prayer, suffering and death in his problem syllabus. There can be no justification for a religious education which is solely concerned with this world and the human dimension of 'love thy neighbour', except in the act of worship. (There is also a very limited value in discussing moral questions in the context of authoritarian schools in which students have no opportunities to make real moral decisions or exercise moral judgements in practice as well as in theory. The effect might be to cause frustration in the course of helping them form opinions and attitudes.)

Most work in the last decade has been in the area of the development of children's religious thinking. In 1964 Ronald Goldman's research was published in a book entitled *Religious Thinking from Childhood to Adolescence* (London) and in 1966 the West Riding produced a new syllabus of religious education which was considerably influenced by it. Since then a number of other agreed syallabuses have taken the 'Goldman-Loukes approach' further. In 1965 Professor Goldman's second book appeared: *Readiness for Religion* (London). Among other things a number of life-themes are outlined on such topics as 'Shepherds and Sheep', or 'Light' some of which were developed in great detail and published by Rupert Hart-Davis. Teachers have had five years in which to use the material and the initial debate which tended to be theological has now become more concerned with the adequacy of the thematic method. Jean Holm (*Learning for Living*, November, 1969) and J. W. D. Smith (*Religious Education in a Secular Setting*, London, 1969) have recently made important contributions. There is a danger that the 'life theme' may be so completely religious that sheep rearing and the work of shepherds in Britain, Australia and elsewhere may be studied only to illustrate the statement: 'I am the Good Shepherd'. Even more seriously the religious conclusion of the theme may be neither natural nor logical and imposed in such a way as to render the work which has preceded it totally irrelevant. The future is likely to witness an increasing use of Ronald

Goldman's findings with regard to religious readiness together with an increasing dissatisfaction with the methods he has advocated. A great responsibility will be placed upon teachers, particularly in primary schools, to discover successful ways of teaching religious education bearing in mind the signposts or warning notices which Ronald Goldman and Violet Madge (*Children in Search of a Meaning*, London, 1960) have provided.

In October 1967 the Department of Religious Studies opened at Lancaster University and the September, 1967, volume of *Learning for Living* contained an article by Professor Ninian Smart: 'A New Look at Religious Studies: the Lancaster Idea'. This article written at a time when the pressure of immigrants in the community was gaining increasing attention and when a number of filmstrips, including those used in the BBC 'Religion in its Contemporary Context' programmes, were becoming available, may be taken to mark the date when World Religions began to be more than an optional element in religious education in schools, colleges and universities. In May, 1970, there were only fifteen university teachers of Comparative Religion in British universities, a handful of colleges of education include the subject as an integral part of the main course, and the Durham Report gives its presence in the syllabus but passing attention though it argues for its inclusion (p. 61). However, all the indications are that certainly in secondary schools and colleges of education world religions will occupy an increasingly important place, and that Christian theologians will give steadily more attention to non-Christian theological concepts and to the relationship between Christianity and the other major faiths.

Though approaches to R.E. have changed considerably during the sixties, as yet no universal agreement upon content and method has been reached and no philospphy has evolved. In common with the rest of English education it is bristling with illogicalities. University and college of education courses are often heavily biblical, at least one B.Ed. theology syllabus rejected the Principles and Practice of Religious Education as part of its content, yet traditionally prepared students are expected to teach the subject in radically new ways. The plea for open-endedness has yet to produce a syllabus whose outlook and approach is not completely Christian implicitly if not explicitly. The concepts and symbolism which have concerned Ronald Goldman and others have either been Christian or have been explored in a purely Christian way. Though syllabuses no longer include as a statement of the aims the making of Christians yet they can only result in people whose knowledge of religion is almost entirely Christian and whose search for meaning has been in one direction only. Perhaps at the end of the seventies we will agree that the underlying assumptions of religious education in this country should be Christian but it is to be hoped that such agreement will have resulted from discussion. At the moment we are taking it for granted and producing new syllabuses which differ from the old in that educational considerations have priority over theological but in no other way. They remain syllabuses of Christian education. The present position may be summed up in the words of the Durham Report, paragraph 118:

> Our argument in ch. 4 will be that, on educational grounds, religious education must set out from some base and that in the schools of England and Wales that base will normally be Christianity. We shall also argue that, where appropriate, opportunities should be provided for the study of other religions.

If other religions are to have a serious position in the R.E. syllabus and to be allowed to form an integral part of it (appearing in primary school topics as well as forming a third year or sixth form slot in secondary schools) a real revolution in religious education will have to occur—unlike the one which modernized the method in the light of educational research and trends but retained the same Christian basis. Syllabus revisers and class teachers will not merely have to decide a theme on 'light' should include reference to Diwali or to the Buddha as the Enlightened One as well as to Jesus, the Light of the World, they will have to recognize that behind their decision lies a totally new idea of what is meant by religious education.

Some teachers may settle for a position typified by the West Riding and Inner London Syllabuses and the Durham Report, the content still being broadly Christian but with educational considerations determining the answers to the questions what, when and how. Other religions would continue to be appendages.

Other teachers may go to the half way position typified by B. Wigley and R. Pitcher in *From Fear to Faith* (Longmans, Green, 1969). Each section ranges broadly in a phenomenological manner but culminates in a statement of the Christian or Jewish-Christian position, for example 3, 'Middle Men', examines the need for holy men, types of holy men—healers, rainmakers, seers, Jesus—the Holy Man, spiritual interpreters,

Jesus the High Priest. Unit 8, 'A Growing Light', traces Religion for Law and order, a searching spirit, the Hebrew, a Chosen Nation, Jesus the Chosen One. Although the text does not lay stress on the finality of Christianity the structure may be said to suggest it and to state that the journey from Fear to Faith ends in Jesus. This position can hardly be called satisfactory. Unwittingly the study of world religions is being used to support the view that they are at best to be regarded as preparatory to the Gospel. Though other books in the series may correct this impression, *From Fear to Faith* has laid bare the danger of the half-way position. There will always be Christians who, ignoring the emphasis which preachers still occasionally put on hell and judgement (fear) and knowing nothing of the wholesomeness as a binding force of preliterate tribal religions, will have no scruples in using the comparative study of religions to emphasize the finality of Christ (faith).

In the long run, however, it appears that once the Bible-based Christian education of yesterday has been rejected there can be no resting place short of the final destination, a subject having some such name as religious studies. In it the study of Christianity will have a place but as part of the whole. Obviously because it is the religion nearest to hand and the one without which Western culture cannot be understood Christianity is likely to enjoy a prominent position but this is not the same as saying that the syllabus will be geared to an appreciation of Christianity. The 'base' desirable on educational grounds will not be Christianity but Religion—or religions.

This will necessitate the study of religious diversity or differences, the aim will not be to search for some sort of common denominator, a religion which lies behind the religions. Teachers will also have to orientate themselves to the view that to teach about a religion does not necessarily demand commitment to it, and that commitment may be more of a hindrance than a help. Traditionally R.E. has been thought of in terms of helping students to discover the meaning of life. Now the term 'meaning' will be different. The whole curriculum may be considered in terms of meaning—an attempt to understand the meaning of the past, of the environment, of science—and so on, in this sense religious studies is concerned with the meaning of religion, what meaning religions have given to such ideas as God and worship, the relationship between man and God and man and man—but it is not the task of religious studies in school to strive for decisions, to offer one religious interpretation of life and to encourage the child/student to accept it or to put a supermarket choice before him and recommend any religion, much less a best buy. To assist the student in his own personal search for meaning is still regarded as the loftiest task the religious education specialist can perform; it is not, in my opinion, one proper to the religious studies teacher in the class lesson in a county school, except in so far as the whole curriculum provides education of such a quality that the meaning of the school, the meaning of society and the place of the individual within it, as well as the meaning of life itself, are subjects for consideration. Meaning in this context differs considerably from challenging the student with the need for meaning and presenting it in an apparently open-ended and liberal but ultimately Christian form.

Having said this it must be repeated that the need for an adequate understanding of Christianity is accepted, it being the religion of the student's own culture. There is no danger of producing people who lack cultural roots—one would have to stand the whole of English education completely on its head to do this! The starting point will always be the native culture. This awareness of the cultural diversity of mankind should begin in the primary years but only assume anything like a significant proportion in the thirteen-plus years. Even in a school which goes wildly oriental in history, art, music, and religion, the major part of the student's time will be spent in his own culture and at 4 p.m. he will return to the Western world. However, far from destroying culture the awareness of cultural diversity is likely to enrich it. W. E. Hocking once spoke of 'reconception', asserting that the study of another's religion makes for a deeper awareness of one's own. This has been my experience and that of many others. Also, there are many who consider that Western culture needs some fresh stimulus. Perhaps the East will provide it—just as the East was itself 'awakened' in the last century by the Western presence. Awareness of cultural diversity, if accompanied by understanding, could lead to a new renaissance.

Conclusion

The future development of religious education seems to lie in four directions with the final one being between 1 and 4.

1. The traditional. Christian Education but with an increasing emphasis upon the understanding of concept rather than the acquiring of Biblical knowledge.

Understandably many humanists will continue to lobby for the abolition of the subject if it is unwilling to interpret the term 'open-endedness' more broadly than this. The next conservative backlash may well result, if not in syllabus changes, at least in a change of teacher-attitudes to a reaffirmation of Bible-based R.E. and world religions will lose their tenuous foothold.

2. World Religions. In a few secondary schools (and there will not be many in the nature of the case) where the subject is given a fair allocation of staff and time, students may be permitted to opt for the traditional R.E. or world religions. In more the teacher is likely to choose world religions as a fourth or fifth form option. In the latter case it is still a mere appendage, in the former an unfortunate distinction is drawn between Christianity and world religions, as though the former were not part of the latter. Already one has heard of people saying 'it's easy now, you don't teach R.E. you teach world religions instead. Anyone can do that!' Presumably they mean that there need be no element of commitment and they hope the questions 'what do you believe, sir?' will not be asked but one shudders at the thought of someone equipped with filmstrip and tape 'doing' Hinduism and the whole subject never becoming real or meaningful.
3. Moral Education. This may become a subject separate from religious education but this is unlikely for two reasons, first the line between religion and morals is arbitrary and when humanist militancy has cooled a little and Christians are more prepared than some are at present to recognize that individual morality is not always dependent upon religious belief the demand may cease. Secondly, in purely practical terms the R.E. man is the one who will be expected to teach moral education though a few schools might try appointing someone who is hostile to religion. The result in either case is unlikely to be the separation of the two.
4. Religious Studies. No detailed syllabus yet exists but a basis might be found in the six dimensions outlined by Ninian Smart in *Secular Education and the Logic of Religion* (London, 1968). They are: doctrinal, mythological, ethical, ritual, experiential and social (institutional).

Of course, it would be naive to suggest that religious studies thus envisaged will not have its opponents (not only among evangelical Christians) for it marks a total break with tradition and some would say sells the Christian pass. However, while the subject will be one through which students can search for meaning it will also be one truly comparable with history or geography, not jingoistic or partisan and seeking to convince but the study of religion. It will also result in a type of religious education which only a specialist can teach. No longer will headmasters be able to economize on R.E. staff by farming out the subject among willing (or not so willing) non-specialists; on the contrary most existing specialists who are prepared to adopt this approach will have to be re-trained.

WOC

43

TEACHING HINDUISM IN PRIMARY SCHOOLS

What do we mean by religious instruction?

IT IS DIFFICULT to talk about teaching Hinduism or Christianity in primary schools without first considering what we mean by Hinduism and religious education. In the words of a Hindu friend, 'The people who populated the fertile plain of the river Sindhu came to be called Hindus and the country of these people came to be called Hindusthan and whatever mode of life, code of morals or ethics they followed came to be called the Hindu religion or Hinduism', so Hinduism is something much wider than we usually think about in the context of R.E. lessons; it has not produced a set of fixed beliefs but a development of values and customs ranging from the most primitive to the most enlightened, with probably as much variation amongst different groups at the present day as between different centuries. It is interesting to read that Ronald Goldman thinks it would be easy to teach (young) children aspects of Hindusim with its animistic assertions, its many gods and pantheistic theology.'[1] There may be some truth in what he says if Hindu stories and myths fulfil a child's need at that stage of his development, but if that is all that Hinduism offers, we can supply plenty of primitive Christian stories to meet this need.

Over the last few years we have seen the change, albeit a very uneven one depending much on the particular school, from teaching the structure of Christianity, the prayer book, the Bible and its history and the church, to a freer interpretation of the Holy Spirit as exemplified in Christ and in the witness of his followers, taking such modern examples as Schweitzer, Martin Luther King and many others. However in society as a whole, apart from the social/cultural/economic activities of Christmas, Easter and Whitsun, in which we all take part, it is unlikely that more than 10 per cent of the population are members of any religious organization, so what is it that parents want us to teach their children—surely not something that is of so little value and is irrelevant in their own lives? Perhaps here our increasing knowledge of the human psyche can help us—its need for love and security, for encouragement in overcoming its reasonable and irrational fears and stresses, for recognizing and expressing its deepest needs and in accepting its inner divinity in relation to the world. Religious growth is not something separate from the rest of a child's development. This is expressed briefly and profoundly by Jeffrey's saying 'Religious truth is normal experience understood at full depth.'[2]

In an infants' school we do not attempt to teach the structure of Christianity but throughout the life of the school we try to demonstrate our attitude of caring for and responsibility towards everyday living, which may be called R.E. when it appears in the garb of a Bible story or myth or Christian festival that has become part of our culture; but much the most valuable contribution is the whole 'atmosphere' of trust, helpfulness and appreciation that we show to the children in their joys and problems. Next come the stories that provide different levels of understanding, so that the child can absorb the greater depth as he is ready; stories in which a child can see himself mirrored and yet be detached from the physical limitations for a time. The world of art, of pictures, sculpture and particularly dance, music and mime, may reach to a deeper level of the unconscious and give him an opportunity to act out some of his basic fears and joys. To give an example, a class of six-year-olds acted out in mime and song the story of Good King Wenceslas, and on the day after our celebration of Diwali, the banishment of Rama and Sita, the brother putting the golden sandals on the empty throne, the overcoming of demons in the forest, and the festival of lights as Rama and Sita were welcomed home to their family, all of which was very popular.

What, then, are these experiences in which we are all involved at a deeper level, and to which we must try to give due recognition before they pass?

1. A cosmic sense of awe and wonder at the mystery of life and the universe.
2. Joy in movement and rhythm, creation and beauty. I am here reminded of Sydney Carter's song 'The Lord of the Dance' and of Shiva Nataraja.
3. A sense of unity with all creation and reverence for life.

4. Recognition of suffering, loss, death and change.
5. Compassion and caring for people, animals, plants, water and the air we breathe.
6. The satisfaction of doing what is right for its own sake, and courage to bear witness to the truth as we see it.
7. A sense of gratitude, loving tolerance and humility.

These experiences are the stuff of everyday living.

What has Hinduism to offer in the primary school?

No doubt Bible stories and experiences can be thought of to illustrate these themes, but there are also Hindu stories which illustrate them. What are the marks of such a story? Hindu mythology can be very intricate and confusing. Where do we draw the distinction between magic and fairy tale? I try to find a rational answer to such stories as the feeding of the five thousand and to say that, though it is rare, some people have the power to heal that Jesus had. There are many instances of nature being friendly to those who respect her, for example, Hanuman helping Rama, the hooded cobra shielding Buddha and Guru Nanak, Daniel in the lions' den, but are these stories to be counted as magic when they seem to illustrate a fundamental truth? The stories I would choose to illustrate these themes would show the means in harmony with the end and the good triumphing or being recognized for what it is . . . but does it always triumph in this world? Now we begin to reach out for answers to problems which often cannot be judged by material values but only in the life of the mind or spirit.

There is no doubt that young children quickly respond to suffering, to sharing and to what seems fair. Their sense of the numinous, of beauty and of joy is spontaneous; there is a sense of awe and satisfaction in simple ritual, of putting hands together and saying simple or even hardly understood prayers, of kneeling before the manger and offering a gift, all of which I have often seen done with moving dignity and reverence. When I have taken some of the Asian children in the woods, they have spontaneously sung hymns learnt in school assembly. 'Daisies are our silver, buttercups our gold, This is all the treasure we can have or hold', or 'Over the earth is a mat of green . . . over it all is the love of God, blessing us everyone.' A Hindu once asked to sing a religious song at an inter-faith service said 'but all our songs are religious!' By the age of ten or eleven children are much less spontaneous but it is easier by this time to discuss with them the apparent triumph of good over evil, the growth of human loyalty and integrity as exemplified in the lives of men and women of many faiths.

Following the tradition of the great teachers of the world, we tell many stories in a primary school based on the children's own experience. Now that we have Hindu, Muslim and Sikh children in our classes and their processions and festivals in our towns, our area of experience is enriched. Quite naturally one hears about mother making chappaties, new shalwars to wear at the festival, and the visit to the Asian films on Sundays. This naturally introduces new food, clothes and customs, the enjoyment of seeing films about India, the nostalgia for a half-remembered home. Even if there are no Asians in the school, newspapers and television are constantly showing pictures and news about Asians in Asia as well as Asians in Britain, and if we included Greek and Norse myths when our world seemed limited to Europe, there is a place for Asian culture now that we are conscious of being members of one world.

The question then arises as to whether Hindu culture has any particular contribution to make in the primary school as the Greek and Norse have done. Hinduism and its stories are particularly rich in their tolerance, in their reverence for all life, in recognising the life of the spirit behind the material forms, in caring for the elderly and in honouring a guest.

Many stories illustrating these themes are published by the Delhi Children's Book Trust (see Bibliography part C). To give a personal example, a few years ago a Hindu friend spent some months with us, and on a bitter night a few days before Christmas a stray underfed dog presented himself at the backdoor and refused to go away. After some heart searching I let him in—much to the dismay of our pedigree bitch, who looked shocked by the visitor. The Hindu said: 'It is a god come in disguise to test your compassion'. Certainly we have comparable stories in our culture but the acceptance of reincarnation and the lack of a welfare state, has left India with a more positive attitude towards honouring God as embodied in a stranger or the aged, and the dog spent a very happy Christmas, adding another dimension to our festivities.

Besides enjoying stories and myths, the upper classes of a primary school can find modern representatives of Hinduism such as Gandhi and Vinobe Bhave, heroes of a modern revolution, of great interest, not only in their own lives but because of the influence such men had on practical Christians such as Martin Luther King. These lives provide stimulating and true stories for the questing minds of the upper primary classes as well as showing people of other faiths who are working for love and justice in their community.

The belief that one's present condition is the result of past actions and that our future state will depend on present actions is more realistic and challenging than the attitude of many who feel they have rights but no responsibilities or say 'why should this happen to me?' So while there are many Hindu stories that express the same truths as ours in 'Shiva's Milk' and Babooshka and the Christmas Visitors or the Loyal Mongoose and the story of Beddgelert, there are also many others which bring into focus truths that we have neglected.

Ways of Approach

It is helpful to do a project on India, to see films of children at home, at school and at play, to collect pictures and make scrap books and collages showing homes, food, animals, acting the stories and listening and dancing to Indian music. Asian parents are usually most co-operative in lending treasures from home to help make a school exhibition. Gratitude and pleasure in these treasures can be expressed at assembly time when one of the Hindu stories can be mimed, the costumes and scenery forming part of the project preparation. In the upper classes of the primary school the project is linked with history, geography, art, language study and wherever possible linked to relevant occasions such as World Children's Day, Gandhi's centenary year, or Guru Nanak's anniversary, when a hero provides a central link and the children can do some of the research by themselves as publicity material is available. This is nothing new of course, but many projects can be static rather than dynamic in that they do not give enough attention to people's beliefs which have led to actions changing the environment in which they lived. A book recently published by Oxford University Press, The Oxford Children's Reference Library, *India and Her Neighbours* (see Bibliography part C) does give attention to this. There are also two new films available from Concord films, 'Gandhi the Silent Revolutionary' and 'Vinobe the Walking Revolutionary' which show modern Hindus who are trying to relate their beliefs to the present needs of India.

The proprietor of the Delhi Children's Book Trust has displayed a typically Hindu attitude by setting his face against producing any sectarian religious books for children. The books published in this series are in an Indian setting, but they are stories for children anywhere; they tell of the visit to the new-born buffalo calf, the boy returning the baby squirrel to its mother, the friendship of elephants and mice. To the youngest they express joy and wonder at birth, they show the realization of a small boy that there is no joy in taking a baby squirrel from its mother, that thoughtlessness can cause pain and co-operation pleasure. Joy, compassion and friendship, these are religious themes. Many stories showing the loyalty and wisdom of animals are found in the *Panchatantra* published by the same firm. At the festival of Pola, oxen are decorated, taken to the temple and given a holiday in thankfulness for their work; once a year at Nagapanchami even the dreaded cobra is respected and given milk, thus recognising its place in the unity of life. These stories need to be absorbed by the teacher, so that she has a reservoir to draw on at the appropriate time.

Examples of Method

Perhaps it would be helpful at this juncture to give a few personal accounts of work in the classroom and at assembly. It did not take long at morning assembly at Diwali to put little coloured lamps on the table in the hall and an Indian classical record on the record player. The children came in silent and wide-eyed on the dark November morning. We sang one of our customary hymns which ends with 'Guard me when mother turns out the light.' We talked about being afraid in the darkness and the joy of candles we have on birthday cakes and at Christmas. I then told them a simplified story of Rama, his banishment, his overcoming demons in the dark forest, how he made friends with people and animals who helped him, and finally his return home when his friends came to meet him with lamps, and people put lamps in their houses as they do today at Diwali. At the end of the story we thanked God for fire and light, prayed that we might not be afraid when it is dark and that we might be brave and helpful to all creatures like prince Rama. After singing 'All things bright and beautiful' the Asian children stood in the middle of the hall while we wished them 'a happy Diwali!' This assembly took about a quarter of an hour, which is about the usual length; the attitude of respect and recognition of another's culture was contained in it, and we shared Diwali with the Hindu children as they shared Christmas with us.

This spring we have been growing bulbs, cress, beans, planting seeds and caring for the small school garden; cutting out the old and accepting death and decay and the compost heap as we feed the ground, looking forward to new growth and thanking God for the joy and wonder of his world, remembering that we must care for and nourish it as it in its turn nourishes us. In our music and movement lessons we are sometimes the wind, the sun, the growing seeds and the swaying trees, sometimes using Indian music for this. A few months ago an Indian friend brought an Indian recording of a song in praise of spring. She danced barefoot, first offering her dance to God and then expressing in many different movements her joy in spring, the wind, the fluttering leaves and the birds, the bee visiting the flower, the flowing river and the waves of the sea. She did this again, slowly showing each of the movements in greater detail as the children tried to do it, using eyes as well as hands, arms and body to express emotions. The children then made up their dance of joy and thanks, offering it first to God. Was this an act of worship? As a *swami* I once met said: 'God looks into the heart of his devotees, so I leave the answer to Him.'

My last example is our World Children's Day project when each child made a book, the cover of which showed Asian children in the class flying or coming by boat from India to England. We painted pictures of our own faces and that of our Asian friends in the class showing the variations of skin, of hair straight, curly, auburn, black, brown or pale straw. The children were shown a number of slides of children in India, showing their homes, clothes, animals and temples, showing them climbing trees, fetching water or feeding chickens. This was followed up by the children painting pictures, making simple models and class collages, putting much of the information they gathered into their special books. These pictures, together with some Indian posters and some pictures painted by children from a school in India, made a very gay and interesting display in the hall which we shared with the parents the week they came to the school 'bring and buy sale'.

Certainly part of our basic teaching is something we now call 'community relations' where we willingly accept people of other cultures and skin colour, the enrichment that they bring as well as the problems they present that have to be faced within the context of respect for the dignity of all men. However, a child looking at the display in the hall asked where the pictures of Jamaica were because that was where he was from, so the next time a project of this kind is undertaken it will be on the West Indies, for we have a number of West Indians in the school.

Many people have been watching the series of television programmes on sex in the primary school in which the importance of establishing attitudes which are wholesome and creative and a sense of loving responsibility early in life is stressed. Attitudes in the primary school are changing, in fact it seems we are becoming more Hindu in our attitude to sex as an expression of the divine joy in the creative spirit. It is interesting to reflect that religious instruction as such is not given in Indian state schools, yet Hinduism is alive and a living reality to the many who sing their morning prayers as they pour water over the head during the morning bath, anointing the god within as later they will anoint the god in the small shrine in the house. Mothers' and grandmothers' teaching and the rituals established over the centuries in a slowly changing society, feed the unconscious in the child with a living force that has more power than the formal teaching of later years. 'Give me a child until he is seven', said the Jesuits, and they were the pioneers of teaching a child with love when the custom was to beat knowledge into a child. Perhaps it is not so strange that within the last hundred years India has produced spiritual teachers of he calibre of Ramakrishna, Vivekananda, Gandhi, Vinoba and Krishnamurti.

EW

Footnotes

[1] Ronald Goldman, *Readiness for Religion*, London 1967. p. 41.
[2] Quoted in *Readiness for Religion*, p. xiii.

44

TEACHING HINDUISM IN JUNIOR AND MIDDLE SCHOOLS

WHAT CAN BE TAUGHT to children aged 9 to 13 and how may it be done? The middle years of a child's education present great opportunities. Basic skills have been mastered, there is enthusiasm and an eagerness to learn. It is the magpie period when almost everything is collected from valuable information to milk bottle tops and if discipline problems arise or boredom is expressed the situation is unnatural enough to warrant serious enquiry. Unsuitable material, some upset at home or a parental attitude is likely to lie at the root of the trouble.

Though I do not wish to advocate specialist R.E. teachers in middle schools (or specialists in similar subjects such as history or geography) yet the education of these children is at far too critical a stage for it to be left to the whim of individual teachers or even heads who *may* include some history or R.E. if they feel like doing so, perhaps in the way currently advocated. In R.E. at least, there is some need for a form of syllabus or programme and for a teacher who is responsible for supervising it and assisting his colleagues. The teaching is likely to be in the hands of the class teacher as is normal in primary schools. L.E.A.'s could well give managerial guidance in recruiting teaching teams to include people competent in art and handicraft, music and dance, the humanities, R.E., French, science, mathematics, etc., to whom allowances could be paid. After all, these schools will be large enough to warrant it and if the education given in these years is not adequate the task of teachers and students in upper schools will be impossible.

The basis and content of religious education in the early years of schooling is likely to be broadly Christian or Christian-humanist in that the values stressed will come under the heading 'love of neighbour' and the numinous dimension of love and awe will tend to be explored and interpreted from a Christian standpoint. This is natural, for we must begin with the familiar and meet the children where they are. We may wish to avoid God-talk but words like God and Jesus and occasions like Christmas will be familiar to them and the teacher must give them meaning. In the West, God is understood in terms of Christianity—even, as I have already said, by atheists. By the age of fourteen the basis will have shifted from Christianity to Religion. If put in diagramatic form it would appear rather like an inverted pyramid. In the early years, as Mrs. Wilson indicates, a start can be made in the movement from one base to another but is likely to be slight in matters of fact, greater, which is more important, in matters of attitude. The middle years provide an opportunity for acceleration.

The main methods of teaching are likely to be the use of theme or topic; in either case Hinduism will be integrated with other material rather than studied as a subject in isolation. A project on India is the obvious and easy starting place. I can see no reason why background topics should be despised, they often provide a basis upon which future work in R.E. and other subjects depends. A teacher who reads the Ladybird book *Flight Four: India* will soon have many ideas and little difficulty in introducing children to India and to its predominant religion. I would have in mind children aged 9 or 10 using it. Good additional material can be obtained from the BBC Schools series 'Man' about an Indian village. This was first broadcast in the summer of 1970 and repeated in 1971. The booklet contains useful pictures, the programmes themselves conveyed the sounds and atmosphere of village life. Twelve-year-olds might derive most benefit from the series but it could be used with younger or slightly older students. Unfortunately the village chosen was one in South India and most Indians settling in Britain come from the north, but this has no bearing on the Hindu content. Perhaps another series will be about life in the Punjab and give more attention to technological development.

Some of the frames in the filmstrips listed in the bibliography can be used but most relate to village or town life and perpetuate the elephant and ox-cart image. Immigrants to Britain are eager to remind us that India is changing, that there are tractors and motor cars, and vast hydro-electric schemes with the highest dam in the world. We do well to listen to them and modify the stories of life in an Indian village which some books give. It is possible to meet Indians whose only encounter with an elephant or a tiger has been in an English zoo and who have never drawn water from a well!

The Hindu content in this topic and throughout the middle years would probably be drawn from the mythological and ritual dimensions of the six dimensions mentioned on p. 141. References to worship would include a visit to the temple, and family religion, a wedding, *puja* in the home, perhaps funerals. Pilgrimages could also be described. A description of one of the festivals would lead into the mythological dimensions and stories of Vishnu or Shiva as Lord of the Dance and the great ascetic. The social aspect of Hinduism would be touched upon in family life, the idea of the extended family and domestic responsibility.

Attention has to be drawn to one problem which can arise in the use of Indian stories. What reaction would there be to someone writing a book of the stories of Adam and Eve, Noah and Jonah and calling it Jewish Fairy Tales—or adding the annunciation, virgin birth and some narratives from the Book of Acts and giving the anthology the title 'Folk Tales of the Bible'? This is what has been done with the religious stories of Hinduism, the *Ramayana* and *Mahabharata* and others which form the foundation of an Indian child's religious education. These are far more than fairy tales or legends. They can be told to our children and should be, but the teacher should be aware of the message they seek to convey. Towards the end of the middle years careful attention might be given to myth, if possible with the co-operation of the English and history specialists. Ideally the art department should also be involved. The use of mythology is a subject for further thought and research. It might be that if the miracles and parables of Jesus cannot be taught, nor, for the same reasons, can the myths of Vishnu and Shiva.

At the younger end in the middle years a topic on journeys might include pilgrimages and so lead to a Hindu festival or journey to Benares. One on caring could show how the extended family functions as well as including the story of Gandhi, champion of the Harijans or Bhai Ghanaya the Sikh 'Good Samaritan'. Mahatma Gandhi is also an example of moral courage as are some of the Sikh Gurus.

Further background material relevant indirectly to Hinduism and capable of being used with under elevens which might be included in topics on farming, food, or clothes are: Indian rice or tea plantations, curry dishes, saris, the costume of temple dancers and the dances they perform, wedding dresses and customs, the conscientious vegetarianism of many Indians. In some immigrant areas it is possible to buy Indian sweets and other foods. The amount of hot fat lying about makes a visit to a sweet-maker's out of the question!

In using background material my aim would be to suggest that India is worth knowing about—and so, by implication, giving the idea that its religion is worth studying. Attitudes form early and it is foolish waiting until a child becomes a teenager before introducing him to Hinduism simply because only then does it become possible for him to understand the concepts. This is particularly important with regard to the religions of India—to a lesser extent with regard to Judaism and to Islam possibly in that order. Indians are dark skinned and belong to the 'third world'. Generations of children in Sunday Schools up and down Britain have collected pennies to send to the 'little black babies overseas'. Indians come into that category. Moreover Oxfam, Christian Aid and other agencies besides TV documentaries have reminded us of the poverty of the subcontinent and Hindus and Sikhs have come here for the better life (materially) which Britain offers. It is going to be difficult to convince some of our secondary modern lads that India has anything to offer, especially if the above pressures and parental prejudice have been at work on them with no contrary evidence being produced in the earlier years of childhood. Mrs. Wilson has had experience of an Indian visitor to her school being called a 'wog' and my youngest daughter was four years old when she returned from her multi-racial infant school singing 'Jew, Jew, dirty old Jews!' Such things will always be, but the teacher has to counter prejudice. One way of doing this is by dispelling ignorance.

The use of books from India with older children is something of a problem. The binding, printing and illustrations are often poor. Librarians, booksellers and college students frequently comment on them and one cannot help wondering what unconscious reaction they produce in any children and teachers who may handle them.

Certain themes definitely belong to the upper end of the middle years. Myth is one (though myths can be used much earlier, especially in a festival context). Another is light. This theme, as presented in the Rupert Hart-Davis series or outlined in some syllabuses, benefits from being used later rather than sooner. Light symbolism is of importance in many religions, the

Buddha is the Enlightened One and in Islam 'God is the Light of the heavens and the earth' (Koran, *Sura* 24), in Hinduism there is the sacred fire present as a witness at marriages, consuming the body at cremation, essential to sacrifice and named Agni, as well as the light symbolism in Diwali and in *puja* in the home. Water is another theme which may be explored phenomenologically.

In *Comparative Religion in Education* (Ed. J. R. Hinnells, Oriel Press, Newcastle, 1970, p. 71) Raymond Johnston concluded that the real problems which had to be overcome before world religions could assume an important position in the school curriculum were educational. I agree with him. The climate of opinion certainly favours the inclusion and teachers of older Juniors are prepared to make the attempt. The help they require is beginning to appear in books such as *East Comes West* by Peggy Holroyde published by the Community Relations Commission and the Ward-Lock series (1970), but it is still far too difficult for them to find imaginative and reliable information of festivals, to obtain visual material, and to attend in-service courses. Enthusiasm must be supported by good materials.

WOC

45

TEACHING HINDUISM IN SECONDARY SCHOOLS

AT THE SECONDARY LEVEL (11–18), serious attempts can be made to present Hinduism in such a way, that children receive a realistic impression of a great religious tradition: a tradition that is intellectually absorbing, emotionally powerful and alive with every form of external expression.

The purpose of this article is to discuss a number of vital questions, viewed against the background of teenage pupils, of either sex, of widely differing ability, and in many different educational situations. These questions are concerned with the principles of education, with the nature of Hinduism, and with the actual learning situation. They are as follows:

1. What educational principles must be applied to the teaching of Hinduism?
2. What are the proper motives for teaching Hinduism?
3. What are the proper purposes of teaching Hinduism?
4. What aspects of Hinduism make suitable material for young people of 11–18?
5. How can these aspects best be taught?
6. What associated activities could provide a natural extension of these studies?
7. What lasting impressions of Hinduism is it desirable to provide?

1. What educational principles must be applied to the teaching of Hinduism?

There are certain principles, ways of thinking or ways of teaching, that apply to all educational disciplines, but especially to the 11–18 age-group, and to Hinduism.

(a) The learning process is firmly based on INFORMATION: the giving, receiving and exchanging of information, sensual, emotional, intellectual, and some would add, spiritual.

The information should emanate from a variety of sources: the teacher, books, teaching aids, other pupils, private research or intuiiton.

(b) The well-informed child is at liberty to accept or reject the information, or to subject it to close scrutiny, and thereby estimate its significance; this could be called SPECULATION.

(c) This active response necessarily absorbs the senses, emotions and the intellect of the child: he undergoes INVOLVEMENT.

(d) He inevitably applies the topic in question to his own situation, and it becomes a part of his own personal EXPERIENCE.

(e) Vivid experience is best worked out in some form of EXPRESSION: again: sensual, emotional, intellectual, aesthetic, practical, literary, or perhaps spiritual, mystical—some form of 'worship' perhaps.

These five concepts: INFORMATION, SPECULATION, INVOLVEMENT, EXPERIENCE and EXPRESSION are the necessary signposts of direction in seeking the answers to the remaining questions. Any materials, any methods, any aims or motives which do not satisfy the demands they make, are bad education, and therefor stand self-condemned. They are the necessary safeguards of the integrity of the subject and the integrity of the child. They also promote the freedom of the teacher to do his work well, and finally, the means whereby everyone may enjoy learning about the Hindus.

2. *What are the proper motives for teaching Hinduism?*

There is a clear distinction between Motive and Purpose in education: motive being the teacher's reasons for wishing to teach a subject; purpose being the end in view, the desired aim of the completed act of teaching. Motive looks back; purpose looks forward.

A devout Hindu might well choose to teach Hinduism to Hindu children in India, from a conviction that for him, and for them, Hinduism is the natural and proper religious tradition to follow. A student of world religions might seek to teach Hinduism because he is attracted to the Hindus and their way of life. This attitude should not be confused with that of the devout convert: in fact, one might suppose that anyone teaching Hinduism without enjoyment might not do justice to the subject.

There may be those who are genuinely fascinated by things

oriental. For them, this exotic curiosity might lead to a lively treatment of Hinduism; but it would be in great danger of being an unbalanced treatment: a powerful treatment of only limited aspects.

Many would find it very difficult to resist the urge to treat Hinduism in comparison with Christianity: perhaps with the preconception about one of the two being nearer to truth and goodness. Such treatment, transferred to the teaching of politics, would be conspicuously lacking in integrity. Is this accusation any less apposite in the teaching of religion?

The immature teenager has his own quota of motives for wanting to learn about world religions in general, and about Hinduism in particular. Many of these, as he grows older, he views with disdain; but one motive: the desire for novelty, is sometimes shared by the teacher; and it has a disturbing ring of natural logic. So much of the maturing personality is dependent upon a variety of experience: novelty, in the best sense, is a natural need of the child, especially the young teenager, who has a lively thirst for knowledge, not only about the world, but about himself too.

It is probably fair to say that none of these, taken in isolation, is a sufficient, or in some cases, an acceptable, motive for embarking on the teaching of Hinduism. The one wholly desirable motive would be the conviction that the study of world religions is a respectable item in the curriculum of the enlightened school: worthy to take its place alongside other humanities, as a valid exploration of aspects of the universal experience of mankind.

3. What are the proper purposes for teaching Hinduism?

For the Guru in the appropriate Indian situation, the purpose is plainly to help children to grow into full understanding and acceptance of the Hindu religious tradition.

The 'world religions' enthusiast will want to commend Hinduism as an attractive and valuable field of study: though once again, not a necessary object of personal faith.

Teenagers have a natural curiosity about the eastern religions; sensible treatment of Hinduism might go a fair way towards, at the same time, satisfying the mere curiosity, and provoking a genuine desire for knowledge.

Comparison with Christianity is inevitable; it need not be treated merely as a tendency on the teacher's part: it will arise in the reactions of the class to first impressions of Hinduism, and in discussion about issues raised by more extended study. The important caveat is that, however much comparison arises, there shall be no *a priori* assumption that one tradition is true, or good, at the expense of the other, and therefore in a position of authority. It is here that the teacher must be content to be an educator, and to set his own personal convictions aside. He may, of course, be invited by the class to express an opinion. If so, he is at liberty to do so: but he must speak his mind only as a contributor to discussion not as an authority whose views have an overriding precedence.

Both teacher and class will enjoy exploring the new fields of thought and experience involved in Hinduism. This exploration will be vivid and memorable if it is undertaken with courage and humility. The ultimate (and immediate) purpose must be to help the child to experience, as far as he is able, what it means to be a Hindu. The experience is itself the aim. This in turn will lead to other benefits: the understanding of the beliefs and customs of Hindu immigrants, the general growth of the ability to make moral judgements, and the development of spiritual maturity.

If children emerge from their study of Hinduism with a profound respect for religious traditions, Christian and non-Christian alike, and an awareness of the significance of the spiritual areas of personality, life and thought, then the teacher may rest on the laurels of having at least avoided inhibiting their educational progress in religious studies.

4. What aspects of Hinduism make suitable material for young people of 11–18?

Nothing less than a balanced and rounded account of the total Hindu experience will satisfy the efficient teacher or the discerning student. So perhaps then, EVERY aspect of Hinduism must be taught? Much depends on what the study of Hinduism is intended to do. If the intention is to create 'world religions experts', then the intention is surely beyond the ability of the child and the brief of the teacher. It remains to be seen what standard of knowledge, understanding and insight would be required from candidates offering Hinduism as part of an Advanced Level Syllabus, or perhaps world religions in general, at Ordinary Level: an interesting problem of assessment. What would be most helpful to university departments, or to colleges of education? Perhaps the intention is to open the child's eyes to new worlds of oriental thought and oriental life.

Perhaps the intention is to lead the child to a new assessment of his own ideas, by approaching them obliquely, from an 'oriental' angle.

With limited time, the choice must lie somewhere between extensive treatment, which may be superficial, and intensive treatment which will necessarily be limited in scope. What is important, is that the basic characteristic features of Hinduism, the things that make it the great religious phenomenon that it is, should be well presented, convincingly experienced, thoroughly understood and sincerely appreciated. A simple but respectable working knowledge of Hinduism is a thoroughly good basis for speculation about God, man, and life. Involvement in the Hindu experience, as far as it is possible, is a powerful induction into the personal spiritual dimension: a mirror for the aspirations of teenagers. Hinduism meets them where they are, and draws them into the religious experience at many points, as befits their needs and demands.

These 'characteristic features' need not be taught together, in one complete and rather large unit. Some aspects are very suitable study material at the 11+ or 12+ stage. Some problems of Hindu philosophy, the political entanglements of the partition of India, and the development of Hinduism in the face of Western influence, these make good 6th form topics. But experience suggests that a full-scale survey is best carried out in the 13+ year. Suggestions about the arrangement of topics at these three levels are given in Table 1.

Such a division into three distinct groups of topics presupposes luxury in terms of time and materials. It is not difficult to refer briefly to Hinduism from time to time in the 11+ year; but for the Sixth-form the tendency in many quarters is to see minority time best used as an opportunity for general Studies, of which religious studies will either be one unit, or they will guide thinking in several wider studies, such as 'Humanities'. What is offered here is an approach to Hinduism as a part of the religious studies of the 13+ age group.

Children of this age are, so to speak, 'just in the mood for a look at world religions'. There seem to be several reasons:

(a) They are beginning to scrutinize many of their assumed loyalities: parental authority, traditional religion, the mere acceptance of knowledge.

(b) They are very acquisitive; they like collecting things, including new knowledge, especially if it involves some new, and very strange-looking words!

TABLE 1

A SCHEME FOR TEACHING HINDUISM

with topics arranged in three groups, to suit ages 11–12; 13+; 16–18.

(i) 11–12:	1. Village life 2. Festivals 3. Mythology 4. Great epics	5. Hatha yoga 6. Gandhi: the man 7. The geography of India
(ii) 13	1. India in general 2. The Indus valley 3. The caste system 4. Gandhi: the Harijans 5. Non-violence 6. Reincarnation 7. Brahman-Atman: all life is sacred 8. The Vedas, the Upanishads and the Gita 9. Family life 10. Birth, marriage and death 11. Indian culture: architecture, art, music and dress 12. Minorities in India: Muslims, Jains, Sikhs, Buddhists, Parsis and Christians	
(iii) 16–18:	1. The modern history of India: the Raj to Gandhi and beyond 2. Population control 3. The cow 4. New industry 5. Gandhi: partition; assassination; enduring influence 6. Various yogic thought-forms 7. Hindu philosophers, reformers and saints 8. Brahman-Atman: mystic philosophy 9. Extreme traditions	

(c) They are looking for themselves: for identity. (This, of course, is precisely what Hinduism is all about.)

(d) They are precise in their working habits (if they are encouraged and helped); they are not nearly as vague in their thinking as they tend to be later!

(e) They are able to assimilate a great deal of unfamiliar knowledge without being carried away.

(f) At the onset of adolescence, the liberation of inhibitions which the study of world religions involves, can be a most welcome therapy.

What follows is a purely hypothetical scheme for fourteen forty-minute lessons, in the 13+ year, with suggestions for homework. It must be hypothetical, for several reasons:

A. Within certain broad principles governing content, a great deal is to be gained by allowing the class to develop its own interest and to follow it up.

B. These broad principles must be based on a particular end in view, such as:
to see Hinduism as the natural expression of the 'religious climate of India';
to promote a deeper understanding of the outlook of Hindu immigrants;
to use Hinduism as an 'avenue of entry into the deeper recesses of the religious dimensions'.

The scheme suggested does provide a rounded survey, which could be adapted to a particular end; it would, however, be a true survey of Hinduism only if the balance of treatment were not upset in the process of adaptation.

C. Some changes may be thought necessary where low-ability groups are in mind. Perhaps there is too much anxiety here: children are frequently underestimated; an advanced intellectual concept, far beyond the normal teenager, can often be appreciated as vividly, often more vividly through senses, or the emotions, through aesthetic appraisal or through sheer cognisance of the effect of that concept on life.

D. Much will depend on the availability of aids, the expertise of the teacher, and the exigencies of the timetable.

The present scheme envisages an allowance of two forty-minute lessons per week, each pair being separated by a thirty-minute homework.

TABLE 2

A SEVEN-WEEK COURSE OF LESSONS ON HINDUISM

Week	*Lesson 'A'*	*Homework*	*Lesson 'B'*
1	1. First glance at India	2. Copy up	3. Hindu immigrants
2	4. The Indian village	5. Hindu village plan	6. God and the gods
3	7. Birth, marriage and death (Information)	8. Hindu love-story	9. Birth, marriage and death (Discussion)
4	10. Life and thought (i)	11. Preparation, or research	12. Life and thought (ii)
5	13. The Hindu mystic	14. Explain Yoga to a friend	15. The other religions in India
6	16. Gandhi	17. 'Gandhi: portrait from life'	18. From the Indus Valley to Calcutta
7	19. Famine and population	20. Revision	21. Assessment

5. How can these aspects of Hinduism best be taught?

It will be convenient to deal with the topics in the scheme (Table 2), in turn; and to offer suggestions about approach, teaching method, expression work, and discussion points. The academic background for each topic is treated in full at the appropriate points in other units. A little will be said about teaching aids; the whole subject of aids is treated more fully in unit 51.

WEEK 1. LESSON A: SCHEME ITEM 1—FIRST GLANCE AT INDIA

Build up a 'sense-picture' of India. Pass round lighted incense-sticks; explain how they are made, and how they are used. Play a little Indian music, perhaps from a *raga*, and explain the form of the music and the shape and structure of the instruments. Mention perhaps that, as in most countries, Indian folk-music is rather different: give an example if possible. Show some large colour-photographs of Indian life: especially pictures with a simple obvious human interest. Pass the pictures round; for this they will need to be firmly mounted on stout card; each picture will need an informative but very straightforward caption. Whilst the passing-round is going on, and with the background of perfume and music, draw a simple map of India on the board, using colour to show the present partition lines, and the 'official' division of religious communities. (The 'map' need not be accurate: this is not what is wanted. It is far more important for it to be more in the nature of a diagram. In any case, a diagram is easier to draw, and quicker too!)

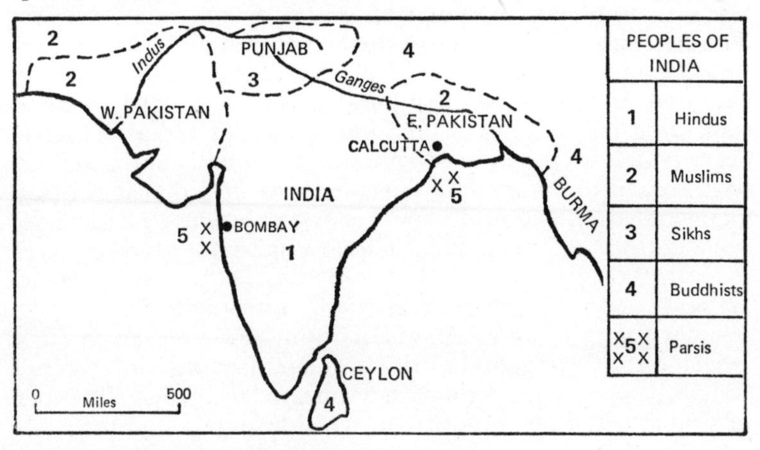

The class make a rough copy of the map, being careful to mark the distribution of religious communities, and the corresponding frontier lines. They should add, in their own words, an explanation of the situation today, and the teacher should help with this.

This introduction to India: setting the scene for Hinduism, and evoking a convincing Indian atmosphere, will provide a lasting backcloth for the presentation of the popular expression of the Hindu way of life, as well as the intellectual concepts of Indian philosophy which are to be found in Hindu texts. It will hold all together in a framework formed by insights into the reality of Indian life.

The involvement of the senses is important: the use of aids can be a tiresome chore for the teacher who has natural gifts of his own; but it is a real and necessary discipline to be obliged to distract the child's attention away from his own person, and let the material of the lesson speak for itself (and also, on occasion, sound, feel, taste and smell, for itself!). Incense-sticks are easily come-by; if the teacher finds difficulty, any of the children will readily supply some! Indian music is available on disc; if time allows, the point about 'classical and popular' should be stressed rather carefully. It is important, for instance, to realize that the Hindu beggar will not know very much about sophisticated *raga* music, or have much opportunity to see classical Indian dancing.

The aids should not be too numerous; the impression easily becomes blurred, and then more harm is done than good.

WEEK I. HOMEWORK SCHEME ITEM 2—'COPY UP'

The class should be asked to write an account of the lesson, and produce a neat version of the map. This 'first glance' needs to be captured and preserved. No great ability is needed to write something on the lines of 'first impressions of India'. There is every reason to be business-like about punctuality and precision with regard to homework. The class must feel that it is being given an expert and professional course of lessons in Hinduism, not a cursory and hesitant account of a half-understood culture.

WEEK I. LESSON B: SCHEME ITEM 3—HINDU IMMIGRANTS

From a glance at the 'cradle of Hinduism', the children pass to a brief look at the Hindus in Britain. A fair-sized body of statistics should be presented, perhaps in duplicated form, and a number of simple and relevant tasks set, which are based on the statistics. The Community Relations Council can help here; the children will find interest in extracting information about numbers of Hindu immigrants, localities of 'high Hindu density', and the numbers of Hindu children in British schools.

From the appreciation of the co-existences of the two communities, the Hindus and the British, an interesting discussion could develop, based on an examination of the aspects of Hindu life which British people might find strange: dress, diet, customs, language; but perhaps an even more penetrating self-appraisal might arise from an examination of precisely what a Hindu might find strange, amusing, offensive or admirable, about the British way of life!

The lesson should not pass unrecorded. A summary-note, compiled jointly by the teacher and the class, should register the presence of the Hindu immigrant-communities, and the need for all concerned to respect their characteristic ways of living and thinking. Intelligent or precocious pupils may raise the relative merits of integration, co-existence or segregation. This could be awkward, especially at the 13+ level; so often, young teenagers ask questions to which the only fair answers would be far beyond their intellectual powers. But in the sixth form, these questions are the very stuff of good general studies discussion. At 13+, a useful and positive way would be to present the various points of view and encourage the class to talk it over on their own.

At this point, a visit to a Hindu community would not be out of place, or a visit from a Hindu who is able to talk simply, clearly, and convincingly, about himself and his home. Extended discussion about worship and beliefs is not appropriate here: it would be better if it were introduced rather carefully, and illustrated later, from real life.

Again, precision is important: the class should be told the proper names for articles of dress, and names of Indian dishes and customs. The very words themselves will spur memory, and crystallize the experience of first meeting them.

WEEK 2. LESSON A: SCHEME ITEM 4—THE INDIAN VILLAGE

The aim here is to conjure up an experience of visiting a village in India. It is the people who make the village, so it is the people who are our centre of interest: the headman, who maybe has the only radio in the village; the priest at his little temple, ministering to the needs of the village people at life's crisis points: birth, puberty, marriage, child-bearing, sickness and death; the family in the family house; old people, retired and leisurely; the widow, loved, but often a problem; the young folk, colourful and gay; the gossips round the well; the travelling tinker with necessities and little extras; the government men with ideas about extending agriculture and reducing families; the men home from a spell of work in a distant city; the craftsmen; the village barber; landowners bathing away defilement in the village pool; the outcaste scavenger.

Lively treatment of all these themes could easily outlast lesson-time, and there is certainly no time for much expression work on the spot. There is also the real risk of confusion, as mental pictures are piled one on another. The answer lies in a diagram of the cumulative kind:

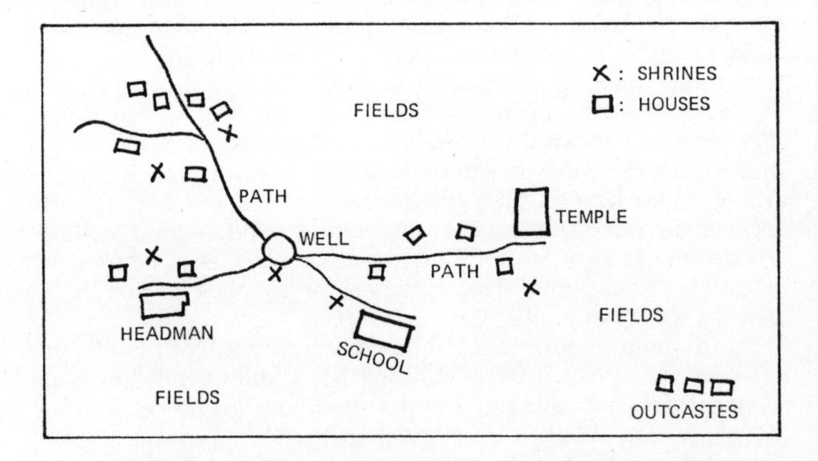

The class can build up their own, and make an improved version for homework. Experience reveals that great interest is aroused by even the most cursory account of village hygiene: the way refuse is disposed of; and the reluctance of villagers to have anything to do with modern toilet facilities. The state of the areas around homes in some Indian villages, and the gruesome tasks of the scavengers are not readily believed; evidence is really necessary here: if possible, quotations from authoritative books on Indian village life.[1]

Children are horrified at the suggestion, expressed by some Hindus, that the use of a handkerchief is unhygienic! But the idea raises unexpected incentives to question the perfection of the Western way of life.

The impression should be conveyed of a way of life that looks neither back to a founder, or a memorable beginning nor forward to a divine intervention, or even a remotest end; this concern with the present, and the significance of the present, is a profound characteristic of Hinduism.

This account of village life is anything but exhaustive; but lessons in world religions can easily suffer from the confusion of too much material covered too quickly. To travel at such a speed leaves no time to feel the soil, breathe the air or exchange glances with the people of the land.

WEEK 2. HOMEWORK: SCHEME ITEM 5—HINDU VILLAGE PLAN

The subject of text-books is not within the scope of this chapter: but it should be understood that children can be expected to carry out research of their own, from class text-books, or from books in the school library, or from any source within their reach.

In their 'plan of a Hindu village', the more enterprising children may be able to supplement the description supplied in the lesson: indeed, deliberate hints to this end may be dropped at the appropriate points in the lesson. The plans themselves should be so well labelled that they are as informative to other children as they are themselves. Any points that need further comment should be explained carefully in a companion-page of footnotes. Finally, an attempt should be made to memorize the plan (something that young teenagers can do, and enjoy doing). Questions could be asked at the beginning of the next lesson, and warning of this might be given.

WEEK 2. LESSON B: SCHEME ITEM 6—GOD AND THE GODS

A strange paradox lurks in the Hindu concept of God, or so it seems to the Western mind, attuned as it is to paradoxes through grappling with the Trinity. At one and the same time, the Hindu will speak of God, and of 'the gods'; and this with no awareness of contradiction! So any lesson dealing with deities must endeavour to convey this notion. Nothing is to be gained by spending 30–40 minutes ferreting about in Hindu mythology; but everything is to be gained by doing two really important things:

(a) looking steadily, but with respect, into the Hindu's devotion to Brahma, Vishnu, Shiva, Krishna, Lakshmi, and perhaps a very few other deities or 'saints', and his insistence that whatever deity is the immediate object of his worship, his life-long devotion, expressed through his worship, is to the one, single, all-pervasive 'BRAHMAN', 'GOD'.

(b) talking about the way that devotion to supernatural beings is a feature of most religious traditions, and the way this devotion has frequently inspired men to great works of art, great deeds of valour, and great courage in times of stress. It would not be out of place to allow the class to talk about the way in which, just as often, if not more often, religious convictions have led men to mutual hatred, persecution, the destruction of works of art, and some of the most terrible wars the world has ever known.

The lesson might conclude, in reverse, with references to the mutual hostility of Hindus and Muslims, and then to the glories of Hindu art and architecture, as also the extent and profound beauty of Hindu sacred literature. This last could have the nature of a preview of future lessons; it would not be out of place to quote, without much comment at this stage, some phrases from Hindu writings which seem to echo passages from the Bible. Two such passages might be:

(i) 'In the beginning, this world was Brahman. It only knew itself. "I am Brahman". Therefore it became the All.' (*Brihad-aranyaka Upanishad* I, 4. Trans. from E. G. Parrinder, *Book of World Religions*, London, 1965, p. 110.)

(ii) 'You do not perceive that the One Reality exists in your own body. But it is truly there.' (*Chandogya Upanishad* VI, 3. *Ibid.*)

Incidentally, it is far better to use one quotation twice, slowly, than any number of quotations which will make no impression. The more compressed and significant a quotation is, the more carefully it must be framed by silence.

If the lesson becomes quite profound, as it may very well do if the teacher catches the children's imagination, it will be difficult to break off for a written record of the proceedings. Are such records necessary? Much of the significance of this lesson might be fed into a later piece of work[2], and thus not be lost for ever.

WEEK 3. LESSON A: SCHEME ITEM 7—BIRTH, MARRIAGE, AND DEATH (i): INFORMATION

Much information to be given here; every reason to begin with a 'preface' about the expression work which is to follow as homework. It is suggested that this expression work might take the form of a short story involving the marriage of two young

Hindus, their growing affection for each other, the sudden death of the husband, leaving a young son, and the widow's retirement in the home of her deceased husband's family. A story of this kind might make reference to the many aspects of Hinduism which arise over the matters of birth, marriage and death. These will include: the caste system, astrology, arranged marriages, wedding customs, funeral rites, reincarnation.

If there seems to be an excess of information here, let it be said that what is needed is little more than a clear, simple, statement of the facts. Many points may arise when the story has been written, and the class meet again to discuss the various fortunes of their heroes and heroines. The important thing is that people feature centrally in the picture, and not the customs and rites in cold abstraction. With the projected story in mind, the children will find themselves linking the information with their own gradually developing plot, and so the information will be remembered precisely for its human interest.

Detailed information is given elsewhere about the topics indicated; sufficient here to make some suggestions about ways of presenting the information effectively.

The Caste System. It is not sufficient to mention the accident of birth into one of the four major castes, or the more numerous sub-castes. Reference must be made to the origin of the system, either in the effects of the Aryan invasions upon the Indus Valley culture, or in the natural divisions of labour in the village, or in the preservation of convenient class distinctions which favour the Brahmin, or at least give the Harijans security of status, even if that status is a low one. Reference might also be made, on the one hand, to the religious sanctions for the caste system to be found in the creation story in the *Rig Veda* (x, 90), and to the work of Gandhi. Discussion might develop about our British class structure; if so, questions might be noted for treatment in a future lesson.[3]

Astrology. The children will be interested to learn that our varying shades of anxiety about horoscopes in this country have their parallels in India, and in the Hindu communities in this country. They will all know their own horoscopes, and might like to discuss whether they will place any importance upon the horoscope of their future wives and husbands.

Arranged marriages. The sincerity of parents, the advantages of arranged marriages for stable society, the looking forward to the love which will blossom after marriage: all these need to be emphasized. Reference should also be made to the recent tendencies among the younger generation, to want love-marriages, but to be hesitant about grieving their less modern-minded parents.

Wedding customs. Brief reference to the ceremony, with the procession round the sacred fire, and the words:

'Come, let us marry; let us beget offspring;
Loving, bright, genial; may we live a hundred autumns.'
(*Ashvalayana Grihya Sutra*).

together with illustrations of the ceremony, will be enough to evoke the atmosphere.

Funeral Rites. The funeral pyre; the disposal of the ashes on running water; prayers for the speedy reincarnation of the dead soul; the provision of a shrine in the home to the memory of the departed; these things could be seen against the background of the general attitude of Hindus to death. Knowledgeable children will mention *sati*, though probably not by name, and the teacher will mention the legislation which ended the custom.

Reincarnation. Belief in reincarnation is the essential companion to contentment with the caste system. It explains what is really not an accident of birth at all. It colours the feelings of young people viewing the prospect of a marriage partner, and it underlies the hopes and fears of every Hindu mourner.

Perhaps it should be stressed again that the lesson has been an occasion for imparting information. At the end, or during the proceedings, questions will be asked, and answered, within the ability of the teacher to do so on the spot. But discussion will be the outcome of the more extended and more profound thought which will accompany the writing of the short story.

WEEK 3. HOMEWORK: SCHEME ITEM 8—HINDU LOVE STORY

Anything more than a brief comment would be out of place. The ground has been prepared; the child goes away to express his new knowledge in terms of people, perhaps young people as he is himself. What emerges will provide discussion material in the ensuing lesson. If the class knows that none of the stories need be revealed to anyone else, they will probably write with considerable personal involvement.

WEEK 3. LESSON B: SCHEME ITEM 9—BIRTH, MARRIAGE AND DEATH (ii): DISCUSSION

If the personal involvement in the stories has been genuine, and based on clear presentation of material in the previous lesson, then the discussion in this lesson will be informed and based on real concern. Discussion is notoriously difficult to bring off in the classroom, and the best discussions are those that appear to be spontaneous. The teacher's task is to engineer spontaneity! It is not advisable to announce a discussion at the outset. There are enough points latent in the material to make a real, as opposed to a contrived, discussion possible.

Perhaps two or three sequences may be suggested here.

A. Did your Hindu couple meet young Hindus of the other sex before their marriage?

Were they of different castes? Do young people in Britain really mix? Aren't class distinctions in Britain really created by money? In any case, aren't people happiest when they are among people with similar interests and backgrounds? Does education sometimes train the mind at the expense of social ease: bringing the boy from an uncultured home into close company with cultured girls, for instance? Is this always good? Is it enough to say, 'We are all equal before God'? Hindus say that in some way God is everywhere, and we are all part of God: does this ring true?

(This sequence, working from the environment to matters of existential thought, is more suited to intelligent 'top streams'!)

B. What do you look for when you are choosing a wife or husband? Appearance? Money? Interests? Horoscope? Religion? Whose advice would you seek? Anybody's? Your parents? A friend? Would you pray about it? What about the Hindu system? 'All happiness comes after marriage: falling in love with your wife, and being blessed with children.'

C. (Having first ascertained that there have not been any recent bereavements in the group.) What do you think about our English custom of visiting family graves? What about the 'lying-in-state' of famous people? Are funerals sad occasions? Why? What instructions will you leave about your own funeral? Do you feel attracted to the idea of reincarnation? What does reincarnation mean for the animal world, or for outer space?

These suggestions are offered in the event of a lack of ideas arising from the children, not due perhaps to a lack of knowledge so much as the absence of quite the right incentive to begin talking.

WEEK 4. LESSON A: SCHEME ITEM 10—HINDU LIFE AND THOUGHT (i)

The work of week four is a carefully structured presentation of some central themes of Hindu thought, expressed in sacred texts, and set against a background of Hindu culture. This combination of simple thought forms, texts and visual material constitutes a pattern of presentation in which the parts support, illustrate, and invigorate each other.

Any treatment of Hinduism that avoids the confrontation of Brahman-Atman, or the concepts of *dharma*, *artha*, *karma*, and *moksha*, would be seriously lacking. Other thought forms may be considered essential to a thorough treatment of the subject; two, *ahimsa* and the various forms of Yoga, are treated in later lessons. For the rest, the limiting factors are time, the interest and ability of the children, and more significantly, the precise degree to which Hindu children of comparable age and ability, know and understand Hindu philosophy. Indeed, the prevailing problem which besets teachers of Hinduism, and incidentally, is not as easily discerned in the teaching of Christianity, is the extent to which children can be taught to know what it is like to have the outlook of an adult! To present thought forms in the abstract would be intolerable, and a sad neglect of the almost unlimited resources of Hindu art and architecture on the one hand, and the fascination of the more homely aspects of Indian life, on the other. The great majority of Hindus appreciate entirely, through contentment with tradition, or emotional reaction to their surroundings, concepts which could be a stern intellectual challenge to the Western mind so inclined to apply reason to what might be instinctive, mystical, or mere impulsive intuition. No, where India is concerned, we do well to let philosophy speak for itself, through art forms.

Let it also speak through literature, as of course it should, though so often this is done badly. Associations are the secret; Christians hear quotations from the New Testament with immediate associations of church and sacrament, or of far-off Sunday School. Let the Hindu texts speak against a background of temple buildings and Indian music; and let the texts be spoken by Hindus: or, since they are to be in English, by English children impersonating Hindus. Hence the three-fold nature of the treatment. It is three-fold in that the children will be involved in the material three times.

In lesson A, a number of things must be done:

(i) A restricted number of really evocative, large, colourful photographs of Indian art and architecture must be shown and explained. This is essential as part of the material for the week's homework, and for lesson 'B'. Examples of appropriate illustrations might be:

(a) Shiva, the great Lord, from the Elephanta Rock Temple.
(b) Shiva, Lord of the Dance. (A bronze image from Madras, Victoria and Albert Museum [V&A].)
(c) Vishnu and his *avatars*. (Eighteenth century painting from Jaipur; V & A.)
(d) The Rajavani Temple at Orissa.
(e) A wheel from the Surya Temple at Konarak.[4]

The need is for a little to be well presented as a guide to the main aspects of Hindu philosophy, and for that little to be much appreciated.

(ii) With the illustrations still on display, a number of texts should be presented: it will do no good at all to present text first and meaning later. The text is the expression of a wealth of meaning, so let the meaning be presented first. Then let the text be produced as the sublime expression of that thought. e.g.—

(a) 'What is God like? How does God help us? Does God live for ever? If God is in heaven, then we are left alone—unless we are God too—or unless we can hope for life for ever too. Perhaps part of me is immortal: is that part really part of God? Is that part the real ME? . . .'

'(Brahman) is the Self within you; the inner Controller; the Immortal.' (*Brihadaranyaka Upanishad*, iii, 7, 3ff. R. C. Zaehner, *Hindu Scriptures*, London, 1966. p. 53.)

The same treatment could be used to give presentation to the following further examples:

(b) 'This whole world is Brahman. Let a man in tranquility revere it as that from which all things are born, into which they dissolve, and in which they breathe and move.' (*Chandogya Upanishad* iii, 14. Zaehner, *op. cit.*, p. 87.)
(c) 'Some say that virtue and material gain are good, others that pleasure and material gain are good, and still others virtue alone or pleasure alone is good, but the correct position is that the three should co-exist without harming each other.' (*Manu Smriti* 2, 224.

Quoted by de Bary, *Sources of Indian Tradition*, New York, 1958. p. 208.)

(d) 'Those who cast off all their works on Me, Solely intent on Me, And meditate on me in spiritual exercise, Leaving no room for others, do me service.' (*Bhagavad Gita* xii, 6. Zaehner, *op. cit.*, p. 301.)

The class should then discuss with the teacher, the arrangements for lesson 'B'. Preparations for this will be the task to be completed in homework time, or at any rate, sometime before the lesson. One group of children should prepare to display the pictures, either those already shown, or a new selection; another, with good voices, should rehearse the reading of the texts, with brief introductions. The rest can be very gainfully employed, being responsible for supplying Indian music for the background, incense-sticks to give a realistic atmosphere, Indian-style clothes for the participants to wear; and perhaps some Indian food for everyone to share at the end.

WEEK 4. HOMEWORK: SCHEME ITEM 11—PREPARATION AND RESEARCH

Briefly, the teacher must help in these ways:

(a) By rehearsing the 'displayers of pictures.'
(b) By rehearsing the speakers.
(c) By giving much needed help over music: discs, tape, background information, and technical instructions.
(d) By giving help with dress: pictures, and hints about ways of obtaining the right effect without labour or expense. Other ideas worth trying are make-up, costume jewellery and a special hair-style.
(e) By supplying incense-sticks (and matches!).
(f) By recommending a simple, but not too exotic, Indian dish: perhaps chapatis are the easiest, especially if the domestic science department is co-operative.

WEEK 4. LESSON B: SCHEME ITEM 12—HINDU LIFE AND THOUGHT (ii)

If all has gone well, then this lesson will be a real experience for everyone, and no more said. With less able children, or difficult circumstances, it might need adaptation. It ought not to need radical change, and it certainly ought not to be omitted altogether.

If a guide is needed to assess the success of week 4, perhaps it could be the knowledge on the part of the children, of something of the significance of Brahman/Atman, and the profound awareness, in the Hindu mind, of the farness and the nearness of God. Perhaps also an idea of the special mystery of life as the Hindu lives it, and the happiness that he longs for, in the present minute, and at the end of time. More intellectual children will enjoy learning words like Veda, Upanishad, and Bhagavad Gita, but even the less gifted ones will derive real pleasure from meeting the words for the first time.

WEEK 5. LESSON A: SCHEME ITEM 13—THE HINDU MYSTIC

Man has always sought ways of coming close to God. In Hinduism, this search for God takes many forms. Ordinary Hindus pray and work, and think, and pray again, day by day, as do devout men of other religions. But Hinduism especially is the traditional home of the kind of search for God which is called Yoga. It has a variety of forms, and one of these, Hatha Yoga, has become very popular in the West. *Hatha Yoga* is simply a way of becoming a better person. Those who practise it seek to become 'better' by attaining something that they cannot find in ordinary daily routine: perhaps relief from physical or mental stress, or a sense of intellectual, emotional or moral well-being, or, in a more specialized, religious sense, the attainment of a profound mood of spiritual quietness or the resolution of a far-reaching personal tension. The Hindu Yogi seeks something beyond any of these: a release from earthly and physical consciousness, and mystic union with the Divine World Soul.

Yoga is, of course, not the whole of Hinduism, nor is it an exclusively Hindu activity. But it is one of India's most precious gifts to the West (and the East), and in its simplest and most easily assimilated form, a vivid and thoroughly proper induction into the 'religious experience'.

What is attempted in this lesson, then, is a glimpse of an elementary aspect of Yoga. What has been said above ought to be said to the class, in simple terms. Reference might be made to the *Gita* (vi, 10–15), but once again, in simple terms. Experience suggests that the following procedure is the most straightforward, the most effective, and well within the ability, and the control, not only of the teacher, but of the children too.

The class should be asked to sit upright, with both feet on the floor, and the hands resting lightly, palms down, on the desk. With their eyes closed, they should direct their thoughts to a single image that has no associations: a pure colour perhaps, or a diminishing light. Two or three minutes (perhaps up to five minutes with a contented group), is quite long enough. The process of recovery should be carefully controlled, and there should be no noise until everyone is 'awake' again. A number of them may be willing to describe their experience, and others will confirm or deny the similarity of their own. Some will mention the Beatles, or the Maharishi, or hypnotism, and useful discussion can ensue. What should be established is the way that some people take naturally to this process, while others find it beyond them, or are frankly unmoved; and the way that, with some particularly well-disposed people, it could have deep and lasting effects.

A number of important considerations should be born in mind:

(i) This 'event' presupposes a good relationship between teacher and class, and a good atmosphere within the class itself. Yoga should not be laid open to abuse, still less to ridicule.

(ii) Inexperienced teachers, and teachers unfamiliar with Yoga, should not attempt any more than what is described here, with a class; they may, however, find unexpected benefits from following up the subject for themselves.

(iii) Teachers with experience of teaching world religions, or personal experience of Yoga, may be tempted to repeat the experiment; in fact, some children may ask for further lessons on Yoga. Anything beyond this first elementary step is more in the nature of a specialized activity, and ought more properly to be undertaken not in a lesson, or in school time, or with the class as a whole. If there seems to be a demand for *Hatha Yoga*, those interested should form a group that meets on a voluntary basis, in out-of-school time, and with parental approval. More important still, the teacher himself should get in touch with a responsible body.[5]

There are moves afoot, among teachers, not only of religious education, but of physical education too, for the introduction of *Hatha Yoga* into the curriculum. As such, it would be an interesting form of subject-integration; but much more careful consideration lies between the idea and its fulfilment.

WEEK 5. HOMEWORK: SCHEME ITEM 14—'EXPLAIN YOGA TO A FRIEND'

This speaks for itself. Diagrams might be encouraged, and if the 'friend' is none too intelligent, the explanation will need to be clear and to the point.

WEEK 5. LESSON B: SCHEME ITEM 15—THE OTHER RELIGIONS IN INDIA

This look at the Muslims, the Christians, the Sikhs, the Jains, the Parsis, the Buddhists and the Jews is necessary. It is not a divergence from the main theme; the intention is to see the place of the groups in the course of Indian history, in such a way that the picture of Hinduism is in no danger of being idealized or unrealistic.

A map of India is the first pre-requisite. It can easily be drawn in simple outline, and added to as the lesson proceeds. In fact, the map should be the focal point, not the teacher's words. It should eventually carry enough information to be self-sufficient and self-explanatory. It can then be copied, and provide the background for the next lesson.

In a way, much of this lesson will echo the first lesson (item 1), but there is no harm in this. The emphasis is different: the clear presentation here, of the origins of the religious groups, and their relations with each other, culminating in the partition in 1947. The communicating of this information will have to be done in twenty minutes, to allow time for copying the diagram; but twenty minutes is probably the full extent of the normal child's concentration, at this age. Gandhi's name is bound to arise, and this is the convenient link with the next lesson.

WEEK 6. LESSON A: SCHEME ITEM 16—GANDHI

In the previous lesson, to be quite fair, the intention ought to have been to help the children to learn what it is to be a Muslim, a Buddhist or a Sikh, in the mixed communities, and during the troubled history of India; this is to some extent outside the aim of the course, though not outside the scope of the course as a whole.

With Gandhi it is different. Here is a controversial figure: of great personal charm, intense devotion to high ideals, much loved, a man whose lasting influence on Indian affairs has been very much a topic of discussion during the past few years which surround the anniversaries of his death and his birth. Should we see Gandhi through Hindu eyes? Through Western eyes? Autobiographically, through the eyes of his own writing? Do the Hindus themselves agree about him? (It was a Hindu who murdered him . . .)

Certainly there is every reason to present the personality of the man whom millions in India admired, and whose death shocked the world. There are many good pictures of Gandhi; his own voice is available on disc; there is also available the eyewitness report of his death. The impact of the man himself, through these audio-visual media, should perhaps constitute the climax of the lesson.

WEEK 6. HOMEWORK: SCHEME ITEM 17—'GANDHI: PORTRAIT FROM LIFE'

The information can be drawn from the lesson, or from private research. The accounts will be better for being illustrated, either with sketches, or with news cuttings. References would probably have to be made to the Indian nationalist movement, *ahimsa* (non-violence), *satyagraha* (non-violent resistance), the Harijans (Gandhi's name for the outcastes), and partition.

WEEK 6. LESSON B: SCHEME ITEM 18—THE INDUS VALLEY AND THE CITY OF CALCUTTA

Another contrast: from emotive biography to archaeology and sociology; the earliest and the latest in India's history. Illustrations are essential: illustrations that provide information that is easy to appreciate, and relevant to the interests of the class.

A glance at the ruins of Mohenjodaro, dating from a time probably before Hammurabi and the beginning of Hebrew history, will reveal the amazingly advanced state of civilisation, in terms of design, and the organization of life and labour, and also in terms of sheer technical skills. The features of the 'man from Mohenjo-daro' in the New Delhi museum, will indicate something of the people of the Indus Valley. The deciphering of the Harappa script will reveal yet more of this early pre-Hindu religious tradition, if and when this takes place.

The comparison with modern Calcutta will be revealing too. The sheer size of the city, set in a mainly village culture; the rather novel concept of thriving Indian industry; the tensions of city-life, the riots of 1946. The biggest changes in India are happening in the cities, bringing education, changes in the position of women, and a new way of life. Is Hinduism strong enough to survive? Young teenagers might find the development of Hindu reactions to the West a little difficult to follow, though they will know a good deal about the great interest of young people in the West in the Oriental way of life, perhaps as a reaction against the pace of life and the growing threat to individuality in the West.

There will be no need for this lesson to be written up: the impressions will be enough to prepare for the next lesson.

WEEK 7. LESSON A: SCHEME ITEM 19—FAMINE AND POPULATION

Carefully managed, this lesson could be a searching discussion of the value of human life. The 'careful management' consists in guiding the logical progression of the 'argument':

(i) To a Hindu, a large family represents a divine blessing;
(ii) Hindus like to have large families;
(iii) Some Hindus would prefer to starve than to limit their families;
(iv) India cannot produce enough food, especially if the monsoon fails;
(v) If the food is limited, should families be limited too?
(vi) How could families be limited?
(vii) Is it immoral to interfere with nature?

Once again, involved discussion is important. Expression work may not be appropriate. Judging the atmosphere of the discussion carefully, the teacher could introduce, quite naturally, and in the Indian context, some information about abstinence, the safe period, mechanical aids to contraception, and the 'pill'.

The last ten minutes should be devoted to instructions about the homework.

WEEK 7. HOMEWORK: SCHEME ITEM 20—REVISION

Almost 7 weeks of Hinduism have passed, or 13 lessons; no mention has been made of tests or of revising a previous lesson or assessing progress. A diligent teacher would perhaps want to do some testing, revision and assessing *en passant*. What is offered here is a brief indication of what might be done at the end of the course; this might also constitute the conclusion of a half-term or a whole-term.

The class is told that the next lesson, the final lesson, will be a careful assessment of the course: particularly an enquiry into the extent to which they have learned what it is like to be a Hindu. Certain areas of work will be recalled, and they will be expected to write, or speak, from their knowledge of the facts, their understanding of the significance of the facts, and their own personal reactions to the Hindu way of life. The course should be briefly reviewed, and ways of revising suggested.

WEEK 7. LESSON B: SCHEME ITEM 21—ASSESSMENT

This will be, in fact, an assessment not only of the children's progress, but a test of the teacher's success, and the helpfulness of the various teaching aids. Four ways of testing are suggested:

(i) A number of direct questions, each involving a paragraph or two by way of an answer.
(ii) A larger number of questions, needing short answers; this is more appropriate for less able children.

(iii) The class impersonate Hindus, and speak in turn on some aspect of 'their' religion—perhaps in interview with the teacher. This might be recorded, complete with introduction and conclusion, and played back later.

(iv) The whole of the expression work of the course could be submitted, on the part of each child, and assessed as a project.

What is being assessed is mainly knowledge, but also appreciation, and to a small extent personal opinions about the topics that have been under discussion. Does a high assessment indicate a full understanding? There are other issues which the next section is designed to accommodate.

6. What associated activities could provide a natural extension of these studies?

There are a number of aspects of Hinduism where special activities could give a greater insight.

(a) India and her people.

1. A tour of India, beginning at Mohenjodaro, and ending at Calcutta, and lasting about 6 months.
2. Where (1) seems unlikely, an afternoon spent visiting a Hindu community: home, school, work, shops, and temple. If a wedding is arranged, permission might be given for a limited number of observers. Children like joining in Hindu worship: they do not have the inhibitions, and the introverted doubts, which cloud the pleasure of their elders!
3. A full-length feature film about India.[6]
4. A visit from a Hindu who is knowledgeable, speaks fluent English, and has a way with children!

(b) Indian art, music and architecture.

1. There are a number of museums in the country with thriving Oriental departments. A visit which is restricted in scope, but well documented, and realistically explained, would be a success with children with an intellectual or artistic disposition.
2. Some children might have contacts with India, or Indians, and could bring *objets d'art*, or simple articles used in Indian everyday life.

(c) Yoga. Something has already been said about this. It might be of use to add that many adults have an interest in Yoga, and the children's parents might be willing to start a group of their own.

(d) Community Relations Work.
The presence of a Hindu community provides a splendid opportunity for mutual sharing of experience. Children from 13 upwards enjoy meeting immigrant children of their own age, or younger: enjoying social activities together, and learning a little of each other's languages. The real difficulty many immigrants find is not so much in picking up enough English to 'get by' in daily conversation, but in learning to write in English, or read English fluently. A party held at school, for immigrant children, would be a fine experience for all concerned, especially if both communities provided food, music and entertainment.

7. *What lasting impressions of Hinduism is it desirable to provide?* Ideally, nothing less than a complete picture. If it cannot be complete, then at least let it be balanced. No major elements should be omitted altogether, though some may not be studied to any great depth. Seen in the context of wider studies in world religions, the particular characteristics of Hinduism are perhaps the following:

(a) An essentially Indian way of life;
(b) A way of living within and surrounded by the supernatural;
(c) A special way of approaching life in nature;
(d) A precise attitude to society;
(e) A discovery of ways to mystic absorption;
(f) An all-embracing love of mankind.

The teacher of Hinduism, or of any religious tradition for that matter, might do well to bear in mind some words of Canon Max Warren:

> 'Our first task in approaching another people, another culture, another religion, is to take off our shoes, for the place we are approaching is holy. Else we may find ourselves treading on men's dreams.'[7]

DGB

Footnotes

[1] e.g. Taya Zinkin: *India Changes!*, London 1958.
[2] See item 8.
[3] See item 9.
[4] Excellent illustrations may be found in V. Ions, *Indian Mythology*, London, 1967.
[5] e.g. The Wheel of British Yoga. (Mr. Wilfred Clark, 8 Poplar Drive, Wootton Hall, Solihull, Warwickshire.)
[6] See the chapter on Audio-visual aids.
[7] Max Warren: Introduction to the *Christian Presence* Series. (London, S.C.M. Press.)

46

TEACHING HINDUISM IN COLLEGES OF EDUCATION

NO ONE MUST LOOK to colleges of education to provide teachers of Hinduism. At present they are under a clear obligation to train men and women the majority of whom will teach children under the age of thirteen. It is university education departments which are responsible for training the graduates in religious studies who will be the secondary school specialists of the future, though the growing numbers of B.Ed. graduates is altering the balance to some extent. In this situation a justification of the inclusion of Hinduism or other non-Christian religions in the main course religious studies syllabuses of colleges of education must be made. It is not enough to point to present syllabuses which include church history or other elements which students will never teach (or certainly not to the extent that they have been taught them) or to comment on the amount of time which the education department may give to the history of education. This is to assert the right to teach irrelevant information on the grounds that others do it!

Negative arguments must be avoided by supporters of CSR as well as opponents. Opposition on grounds of difficulty or time are negative. If they can study the philosophy of Plato who was not a Christian or the ideas of Augustine and Aquinas whose pre-Copernican thought world is far away from our pluralistic age, how can it be said that Hinduism is beyond them unless we are unhappy about the theological problems that might be raised or unless the students are of such calibre that they find everything difficult—in which case we should not entrust the care of the minds of our young children to them. The question of time (what has to go?) is one which probes to the very roots of the main course, and of the whole curriculum of teacher training. Some things cannot be done in three years, the course is an *initial* training course after all. But surely its purpose is not simply to impart knowledge. Rather it is to teach students how to study and how to express themselves, and with regard to content concern should be with understanding concepts rather than accumulating facts which can easily be obtained from books. My answer to the time problem is to urge for a restructuring of the course along lines to be suggested later.

There are a number of excellent reasons for including other religions in the religious studies syllabus, and Hinduism in particular as the oldest and an example of one that is non-Semitic. (The others to be studied in depth might be Judaism, Islam and Buddhism. To cover all religions adequately is impossible but these four plus Christianity provide a more than sufficient basis for acquiring techniques which can be used in other areas.)

First there is the world situation. When Vietnam and the trendy young Buddhists of Oxford Street are forgotten, despite the 1968 Commonwealth Immigrant Act, there will be Sikhs, Muslims and Hindus in our large towns, living witnesses to a multi-religious world. In 1970 the various TV channels put out at least six series which included some reference to the major religions and the next series on 'Civilization' may well cross the Bosporus! It is not simply to be 'with it' to teach world religions, it is to be realistic. We live in a multi-religious society.

It is hard for anyone in a Western Christian society to view his faith and culture objectively. Even atheists in Britain are Christian atheists whether they like it or not—the God they say does not exist is the Christian concept, not the Muslim or Hindu! The student of religion will still be over-ready to make value judgements about other religions from the standpoint of his own. What he finds worthy of respect in Hinduism is likely to be that which mirrors the Christian idea of good. In spite of this one way, and for some people the best, of taking a cool look at one's own beliefs is to examine the faith of someone else. It is rather like learning a strange language, for the first time in one's life one notices the peculiar idioms and construction in one's own. In other words, the study of another religion can stimulate a religious self-awareness which is necessary for spiritual development. For example, the study of the *Purusha Sukta* (*Rig Veda* x, 90) has influenced some students in their thinking about the Christian idea of atonement. An examination of initiation rites, noting their cultural significance, may well draw attention to the fact that confirmation has no social function and yet still tends to be a 'puberty rite' and so point to one of its weaknesses.

It is to be hoped that the study of world religions will result in tolerance but at least it should produce teachers who are well informed and cannot tell the old tales—that Hinduism is polytheistic, that only the presence of the British in India stopped the practice of *sati*, that a Hindu can be as immoral as he likes because he has many lives in which to gain salvation whereas the Christian only has one. Teachers are influential members of society, they can provide the young with accurate information and try to remove the prejudices which white Christianity has helped to foster—but only if they have been prepared for the task.

Returning to the question, what has to go? We must note the movement in education from teaching facts for their own sake to the understanding of concepts. There is still a long way to go, perhaps because we who teach have not always been trained to examine concepts. Consequently students are still told the things they could discover from books. By broadening the syllabus and recognizing the impossibility of teaching everything about five religions we are soon forced to consider what are the essentials. We discover that we are making fundamental inquiries into such things as the nature of God—is he in some way destroyer as well as creator; is there a creative element in apparent acts of destruction; should we refer to God as 'he'? If we think of God as a mother what effect has it upon our piety? From Vedic sacrifice, asceticism and yogic meditation it is possible for a discussion of the relationship of man with the Beyond to take place in a way which enables us to consider the whole concept of communion in a way which is free from the inhibitions which might be placed upon it if studied in a Christian context. Furthermore, if the subject is religious studies and not Christian studies it must be recognized that it is not enough to consider only Christian concepts. And an understanding of religious concepts is something which the primary school teacher needs as much as, if not more than, the university lecturer.

With regard to content the first pitfall to avoid is making the study of Hinduism an examination of the texts; the second is to regard Radhakrishnan as a typical, representative Hindu. Because Christianity is the religion of a book and because education is chiefly concerned with the intellect there is a temptation to turn the religion of Hinduism into a philosophical study based on the Upanishads. The literature of piety is, however, the *Gita*, the *Ramayana* and the other epics mainly of Vishnu or Shiva. Through these, often in conjunction with an introduction to Indian art and architecture, the student can obtain the feel of Hinduism.

Having said that religious studies ought to be concerned with the examination of concepts rather than the accumulation of knowledge I would obviously like to dispense with the traditional approach of Old Testament, New Testament, Christian Theology, Judaism, Hinduism, Islam, Sikhism and Buddhism. I would like to examine the impact of sociological, environmental, historical conditions upon religious belief and the development of religious organization by looking especially at the life and times of certain important figures such as Moses, the Buddha, Jeremiah, Jesus, Muhammad, Guru Nanak and by examining what became of their work in the centuries after their deaths with changed circumstances—how did each of these view God, what had each to say about corporate and individual communion with God in worship? What methods of communion they devised; the impact of the religious beliefs upon culture, literature, art, science, their attitudes towards other religions and cultures with which they came in contact, would form another section. It is also important to examine tendencies towards sectarianism, protestant, heretical and revivalist movements and finally to look at the state of the chosen religions, as they exist in the twentieth century. There are of course other topics which will receive mention here and there and which might become sections in themselves depending upon the interest of the tutor or student, for example, holy places (viz. Arthur and Mina Klein's study of the site of Solomon's Temple in 'Temple Beyond Time'). In short it seems that the six dimensions of religion, doctrinal, mythological, ethical, ritual, experiential and social described by Ninian Smart in *Secular Education and the Logic of Religion* chapter 1 provide an appropriate framework.

Some might opt for a self-contained study of Hinduism using for convenience an historical approach. The following is part of the outline of a supporting studies course of three hours per week lasting two terms. The course is entitled 'Commonwealth Studies' and includes sections on the Caribbean. It has two purposes: to introduce students to the cultures from which immigrants to Britain come and to give them experience of a cross-subject approach to education. The sections relevant to Hinduism are:

1. Geographical introduction to the Indian subcontinent.
2. Human migration—causes and effects, the Aryan invasion and developments in India to the second century A.D.
3. Religious developments from the Vedas to Buddha.
4. The caste system.
5. Popular Hinduism—Vishnu, Shiva, mythology.
6. Indian art.
7. The Muslim invasion of India, prefaced by an introduction to the rise of Islam.
8. The Sikhs.
9. The Mughal Empire—Islam in India.
10. European Expansion to India. Its influence upon Europe and upon India.
11. Hinduism from AD 1800 to the present day.
12. Imperialism, India under the Raj.
13. Indian Music and Dance.
14. Literature of and about India—E. M. Forster, John Masters, Kipling, Narayan, etc.
15. The End of the Indian Empire—India and Pakistan: the Republic of India, problems and prospects.
16. Indian immigration to Britain. Indian immigrants (Hindu and Sikh) in Britain.

Although the course is not specifically geared to Hinduism and involves staff from the history, geography, English and art departments as well as a few visiting lecturers and myself, it is one which I put forward for consideration because I believe that all religions need to be studied in their general context, Hinduism perhaps more than any other. Indian dance is more than a theatrical display: it is a religious offering; Yoga is more than a series of keep-fit exercises, the *Ramayana* is more than a fairy story of folk tale, the beautiful sculptures in the Victoria and Albert or British Musuems are not merely works of art, the caste system and reverence for the cow are complexities which need to be placed in the context of Indian life and history and not presented as oddities. Approaches may differ. The content in the end will probably be much the same, any variations depending upon particular circumstances—the interests of the tutor and students, the overall policy of the department, the local presence of Hindu and Sikh immigrants, for example.

There are a number of problems which are likely to confront the teacher of Hinduism at any level. They deserve the attention of those who are training teachers as well as those who, like the

Shap Working Party, are encouraging the inclusion of religions other than Christianity in religious studies syllabuses. Some, the 'third world' and literary problems have already received sufficient attention in the section 'Hinduism in the junior and middle schools'. Students need to be prepared for coping with them.

Attention also needs to be given to problems which may arise in the classroom and ought, anyway, to be present in the minds of college students. One is the place of Christian missions. Should they exist, if so, what should their purpose be? Related to this is the place which should be given to the story of Christian mission in the school syllabus. The command to preach the Gospel and the obedience of Christians to this injunction and the consequences of it are essential aspects of the religion, as of Islam and Buddhism, the place for examining them is in a topic such as 'What is the Church?' or individuals may be used as illustrations of courage or caring, for example, Father Damien. Xavier's grave is in India; it may be argued that his story is part of the story of religion in the East but will children see it this way? The work of Carey and Xavier in the context of a topic on India may give the wrong impression.

There is also the question of the Christian attitude to Hinduism. Raymond Johnston considers it in his chapter 'A Christian Approach to the Comparative Study of Religion in Schools' in the first Shap volume. Dialogue between religions is still in its infancy. As yet we hardly know what the other person believes. This has not stopped Christians and Muslims from condemning the views of the other without even knowing the strength of the authority of the Bible or the Koran. Students and children are prepared to follow this tradition. In college the problem must be faced. In school it may arise and the teacher must have given it thought beforehand.

The final problem is of another kind. Visual aids are essential in studying such a different culture as that of India. Films have often been produced with tourism in mind, seldom with the intention of aiding the student of religion. Opportunities for R.E. teachers to use films have been rare in the past, with the development of integrated studies the prospect is brighter. In a team effort involving a year, group time and facilities for using films are likely to become available. It is to be hoped that some film maker will be prepared to meet the demand. Film strips and slides are listed in the bibliography. All of them are introductory. Anyone who wishes to go into further detail on some such topic as Hindu gods, temples, holy men, light or water symbolism, must do it himself. There is a need for short sets of twelve or twenty slides on more specialist themes. At the time of writing I know of no pictures about Hinduism which can be obtained commercially in Britain. One has to cut up tourist brochures and art books and write begging letters to travel agents or to some of the businesses belonging to our Indian immigrants. Christianity, and to some extent Judaism, are well served; it is to be hoped that publishers will now turn their attentions to the other religions. Children cannot imagine being in India, they need the assistance of good audio-visual material.[1]

WOC

Footnote

[1] Since the writing of this article the Shap Working Party and Lancaster University in conjunction with Mr. B. Peerless are looking into the possibility of producing sets of slides on Hinduism. Teachers may also like to know of a series of 16 mm movie films on Hindu religious practices produced by Dr. Smith of Syracuse University, U.S.A.—*Editor*.

47

TEACHING HINDUISM IN THE UNIVERSITY

To TEACH RELIGION is not the task of a university, though some of its attitudes may be derived from a religious tradition. The study of Christianity is commonly termed theology or divinity, and is broadly sub-divided into languages, history and philosophy. The study of Hinduism is even more complex and one is aware of the warnings given by Cantwell Smith that the term Hinduism is 'a particularly false conceptualization.' But his statement that modern students have abandoned the use of Hinduism and tend to use titles such as Brahmanism, Vedism and Charvakism needs modification. Eighty years ago Monier-Williams wrote a standard work on *Brahmanism and Hinduism*, but the discovery of the Indus Valley culture has radically changed the assessment of Hinduism as later than Brahmanism. Smith admits that for the early period 'the religious life of ancient India' is perhaps the only valid designation. Even this cumbersome title however would include Jainism and Buddhism and if, for the sake of economy, they are to be omitted or left for separate study, we are back with Hinduism as a convenient label for the ancient and modern periods of the dominant religion of India. There is value in using omnibus words for ordinary purposes, as long as we are clear as to what we are doing.[1]

Teaching *about* any religion at university level runs immediately into the problem of language. Is it desirable, or even possible, to learn about a religion, especially one so different as Hinduism, without a knowledge of the classical language, in this case Sanskrit? Further, can it be taught without such a knowledge? This problem has divided linguists and orientalists from theologians and philosophers. In a discussion some years ago about a master's degree in religious studies, which was to include as one paper out of three (plus essay) a study of a major religion, a great tussle took place. The professor of Sanskrit declared that it was impossible to study any religion, especially Hinduism and Buddhism, without a working knowledge of the classical languages. No texts had been translated adequately and the philosophy was too remote from European understanding. The professor of philosophy retorted that this was nonsense, the Pali Text Society had provided many sound translations, and anyway Theravada Buddhist philosophy was not all that difficult. The linguist conceded that an exception might be made for Theravada, but still ruled out Mahayana Buddhism and Hinduism. Since the translation of the *Bhagavad Gita* then in favour was Radhakrishnan's often paraphrasing version there was some justification for this criticism, but both Hill and Edgerton were already available with their much more faithful translations, and since then Zaehner has produced both translation and full commentary.[2]

The problem of language has long troubled the syllabuses of Christian theological degrees. For many years London university insisted that however good a candidate might be in philosophy or history, he could not obtain an honours B.D. without both Greek and Hebrew. Compulsory Hebrew has been dropped since 1969 but Greek retained, though there appears to be a weakening in some other universities over compulsory Greek. Of course Greek is not essential to an understanding of Christianity; millions of Greekless people have understood it much better than most theologians, but it is maintained that for academic study of the documents some knowledge of the original language is essential. But if a further language were to be demanded now in the B.D., adding Sanskrit or even Pali or Arabic to an already heavy and wide-ranging syllabus, the study of theology would become impossible, or at least any extension of it into the field of comparative religion.

In oriental schools the contrary process has been at work. So much emphasis has been placed upon languages that theology and philosophy have had very little place, and to some extent these institutions have deserved the title of grammar schools. This criticism was suggested by the Hayter Report, which considered that too much attention was paid to ancient periods and classical languages, and too little to modern languages and cultures. Some attempts have been made to counter such criticisms since Hayter; more emphasis is given to modern languages, and provision is made for open lectures on a wide range of subjects. It remains generally true, however, that a student cannot take a first degree in Hindu, Buddhist or Islamic doctrine or philosophy in the oriental schools, as he can take a first degree in Christian theology and European philosophy in numerous universities, not all of which demand Greek.

The oriental schools provide intensive three year courses leading to a B.A. in Sanskrit, Pali, Arabic, Chinese, Mongolian, Turkish, and so on. In these courses the texts prescribed for special study may well be religious, for example, chapters from the Qur'an, but usually such chapters are studied from a strictly linguistic point of view, with attention to fine points of grammar or lack of it. Little or no exposition is given of the religious and doctrinal content of the chapter, which after all has been its chief claim to attention for many centuries. In addition to the dominant language papers, there are a few other subjects which may be offered, but these generally refer to history, archaeology, art or law, and avoid the thorny and complex subject of religion.

Some broadening of approach may be seen among orientalists at the post-graduate level, though here the pressure towards specialization tends to concentrate again upon language, and the production of meticulous and unreadable theses upon the difficult points of little known texts. However, the introduction of one-year M.A. courses has effected some changes. This has not been done without stiff opposition, broadly from two opposite camps, anthropological and linguistic, which hold that it is impossible to take a master's degree in one year when coming from another discipline. Illustration of the difficulties involved may be given from the M.A. in Area Studies which has been introduced in London. For entry these courses demand a first or second class honours degree, or its equivalent, without restriction of subject, though a qualifying examination may be demanded in some courses. The areas studied are: Africa, the Commonwealth, Eastern Europe and Russia, Far East, Latin America, Near and Middle East, South Asia, South East Asia, and the United States. Each area is sub-divided into subjects, such as: anthropology, geography, history, law, literature, music, politics and sociology. Since religion has played an important role in human life it is surprising how little it appears here, though the omission is partly symptomatic of uneasiness about how to deal with it. In the first draft of this degree course only the African section offered religious studies, a change from the neglect of African religion in the early days! When it was suggested to the orientalists that there had been quite a lot of religion in Asia, they began to look at their syllabuses again. South East Asia now provides 'the iconography of South East Asian religions' under archaeology, but nothing further on Buddhism despite the Pali Text Society's translations. South Asia, a modern term for India and its neighbours, has introduced religious studies, with two papers on 'Introduction to Hinduism', and 'Hinduism and its role in Indian society.' However there are restrictions. The examination consists of one major subject, with two minors, plus an essay. These two papers can only be taken as minors, along with a major such as law, music or history. 'Indian Religion' can be taken as a major, but only by candidates equipped with 'adequate' knowledge of Sanskrit. This means in effect that the candidate must have a first degree in Sanskrit, in which case he would probably not wish to take such a broad master's degree, or he would be required to take an introductory course in the language, lasting at least a year, which would lengthen this first master's degree from one to two years which is against the general pattern of the degree in other subjects.

Nevertheless there has been a trickle of students for the minor subjects of this Hinduism course, and that has involved a further development. The great School of Oriental and African Studies, which for many years had no regular courses on Hinduism, or for that matter on most other religions, has for the past four years provided a series of weekly lectures on 'the Religions of India, Pakistan, Ceylon and Nepal.' These are open to its own graduates and students from other colleges. During 1970–1971 nineteen lectures were arranged, given by fifteen members of staff, with the following titles: Religion in Mohenjo-Daro and Harappa; Hindu Ethics; the Caturvarga; Indian Logic (Nyaya); Indian Aesthetic Theory; Jainism; Origin and Development of Buddhism; Later Buddhism; the Buddhist Heritage in Tibet; the Sangha in Ceylon; Vedic Ritual (two lectures); Is there a Philosophy of the Upanishads?; The Philosophy (and Religion?) of Samkhya and Yoga; the Poetry and Thought of Kabir; Sikhism; Devotionalism in Indian Music; Jagannatha-cult at Puri; Christianity in South India; Mysticism in Urdu Poetry. Ten of these lectures can be said to deal strictly with Hinduism.

In addition to this welcome development the School of Oriental and African Studies arranged in 1971 a Seminar on South Asian Religion. In preparation for this papers were presented during the previous two years by local and visiting scholars. This is at an even higher level, for university teachers and advanced graduates, but it is evidence of a widening scope in oriental studies from which students of Hinduism can expect much benefit.

On the other wing, in the theological schools, there is a demand for first degree courses which include comparative religion, and the preoccupation with theology and philosophy leads to a playing down of linguistic requirements, as much through lack of time as by deliberate policy. But few denominational training colleges pay any attention to comparative religion, and even in those universities which make provision for it this is normally as an optional rather than a compulsory or basic subject. So considerably less than half the students of theology have any knowledge of another religion beside their own, and many of the clergy receive no training in subjects which occupy the minds of many in their congregations.

The desire to provide some knowledge of other religions to theologians has led to the formulation of various syllabuses, and since these differ widely from one university to another I must confine my remarks to experience of London. Up to 1962 comparative religion, as it was then called, consisted in the B.D. of one optional paper on a wide range of religions: Judaism, Zoroastrianism, Brahmanism, Hinduism, Buddhism, Confucianism, Taoism, Shinto and Islam. These had previously been taught in all three theological schools, when Sidney Cave was at New College, Eric Waterhouse at Richmond and E. O. James at King's. But since their time all the teaching in this subject has been given at King's College, which means that few students from the distant Richmond College attend these lectures. Comparative religion was entrusted to one lecturer, who was supposed to cover all these religions in two years, with little study of the texts, and some colleges gave no essay work.

In 1962 two new degrees, B.D. (pass) and B.D. Honours were introduced and the subject in question, still an option, was renamed study of religions, with one paper in the pass degree and two in the honours, the latter including texts. Six religions were now listed: Judaism, Islam, Hinduism, Buddhism, Chinese and Japanese Religions, African Religions. Three of these were to be selected for study, and one of them chosen for special texts by honours candidates. The addition of African Religions was a sign of the times, though experience of teaching led to the conclusion that it is difficult to teach to undergraduates, because of lack of texts and time, as well as the wide field involved, and it soon became reserved for post-graduate research.

After several years' experience of these degrees pressure from the university led to the return to a single B.D. degree, with both pass and four honours grades. This was inaugurated in 1969. In study of religions the pattern is still similar, with the exception that Judaism has followed Zoroastrianism in being omitted. The reason for abandoning Zoroastrianism was that of its small size and few modern followers, compared with the other great living religions on which emphasis is placed. Judaism was left out for different reasons; there was already a considerable place given to the Old Testament in the B.D., despite Hebrew becoming optional, and those who wished to proceed to study rabbinic or medieval Judaism should do so after graduating.

Experience of teaching *three* religions had proved awkward, involving a term or a term and a half each, and covering too wide a field of study. Already before the new degree was introduced the old regulations were amended to require only *two* religions and this has proved much more helpful for teaching, with a full year at least devoted to each religion, and two years for a special choice with texts. Study of religions is still taken as either an Option or a Special. Option involves one general paper on the two religions, and Special involves the same first paper and a further paper on the texts of one of the chosen religions.

The choice of two religions out of five depends upon the interpretation of the purpose of this course in a theological degree, and upon the preferences and qualifications of the teacher. Hinduism and Buddhism clearly would go well together, or Buddhism with Chinese and Japanese Religions. But there is a strong case for the inclusion of Islam, as a useful bridge between biblical studies and those of the Farther East, as a major though often neglected member of the great Semitic religions, and as dominant not only in the Middle East but in many other parts of Asia and Africa. For these and personal reasons the two religions studied at present in the London internal B.D. are Islam and Hinduism, and at least one year is devoted to each, with additional non-examinable lectures on Buddhism in the first short summer term. These lectures are given to both Option and Special students, who have a common paper on the two religions in the B.D. It may be remarked again that there is still only one lecturer provided for this course, with care of undergraduates and graduates, covering both lecturing and tutoring.

Study of religions in the B.D. has always been on English translations of selected texts, with no knowledge required of Arabic or Sanskrit, though technical terms are used and explained. The Hinduism course covers twenty weekly lectures on the following subjects: Introduction; Indus Valley religion; the Vedas (two periods); the Upanishads (three); the Systems of Philosophy (two); Teachings on Man and Society; the Epics; the *Bhagavad Gita* (three); the Puranas and Bhakti; Shiva and Shakti; Kabir and the Sikhs; Home and Temple Worship Modern Hinduism (two). Like the lectures given at the School of Oriental and African Studies this course is largely doctrinal and philosophical, though with some history and sociology where possible.

The second paper on Hindu texts is for those who choose the Study of Religions as their special subject, usually seven or eight students each year, men and women, ordinands and laymen. These have a weekly seminar in their third year, following the year's introduction to Hinduism, in which the texts are expounded and discussed. The texts are selected from F. Edgerton's *Beginnings of Indian Philosophy* and R. C. Zaehner's *Hindu Scriptures*. These books have the advantage that they largely overlap and the translations of technical terms can be compared. Selections are taken from the translations of the *Rig Veda*, four of the Upanishads, and the whole of the *Bhagavad Gita*. The value of Zaehner's commentary on the Gita for such a course will be evident.

Experience has shown that this kind of course is workable and useful. Naturally it is invaluable for the university teacher to have a knowledge of the language of his texts, and here important assistance can be found in courses provided by the oriental schools. For post-graduate students the problem of language becomes more acute than for undergraduates. Wherever possible some study of the language involved is insisted upon, and otherwise restriction of the field of research is generally made to those aspects of modern religious thought where the sources are mostly in English, e.g. Gandhi or Aurobindo.

University teaching tends to be chiefly by means of lectures and tutorials. Essays are written by both Option and Special students in the above courses, and discussed in tutorial classes, with emphasis upon wide reading. Additional lectures are given occasionally on other aspects of religion by visiting lecturers, sometimes film slides or strips are used, and visits to the great museum collections are encouraged. The Oriental School welcomes graduates to its open lectures. Some students following the study of religions courses have already had some experience of or interest in certain Asian or African countries and others visit them during vacations, so gaining first-hand views which are interpreted by and help to enlarge the formal lecture and reading work.

A year's course on comparative religion figures also in general A.K.C. lectures provided at King's College for non-theological students, coming every third year in the syllabus. This follows roughly the older wide-ranging survey of the world's religions, and with lack of class and essay work for the hundreds of students who attend it is difficult to do any text work, though those who have special interests are advised on wider reading. Teaching of comparative religion in colleges of education is beyond the scope of this chapter, though it is clearly of great importance. The faculties of theology will provide some future teachers of comparative religion, since there is a declining number of ordinands but no lack of lay students in this subject, and there is a great need for the expansion of this subject in the universities. A recent attempt was made to introduce a wider degree in the study of religions in London, the syllabus for which had secured the approval of orientalists, anthropologists, sociologists, theologians and philosophers. This was approved by the Academic Council but has been deferred indefinitely because of the lack of funds for such a development in particular colleges and the restriction placed on the quotas of student admissions to all courses in the present economy drive.

EGP

Footnotes

[1] W. C. Smith, *The Meaning and End of Religion*, New York, 1962, pp. 61, 249f.

[2] S. Radhakrishnan, *The Bhagavad-Gītā*, London, 1948; W. D. P. Hill, Oxford, 1928; F. Edgerton, Harvard, 1952; R. C. Zaehner, Oxford, 1969.

PART THREE

APPENDICES

48

NOTE ON LANGUAGE AND PRONUNCIATION

The sacred language of Hinduism is Sanskrit, an Indo-European language related to Latin and Greek, and the direct ancestor of Hindi, Gujerati, Bengali and other modern Indian languages. The Sanskrit alphabet (called *devanāgarī* in its commonly written form: the name is of uncertain meaning) has 49 letters, in phonetic order, as follows:

Letter	*Approximate pronunciation*
a	c*a*t
ā	c*a*rt
i	p*i*n
ī	b*ee*n
u	r*u*n
ū	m*oo*n
ṛ	w*ri*t
ṝ (rare)	*rea*son
ḷ	angl*e*
ḹ	(no equivalent in English)
e	br*a*ve
āi	r*ai*n
o	c*o*ne
āu	ar*ou*nd
ḥ (final)	(no equivalent)
ṃ or ṁ	ha*ng*
k	*k*ick
kh	blo*ckh*ole
g	*g*ood
gh	bi*gh*ead
ṅ	ma*n*y
c	*ch*urch
ch	coa*chh*ouse
j	*j*oy
jh	brid*geh*ead
ñ	si*ng*ing
ṭ	*t*ry
ṭh	boa*th*ook
ḍ	ba*d*
ḍh	ma*dh*ouse
ṇ	*n*un

t	as ṭ (in West: there is a difference in Indian pronunciation, too slight for most Westerners to follow)
th	as ṭh
d	as ḍ
dh	as ḍh
n	as ṇ
p	*p*ut
ph	cu*ph*ook
b	between *b*ail and *v*eil
bh	a*bh*or
m	*m*ain
y	*y*outh
r	t*r*ill
l	*l*ip
v	either *v*et or *w*et (may be transliterated in either way: *swami* or *svami*)
ś or ç	*sh*oot
ṣ	*sh*oot
s	*s*it
h	*h*ouse

In this book the general rule is that precise spellings (with diacritical marks) are given only in the glossary, and when the context demands it. Commonly Anglicized forms (Brahmin, Vishnu, Krishna) are used throughout).

49

THE HINDU CALENDAR

Solar Months	*Lunar Months*	*Seasons*	*Fixed times for annual festivals determined by lunar calendar*
March			Birthday of Rāma. 9th day of Caitra
	Caitra (New Year South)		
April			
May	Vaiśākha Jyaiṣṭha	Summer	Worship of goddess of Ganges (Daśarā): 10th lunar day of bright fortnight of Jyaistha.
June			
July	Āṣāḍha	Rainy	Car festival of Jagannāth (Rathayātrā): 2nd day of bright fortnight of Asadha.
August	Śrāvaṇa		Swinging the Lord Krishna (Jhulanayātra): 11th–15th day of bright fortnight of Sravana.
September	Bhādrapada	Autumn	Krishna's birthday, Janmāshṭami: 8th of dark fortnight, Bhadrapada.
October	Āśvina		Durgā-Pūjā: 7th–10th of bright fortnight of Asvina. Next full moon day: Lakshmi-Pūjā. Next new moon: Kālī-Pūjā.
November	Kārttika (New Year North) Āgrahāyaṇa	Winter	Diwali. Dusk of night of new moon of Karttika. Full moon day of Karttika: round dance of Krishna with *gopis* of Vrindaban.

December			
January	Pauṣa	Dewy	
February	Māgha		Sarasvatī-Pūjā: 5th day of bright fortnight of Magha.
March	Phālguna	Spring	Śivarātri, festival to Shiva. 14th day of dark fortnight of Phalguna. Full moon day of Phalguna—Holi (Dolayātrā), with scattering of coloured powders to Krishna and Radha in celebration of Spring.
	Caitra		

N.B. There is an additional lunar month every thirty months to correct the difference between the solar and lunar calendars.
Cf. A. L. Basham, *The Wonder that was India*, Appendix III, pp. 494–497.

50

BIBLIOGRAPHY

PART A. BOOKS ON WORLD RELIGIONS WITH SECTIONS RELEVANT TO THE STUDY OF HINDUISM

The editors are indebted to Mr P. Woodward of Borough Road College, Isleworth, Middlesex and Co-ordinating Secretary of Shap Working Party for permission to use and adapt the Shap Working Party Booklists in Bibliographies 1, 2, 3 and 4. The prices given are 1970 prices and may, of course, be subject to change. It is hoped they will nevertheless provide a useful guide.

1. Noss, J. B. *Man's Religions*. 1963. Collier-Macmillan. £3·15.

   For many years this has been the major text book used in survey courses in the U.S.A. and has run into three editions and a number of reprintings. It is quite useful, and mainly concentrates on living religions.

2. Ling, T. O. *A History of Religion East and West*. 1968. Macmillan. 496 pages. £4 and paperback £1·50.

   This is a most excellent text book which is also genuinely comparative in that the author compares aspects and phases in the development of the different religions. Its title indicates its scope, there being no treatment of, e.g. African Religions other than African Islam. Probably this is the best single source for an overview of the major religions.

3. Ringgren, H. and Ström, Å. V. *Religions of Mankind, Yesterday and Today* (translated by J. C. G. Greig). Oliver and Boyd. 492 pages. £3·15.

   A wide ranging, often dull and sometimes inaccurate survey, this nevertheless can be used as a reference work. It includes quite a lot of material on ancient religions and on 'primal' religions.

4. Zaehner, R. C. (ed.) *A Concise Encyclopaedia of Living Faiths*. 1964. Hutchinson. 432 pages, 98 illustrations. £3·15.

   This contains useful chapters on different religions by various scholars. The quality overall is high, and the chapter on Hinduism is outstanding. The contribution on Marxism by the editor is speculative.

5. Smart, N. *The Religious Experience of Mankind*. 1969. Scribners. $10. Fontana paperback, 1971, 75p.

   A general history of religions and modern 'quasi religions' with the accent on religious experience. Unreliable in parts, but well illustrated.

6. Finegan, J. *Archaeology of World Religions*. Oxford. 3 volumes. Paper £3·50 set illustrated; bound £7·15 set; 672 pages, 156 plates, 9 maps.

This book is beyond the reference of its title, though the accent on archaeology is strong. It is a very useful source of information about the origins of major religions.

7. Brandon, S. G. F. (ed.) *A Dictionary of Comparative Religion.* 1970. Weidenfeld & Nicolson. 704 pages. £5·50.

   This contains contributions by a number of scholars, and sectional editors, and has a good system of cross-referencing and indexing. Though it could have been more systematic in the comparative entries, it is extremely good value as a reference work as you get about 5,000 words for a shilling. In its field, at the present time it is without rivals.

8. Adams, C. J. (ed.) *A Reader's Guide to the Great Religions.* 1965. Collier-Macmillan. £3·75.

   An excellent bibliographical survey with sections on primitive religion, China, Hinduism, Buddhism, Japan, Judaism, Christianity and Islam. All these sections are good, but the one on Buddhism is superlatively so (by Richard Gard).

9. Hastings, James (ed.) *Encyclopaedia of Religion and Ethics.* T. & T. Clark, 13 volumes cloth £4·75 each; leather £5.

   This multi volume work still contains many useful articles and is to be found frequently in libraries and in second-hand bookshops.

10. Edwards, P. (ed.) *The Encyclopaedia of Philosophy.* 1967. Collier-Macmillan. 8 volumes, each 500 pages £117 set.

    This American publication, which is beyond most people's means, nevertheless is to be found in most university libraries, and contains articles—slanted towards philosophical interests, naturally—on major religions and major religious figures.

11. Eliade, M. *From Primitives to Zen.* 1967. Collins. 645 pages. £3·50.

    A useful source book on religions, somewhat geared to Eliade's teaching interests.

12. Parrinder, E. G. *Worship in the World's Religions.* 1961. Faber. 240 pages. £1·25.

    This is a useful, indeed a unique source of comparative information on the topic.

13. Spencer, S. *Mysticism in World Religion.* Allen & Unwin, new edition 1967. 363 pages. £1·75; Pelican 40 p.

    For its size this is a masterpiece of compression and contains an excellent introduction to the theme.

14. Bowker, J. *Problems of Suffering in the Religions of the World.* 1970. Cambridge. 318 pages. £3·50.

    I cite this as an example of recent work in the thematic approach to the religions. It is full of excellent detail and could be a useful source book to brief those who wish to teach about this theme. It does however presuppose some knowledge of religions, although the author includes introductory material as well.

15. Hinnells, J. R. (ed.) *Comparative Religion in Education.* 1970. Oriel Press. £1·25.

    The 'foundation document' of the Shap Working Party.

Journals

Of the various theological journals available widely, probably *The Expository Times* is best value in terms of the content of the reviews on other religions than Christianity. The excellent *Religious Studies*, though the majority of the articles are on philosophy of religion, contains some on the history of religions. *Religion, a Journal of Religion and Religions*, published by Oriel Press, is explicitly devoted to work in the study of religions by various relevant disciplines, and contains extensive survey articles on recent work in various areas together with reviews.

Numen, the journal of the International Association for the History of Religions, published by E. J. Brill, Leiden, The Netherlands, and *The History of Religions*, published by Chicago University Press are important journals in this context.

NS

PART B. BOOKS ON HINDUISM

This bibliography was prepared with the teacher in mind. It therefore concentrates on those books which are most likely to be available in bookshops and libraries, and which have a general bearing on the understanding of Hinduism. Specialist bibliographies are added to the individual units in the body of this book.

A very full bibliography, which may be used to supplement this information, is Mahar, J. Michael, *India: A Critical Biography*. Tucson, Arizona: University of Arizona Press 1964, 119 pages.

A book for classroom use, which may be used in conjunction with this volume, is expected to be published during 1971: Eric J. Sharpe, *Thinking About Hinduism*. London, Lutterworth Press.

1. Walker, Benjamin. *Hindu World: An Encyclopaedic Survey of Hinduism*. 1968. George Allen & Unwin. 2 volumes, 608 and 695 pages. £10·50 the set.

   The only available 'encyclopaedia' of Hinduism. Useful in many ways, but tends to over-emphasize some features of Hinduism at the expense of others.
2. Basham, A. L. *The Wonder that was India*. Macmillan, 1954 and later editions. 568 pages, 116 illustrations (3 colour). £2·25. Fontana paperback, 1971, £1·50.

   As the title indicates, this magnificant book deals with much more than Indian religion. Invaluable for an understanding of Indian history and Indian culture.
3. Basham, A. L. 'Hinduism', in Zaehner, R. C. (ed.). *The Concise Encyclopaedia of Living Faiths*. 1959, 1964. Hutchinson. 432 pages, 98 illustrations. £3·15.

   An excellent concise survey of the subject.
4. Farquhar, J. N. *A Primer of Hinduism*. Oxford, 2nd edition, 1914.

   Inevitably dated, and long out of print, but still valuable in many ways. Has a useful bibliography of older literature.
5. Konow, Sten and Tuxen, Poul. *Religions of India*. Copenhagen: G.E.C. Gad, 1949.

   Translated from Danish, this is undoubtedly the most scholarly of the smaller books, and is warmly recommended. However, it may not be easily obtainable. The English is sometimes a little eccentric.
6. Bouquet, A. C. *Hinduism*. 1966. Hutchinson University Library. 152 pages, cloth £1·50; paper 65p.

   Originally published in 1949, this is the most popular of popular introductions, and is readily available. Weak in parts.
7. Sen, K. M. *Hinduism*. 1961. Pelican A 515. 20 p.

Written by a disciple of Rabindranath Tagore, this book is selective and impressionistic, and not always accurate. Difficult reading for the beginner.

8. Zaehner, R. C. *Hinduism*. Oxford, 1962. (Home University Library). 282 pages. 65p. Oxford, 1966 paperback 40p.

   Professor Zaehner writes with elegance about important concepts in Hinduism—Veda, Brahman, Moksha, God, Dharma, Bhakti. Little account is however taken of 'popular' Hinduism.

9. Morgan, K. W. (ed.) *The Religion of the Hindus*. New York. Ronald Press. 1953. $6.

   A symposium written entirely by Hindus, containing a great deal of valuable information, and conveying more of the atmosphere than most books. Also has a selection of Hindu scriptures.

10. Bhattacharyya, H. (ed.) *The Cultural Heritage of India. Volume IV: The Religions*. Calcutta; The Ramakrishna Mission, Institute of Culture. 1956. Luzac. £4.

    Another, larger symposium, originally part of a project to commemorate the centenary of Ramakrishna's birth (1936). Contains 46 essays by Indian specialists on various aspects of Indian religious history. A mine of information, though understandably uneven in quality.

Among histories of the oldest period in India (that which dates the older books on Hinduism most clearly), may be mentioned:

11. Wheeler, Sir Mortimer. *Civilizations of the Indus Valley and Beyond*. 1966. Thames & Hudson. 144 pages, 23 colour illustrations. Cloth £1·50. Paper 75p.

    Beautifully illustrated, an excellent introduction to the pre-Aryan culture of India.

12. Piggott, Stuart. *Prehistoric India to 1000 B.C.* 1950. Pelican Books A205, Cassell 1962. 296 pages, 42 illustrations. £1·05.

    Sound and sober archaeology, though to some extent superseded by:

13. Allchin, Bridget and Raymond. *The Birth of Indian Civilization*. 1968. Pelican Books A950. 367 pages, 32 illustrations. £1·12.

14. Dowson, John. *A Classical Dictionary of Indian Mythology*. 1968. 11th edition. Routledge & Kegan Paul. 432 pages. £1·75.

    An old warhorse, still eminently useful as a work of reference on the great mythological tradition of India.

15. Farquhar, J. N. *An Outline of the Religious Literature of India*. Oxford, 1920. 480 pages, recently reprinted by Munshiram Manoharlal, Delhi.

    An older standard work of reference, much too detailed for the beginner, but worth its place in any reference library.

The student naturally requires selections of Hindu scriptures for ready reference. Regrettably, the situation in this field is still far from satisfactory. Many important scriptures have either never been translated, or translated so badly that they are best left alone. Anthologies are few. See, however:

16. MacNicol, Nicol. *Hindu Scriptures*. 1938. Everyman's Library.

    Now out of print. Contains useful selections from the Vedic hymn, five Upanishads and the *Bhagavad Gita*. Replaced in the lists by:

17. Zaehner, R. C. *Hindu Scriptures*. 1966. Everyman's Library. 328 pages. 90p.

Certainly the most accessible collection. Differs from its predecessor in having fewer Vedic hymns, more Upanishads and a new verse translation of the *Bhagavad Gita*.

18. Renou, L. *Hinduism*. 1961. Prentice-Hall International. £1·25.
Out of print, but potentially the best of the anthologies, with a much wider selection of texts, and good introductory material, but too short. Covers (or attempts to cover) the whole of Hindu history.

18a. De Bary, W. T. *Sources of Indian Tradition*. 1969. Columbia University Press. 2 volumes, paperback, each £1·50.
An outstanding collection of texts relative to the history of Indian culture.

Among separate editions of individual scriptures, there is a great preponderance of editions of Upanishads and the *Bhagavad Gita*. Among these, see e.g.

19. Radhakrishnan, S. *The Principal Upaniṣads*. 1953. Allen & Unwin. 1968. 958 pages. £2·50; paperback £2.
Has the advantage of having a transliterated Sanskrit text together with the English translation. The commentary is that of a modern Vedāntin.

20. Hume, R. E. *The Thirteen Principal Upanishads*. 2nd edition, Oxford, and later printings. 604 pages. £1·70.
A standard work.

Editions of the *Bhagavad Gita* are legion. Probably the most useful are:

21. Hill, W. D. P. *The Bhagavadgītā*. 1968. 1st edition. Oxford, 1928; 2nd abridged edition 1953. 242 pages. £1·50.
Moderate and scholarly, with good introduction.

22. Zaehner, R. C. *The Bhagavadgītā*. 1969. Clarendon Press. 480 pages.
At £4·40, rather over-priced, but a better translation (prose) than in the same author's *Hindu Scriptures*.

23. Chidbhavananda, Swami. *The Bhagavad Gita*. 1967. Tapovanam Publishing House, Tiruparaitturai, S. India.
Remarkable value for money. Over 1000 pages—Sanskrit text, translation and commentary from the angle of the Ramakrishna Mission. Costs only £1 from Independent Publishing Co., 38 Kennington Lane, London S.E.11.

Editions of the more popular Hindu religious writings are hard to come by, but are in many ways more important than the philosophical books.

24. Narayan, R. K. *Gods, Demons and Others*. 1965. Macmillan. Heinemann. 256 pages. £1·25.
A retelling by an outstanding Indian author of some of the most famous of the mythological stories. Also has an introduction about the role of the storyteller in Indian village life. Highly recommended for use in schools.

25. Dutt, R. C. *The Ramayana and the Mahabharata*. Everyman's Library No. 403. 352 pages. 55p; paperback 40p.
Condensed version of the two great epics, translated (by an Indian) into rather precious Victorian verse. Still succeeds in conveying something of the flavour of the original.

26. Rajagopalachari, C. *Mahabharata; Ramayana*. 1968. Bharatiya Vidya Bhavan, Bombay. Condensed prose versions, available, at only 40p each from Independent Publishing Company. (See 23).

The philosophically-minded would find no difficulty in compiling a library of books on Indian philosophy. To choose is extraordinarily difficult. Nevertheless:

27. Radhakrishnan, S. (ed.) *History of Philosophy Eastern and Western.* 1953. George Allen & Unwin. 617 pages and 462 pages. (Out of print.)
    A two-volume work, with a useful account of Indian philosophy in volume one.
28. Smart, N. *Doctrine and Argument in Indian Philosophy.* 1964. George Allen & Unwin. 255 pages. £2.
    For the more advanced student. Written from the Western point of view, but sympathetic and sensitive.

29. Ions, Veronica. *Indian Mythology.* 1967. Paul Hamlyn. 144 pages, 124 illustrations (24 pages of colour). 90p.
    Eminently suitable for school work. Well illustrated account of the outstanding themes of Indian mythology. For 90p this is very good value indeed.
30. Kramrisch, Stella. *The Art of India through the Ages.* 1965. Phaidon. (3rd edition), illustrated. £2·40.
    An understanding of Indian art and Indian architecture is a 'must' for the student of Hinduism. Many books on the subject are expensive. This is only moderately priced at £2·40. Many plates, mostly in black and white.

30a. Rowland, B. *The Art and Architecture of India.* 1970. Penguin Books. Paperback ed. £2·25.
    A standard work, now at a very reasonable price.

The recent history of Indian religion is a subject in itself. Apart from the writings of, and books about, modern Hindu religious leaders, the following may be mentioned as general works of reference:

31. Farquhar, J. N. *Modern Religious Movements in India.* 1915. Macmillan. Illustrated (out of print). Reprinted edition by Munshiram Manoharlal, Delhi, 1967.
    An indispensable work of reference which is at the same time thoroughly readable. Written from a Christian angle, but sympathetic to all except Theosophists.
32. Sarma, D. S. *Studies in the Renaissance of Hinduism in the Nineteenth and Twentieth Centuries.* 1944. Benares Hindu University.
    Modern Indian religious history from the Hindu point of view. Somewhat difficult of access, but well worth reading.
33. Zinkin, Taya. *India Changes!* 1958. Chatto & Windus (out of print).
    Highly readable account of the modern Indian scene, written by a sympathetic observer. In some respects already a little dated.

Among books by modern Hindu writers, two in particular may be recommended:

34. Bhave, Vinoba. *Talks on the Gita.* 1960. Allen & Unwin (out of print).
    In the form of a commentary on the Gita, but covers a wide range of Hindu devotional thought. Written by a well-known disciple of Gandhi.
35. Radhakrishnan, S. *The Hindu View of Life.* 1960. Unwin Books. 92 pages. 55p; paper 25p.
    First published in 1927. Four lectures interpreting a philosopher's view of the essence of Hinduism. Representative of 20th century Vedanta modified by contacts with the West.

The Christian student may wish to know something about Christian attitudes to Hinduism. This again is a wide field. See however:

36. Hogg, A. G. *The Christian Message to the Hindu.* 1947. S.C.M. Press. 104 pages (out of print).
37. Boyd, A. J. *Christian Encounter.* 1961. Edinburgh: St. Andrew Press. 122 pages. 40p.
38. Stewart, W. *India's Religious Frontier.* 1964. S.C.M. Press. 184 pages. 80p.
39. Panikkar, R. *The Unknown Christ of Hinduism.* 1964. Darton, Longman and Todd. 180 pages. £1·25; paper 65p.
40. Thomas, M. M. *The Acknowledged Christ of the Hindu Renaissance.* 1970. S.C.M. Press. £3·15.
41. Klostermaier, K. *Hindu and Christian in Vrindaban.* 1970. S.C.M. Press. £1·05.
Although written by a Christian, I know of no better book for conveying the atmosphere of Hindu life and worship. Should be on every teacher's bookshelf.

EJS

PART C. BOOKS FOR USE IN THE PRIMARY SCHOOL

Choice based on notes supplied by the Children's Book Trust of India. Orders to: Helping-by-spelling Project, Oxfam, Banbury Road, Oxford OX2 7DZ. Trade terms are available, and school discounts for orders over 50 books.

A. Books showing small Indian children enjoying the same things as children in Britain.

1. *Animals and their Babies.* 28 pages, soft covers, 17½p.
How animals, fish and birds have their offspring and care for them. For 6–9 years olds. Pictures on each page.
2. *Ashok's Kite.* 28 pages, soft covers, 20p.
'Your kite is very big and strong,' said Sona, 'But I held it tight.' Adventures when brother and little sister fly a kite. For the very young. Colour illustration on every page.
3. *Home.* 28 pages, soft covers, 20p.
A charming picture book describing the security and neighbourliness of domestic surroundings. Staged in India, but the sentiments of children everywhere. For the very young. Full colour illustration on each spread.
4. *Mara Mouse.* 28 pages, soft covers, 20p.
A kitten and the mice of the house become firm friends . . . until a tom cat arrives. For infants. Full colour pictures on each page.
5. *Shobhana.* 28 pages, soft covers, 20p.
Some road safety on the way to a nice new friend. For the very young. Full colour pictures on each page.
6. *Three Fish.* 12 pages, soft covers, 12½p.
The clever fish escape the fisherman; the one that panics is killed. For the very young. Full colour illustration on each page.
7. *Two Little Chicks.* 28 pages, soft covers, 15p.
Raju gets two new friends—and learns about chicks. For infants. Pictures on each page.
8. *What Shall I Be?* 28 pages, soft covers, 17½p.

A mechanic? Farmer? A doctor to keep everyone strong and healthy? Sunil examines the possibilities. Uncle says he can be anything he likes, but first he must study hard. For infants. Colour pictures on each page.

B. Books having a special quality of courage and compassion.

9. *Bommakka.* 28 pages, soft covers, 22½p.
   She was a buffalo, and most courageous in what she thought was right. For 8–10 year olds. Illustrated on every spread.
10. *The Elephants and the Mice.* 36 pages, soft covers, 22½p.
   An old Indian fable about the need for harmony between the large and the small—portrayed by some very grand elephants and a community of most friendly mice. For 5–8 year olds. Illustrated on every spread in colour.
11. *Mahagiri.* 28 pages, soft covers, 20p.
   He was a big, courageous elephant who wouldn't do as he was told. But everyone loved him when they found out why . . . he would not have hurt a little cat! For infants. Colour pictures on each page of temple, priest, etc. Very good.
12. *Mother is Mother.* 28 pages, soft covers, 20p.
   A small boy makes a pet of a baby squirrel, but soon learns the squirrel's real home is with its mother. For infants. Full colour illustration on each page. Very good.
13. *Swarup Returns.* 24 pages, soft covers, 15p.
   The villagers were poor, but they could make curtains, tablecloths, and blouses if the city folks would buy them. Swarup's honesty with the customer brings more income for all . . . and good food! For 8–10 year olds. Illustration on each page. Gives useful background to monsoon and flooded village.

C. Good tales with an Indian background suitable for children over 7.

14. *Four Brothers.* 28 pages, soft covers, 22½p.
   Jealousy and greed divide four brothers and their wives, but their wise old father reunites them. For 8–10 year olds. Illustrated on every spread.
15. *Hari and Other Elephants.* 64 pages, hard covers, 47½p.
   Six sensitive stories about elephants—what they feel, how they think and behave. For 8–10 year olds. Colour illustrations throughout.
16. *Tiger Tales.* 56 pages, hard covers, 22½p.
   Reading these dramatic short tales about tigers, you also learn about everyday life in India, almost without realizing it. Some stories are funny, some a little sad, all are thrilling. For 8–10 year olds. Illustrated.
17. *Life with Grandfather.* Very helpful Indian background of temple, caste and crocodile.
18. *Panchatantra*, 1, 2 and 3. 47½p, hard covers, 6–8 year olds.
19. *Indian Classics*, 1 and 2. 47½p, hard covers, 8–10 year olds.
20. *The Cave that Talked* (Infants).
21. *Maya of Mohenjo-Daro* (for Juniors).

Set of one each of 18 books £3·62½.
Please add 3p towards postage and packing when ordering single copies of books.

Also recommended:
The Story of Vivekananda: Illustrated, from *Advaita Ashrama,* Dehi Entally Road, Calcutta. Rs 3.75.
Story of Stories. C. M. Kay, Volturna Press.
India and her Neighbours. Taya Zinkin, Oxford Children's Reference Library.
Indian Mythology. V. Ions, Paul Hamlyn 90p.
Bala, child of India. Methuen's 'Children Everywhere' Series.
From Long Ago and Many Lands. Sophia Fahr, Beacon Press, Boston.

EW

PART D. BOOKS ON HINDUISM AND INDIA FOR THE JUNIOR AND THE OLDER CHILD

* indicates suitability for use by or with junior children.
** indicates a largely adult vocabulary but suitable for reading or telling to younger children.

* *India*, Brown, J. D., Life World Library, £1·80.
* *Historic India*, Life, Great Ages of Man, £2·05.
* *Life and Times of the Buddha*, Sugana, Hamlyn, 90p.
* *A Hindu Family in Britain*, Bridger, P., R.E.P., (flexi) 75p.
* *Cradles of Civilisation*, Marshall Cavendish, 45p.
* *Asia—Dawn of History*, Marshall Cavendish.
* *Flight Four—India*, Ladybird, 12½p.
* *Indian Tales and Legends*, Gray, J. E. B., O.U.P., 80p.
* *Folk Tales of the World—India*, Crown, A. W., E. J. Arnold, 47½p.
* *Indian Tales*, Thapar, R., Bell, 75p.
* *Indian Fairy Tales*, Turbull, C., Muller, 75p.
* *Fairy Tales of India*, Wilson, R. K. Cassell, 30p.
* *Story of the Pandavas*, Picard, 80p.
* *The Story of Guru Nanak*, Singh, Mala Heinkunt Press, 1E/15 Patel Road, New Delhi, 8.
* *What then, Raman?* Arora, S. L., Blackie, 75p.
* *White Shirt*, Arora, S. L., Blackie.
* *Gopal, His Life in India*, Darbois, D., Chatto, 75p.
* *Indian Delight*, McGregor, R. J., Brockhampton, 17½p.
* *Rama and His White Bullock*, Plummer, M., Oshams, 75p.
* *Ramu: a story of India*, Melita, R., Angus & Robertson, 80p.
* *A Letter from India*, Papas, O.U.P., £1·05.
* *Taresh, the Tea Planter*, Papas, O.U.P., 90p.
* *Rishi: the story of a Childhood in India*, Zinkin, T., Methuen.
* *Rishi Returns*, Zinkin, T., Methuen.
* *Chendru: the Boy and the Tiger*, Sucksdorf, A. B., Collins, 80p.
* *Geeta and the Village School*, Thampi, P., Gollancz.
* *The Children of Bird God Hill*, MacFarlane.
* *Black Warrior*, Garbult, D. M., Abelard-Schuman, 90p.
* *The Story of Guru Nanak*, Wylam, P., Children's Book Trust, 25p.
* *Cradle Tales of Hinduism*, Sister Nivedita, Advaita Ashrama, 62½p.
* *Let's Visit India*, Caldwell, J. C., Burke.
* *Ricefields of India*, Hardman, T., Longmans.
* *India in Pictures*, Katz, E., Oak Tree Press.
* *India* (Oxford Children's Reference Library), Zinkin, T., O.U.P. 62½p.
** *The Sikhs of the Punjab*, Mcleod, W. H., Oriel Press, 30p.

Folk Tales and Mythology

** *Indian Tales and Fantasies*, Oxford, 93p.
** *The Story of Rama and Sita*, Pickard, B. L., Harrap.
** *How the Birds Choose their King*, Clark, L., Pergamon, £1·25.
** *The Faithful Parrott*, Zinkin, T., Oxford, 43p.
The Blind Men and the Elephant, Galdone, P., World's Work, 93p.
Tales and Legends from India, MacFarlane, I., Chatto, 75p.
** *Listen and I'll Tell You*, Korel, E., Blackie, 80p.
** *Indian Fairy Tales*, Jacob, J., Dover- Constable, 95p.
** *Olive Fairy Book*, Lang, Oliver-Constable, 95 p.
** *Hindoo Fairy Legends*, Frere, M., Dover-Constable.
** *Stories from the Indian Classics*, Naravane, V. S., Asian Publ. House.
** *Three Bags of Gold*, Kunhappa, M., Asian Publ. House.
** *Myths and Legends of India*, Macfie, T. & T. Clark, 40p.
** *Tales of Hindu Gods and Heroes*, Beswick, E., Jaico Publ. House, Bombay.
** *The Elephants of Saragabal*, Guillot, R., Oxford, 38p.
** *Storm over the Blue Hills*, Jenkins, A. C., Oliver, 75p.
** *Kingdom of the Elephants*, Jenkins, A. C., Blackie, 75p.
** *The Lyre and the Lotus*, Lyons, I., Harrill, £1·50.
** *Judy and Lakshimi*, Mitchisom, Collins.
** *One Rupee and a Bundle of Rice*, Plummer, M., Odhams.
** *Bala: Child of India*, Silverstone & Miller, Methuen, 63p.
** *Ghurkas and Ghosts*, Silverstone & Miller, Methuen, 68p.
** *The Road to Agra*, Summerfelt, A.
** *Shanta*, Thoger, U.L.P.
** *Gay Neck*, Dhan Gopal Mukerji, Angus, 90p.
The Dance of Siva and other Stories, ed. Ghosh, Signet, 45p.
Popular Tales of Rajasthan, Birla, L. N., Independent Publ. Co.
The Maneater of Malgudi, Narayan, R. K., Heinemann, 80p.
Gods, Demons and Others, Narayan, R. K., Heinemann, £1·25.
The Sweet Vendor, Narayan, R. K., Bodley Head, £1·05.

Information

India and Her Neighbours, Zinkin, T., Oxford, £1·05.
Pakistan, Feldman, W., Muller.
India, Beney, R. and Menen, A., Thames & Hudson, £8·40.
Indian Painting, Randawa, M. S. and Galbraith, J.K., Hamish Hamilton, £7·35.
World of Premchand, Tr. Rubin, D., Allen & Unwin, £1·75.
Young India, Norris, M., Wheaton, 53p.
Classical Dances and Costumes of India, A. & C. Black, £1·75.
Slowly Down the Ganges, Newby, E., Hodder & Stoughton, £2·50.
Between Oxus and Jumna, Toybee, A., Oxford, £1·05
Common Sense about India, Pannikar, K. M., Gollancz, 75p.
India, Zinkin, T., Thames & Hudson, £1·50.
Visual History of India, Jeffries, A. B., Evans.
Introducing India, Thapar, R., Asian Publ. House.
Everyday Life in Early India, Edwardes, M., Batsford, £1·50.
Getting to Know India, Muller, 53p.
India, Indian Tourist Board.
Hindu and Christian in Vrindaban, Klostermaier, K., S.C.M., £1·05.
The Hill of Devi, Forster, E. M., Penguin.

Passage to India, Forster, E. M., Penguin.
The Deceivers, Masters, J., Penguin.
A Backward Place, Jhabrala, R. P., Murray, 75p.
The Householder, Jhabrala, R. P., Murray, 70p.

Forthcoming
A Sikh Family in Britain, Cole, W. O., R.E.P., 1971, 75p.

A further list can be obtained from the Ramakrishna Vedanta Centre, 54 Holland Park, London, W.11, containing many books of use to Primary school teachers.

Selected reading lists for Advanced study are available from the Commonwealth Institute: Kensington High Street, London W.8.
leaflet 5 on display material (maps, posters, etc.),
leaflet 6 on books and leaflets,
leaflet 8 on loan services.

WOC

51

LIST OF AUDIO-VISUAL AIDS TO HINDUISM

In drawing up this list I have excluded specialist books on Hinduism but included general works of value to child, student or teacher.

Anyone wishing to look further should turn to the following:

Commonwealth Institute: Kensington High Street, London W8, for selected Reading Lists for Advanced Study—India; leaflet 5 on display material (maps, posters, etc.), leaflet 6 on books and leaflets, leaflet 8 on loan services.

Mr. Bury Peerless, 22 King's Avenue, Birchington, Kent, for lists of further film strip/slide studies in process of production.

Community Relations Commission, Russell Square House, London WC1, for their Audio-Visual Aids booklet.

Peter Woodward, Religious Studies Dept., Borough Road College of Education, Isleworth, Middlesex, for general book lists, visual aids lists, and a calendar of important dates. Hinduism is, of course, included in all these. (Please send 15p to cover costs.)

A. Filmstrips

Hinduism: Life. Available from the U.S.A. (427 West 42nd Street, New York, N.Y. 10036). The colours could be better, and the captions under almost every frame are annoying.

Encounter with Hinduism: BBC Radiovision (with tape or record). Intended for use with a schools broadcast at sixth form level, most frames can be used with younger age groups. Good.

Hinduism: Concordia (117/123 Golden Lane, London EC1) (with taped commentary). Contains many excellent frames. The commentary is too advanced for most children but the technique of accompanying a child through his religion is unlikely to appeal to fifth and sixth formers. The detail covered is far too much for one session. Nevertheless, highly recommended.

Hinduism: Educational Productions (East Ardsley, Wakefield, Yorks. £1·80 each). Much simpler altogether, the middle frames are valuable for their illustration of domestic religion but early ones devoted to earth, water, light, wind, fire, rain, lightning and storm serve little useful purpose. The many pictures of temples though adequately justified in the notes, are merely repetitive to children.

Hinduism: Gateway (470 Green Lane, Palmers Green, London N13). At the moment of writing this filmstrip is not yet on the market. The frames devoted to *puja* and festivals and the general high quality of the strip make it a welcome addition to the material already available.

India—Religion: Gateway. Misleading. No Parsis, Buddhists or Jains, though the Christian minister is an Indian. Sikhs do a little better (2 frames) and Muslims a few more. However, good photography and additional useful pictures of Hinduism.

Hinduism—Religions of India: (Norstedts, Drottninggatan 108, P.O. Box 45120, 10430, Stockholm 45, Sweden).

India—the People: Gateway. Many frames would go well with the BBC schools radio programmes on India in the 'Man' series. No wedding ceremony—a disappointing omission. By concentrating on ethnic variety the filmstrip becomes too diffuse.

India—Village Life: Gateway. Indians would not like the stress on poverty and 'backwardness'.

India—Town Life: Gateway. Goes some way to correcting the picture of the previous set. Modern buildings and 'buses, but the second half returns to rickshaws and beggars.

India—Architecture: Gateway. Mughul and modern contributions as well as ancient Hindu temples. Further frames of the post-independence period (e.g. Bhakra Nangal Dam) would have been welcome.

Everyday Life in an Indian Village: Educational Productions. Outlines the variety of activity most interestingly and effectively—ploughing, making, pottery, building, but not a tractor in sight. Again useful in conjunction with the 'Man' series on India.

Everyday Life in the East: Educational Productions. Misleading title. The East here is Pakistan. Considerable variety and, perhaps because the Government of Pakistan provided assistance and facilities, such things as modern schools and the education of women are shown. The text notes the changes which were taking place when it was written (1952).

Encyclopaedia Britannica (Instructional Materials Division, Dorland House, 18/20 Lower Regent Street, London SW1) produce three relevant filmstrips at £1·90 each.

8571. *Bombay. Gateway to India.* It depicts life and industry in a modern city. The comments under each frame are satisfactory and a good impression is given of a busy, developing community.

8572. *A Village in India.* Chhattarpur is in north India and has two schools. Pottery, cloth making and sugar cane cultivation are illustrated and life is shown as very different from that in a village in the West, but not as quaint! Comments are given under each frame.

10985, *Family of India.* The family lives in a modern house on a tea plantation owned by an Englishman. Its members are shown at worship in the home, at work, at play, dancing and at school. The teaching notes state the obvious and no further help is given towards answering the difficult questions which this interesting strip might provoke.

All three are background filmstrips and as such to be rated as good, but they include very few frames about religion.

The Sikh Religion: Concordia. This filmstrip concentrates entirely upon Sikhs living and worshipping in Britain.

B. Slides

Meet the Hindu: Church Missionary Society. Available on loan. The slides are useful but the commentary is, as one should expect, Christian and missionary.

Art Treasures of India: Miniature Gallery (60, Rushett Close, Long Ditton, Surrey). Excellent studies in the art of the sub-continent for use by specialists with fourth, fifth and sixth forms.

From Mr. Bury Peerless, 22 King's Avenue, Birchington, Kent, a number of excellent studies are available in strip or slide form with taped commentary or notes. Relevant to Hinduism are:

India of the Hindus, *India of the Mughals*, *The Emergence of Modern India* (each 100 frames). Studies in preparation are *Pakistan and Archaeological Sites of W. Pakistan (including the Indus Valley)*. For the serious study of Hinduism this is undoubtedly the most satisfactory source for visual material.

(Other, short thematic studies of 12 or 20 slides by Mr. Peerless are being planned. Details of these and of a series of wall pictures now under consideration, will be made available through the Shap Working Party and the Religious Studies Department of Borough Road College of Education.)

Miniature Gallery, 60 Rushett Close, Long Ditton, Surrey, can provide a number of slide sets—but these have as their purpose the study of art not theology, consequently their value is considerable but indirect. Some sets are: *Art Treasure of India*, 2 vols. of 21 slides each, at £2·97½ each volume: *India*, £2·97½ (21 slides).

C. Artefacts

Bronzes, pictures, yantras and also records are available from Indiacraft, Marble Arch (533 Oxford Street), London W1. No catalogue is available. It is best to make a visit.

Central Cottage Industries Emporium, Janpath, New Delhi, 1, for a wide range of artefacts. Catalogue available.

D. Records

Available from Universal Record Shop, 40 S. Molton Street, off Oxford Street, London W1.

Settings of Sections of the Gita. Ravi Shankar, World Pacific, WPS 21466.
Music of India (introduced by Menuhin), EMI, ALPC 2.
Music from India, Ravi Shankar and Akbar Khan, EMI, ALP 2304.
Gandhi, BBC Radio Enterprises.

E. Films

I am indebted to my friend Mr. Derek Webster of Bretton Hall College of Education for this selection. They are to be obtained from the Indian High Commission, Film Section, Information Service of India, India House, Aldwych, WC2.

Mr. Webster's selections are, especially, *Radha* and *Krishna* and *The Sword and the Flute*. Also *Jain Temples of India*, *Cave Temples of India* (largely Buddhist), *Saga in Stone* (temples at Orissa), *Kathakali*, *Himalayan Heritage* (useful as background for children), *Festival Time*, *Family of Faiths*, *Invitation to Enchantment* (which lives up to its name), *An Invitation to an Indian Wedding* (of rather well-to-do Hindus), *Holy Himalayas* (a pilgrimage to Badrinath), *Vinoba Bhave*, *Swami Vivekananda*, *Rabindranath Tagore*, *Bhoodan Vatra* and *Glimpses of Ghandhiji*.

Mr. Webster has not seen every film in the catalogue. He and his students have seen those listed and consider them valuable in the college or secondary school situation.

WOC

52

GLOSSARY AND INDEX

The following glossary includes technical words not used in this book so that readers may be enabled to use technical books which do not translate the terms. The glossary and index are combined for the sake of convenience.